D0195090

REDEFINING

THE CORPORATION

*Stakeholder Management
and Organizational Wealth*

JAMES E. POST

LEE E. PRESTON

SYBILLE SACHS

STANFORD BUSINESS BOOKS
An Imprint of Stanford University Press

Stanford University Press
Stanford, California

© 2002 by the Board of Trustees of the
Leland Stanford Junior University

Printed in the United States of America
on acid-free, archival-quality paper

Library of Congress Cataloging-in-Publication Data

Post, James E.
  Redefining the corporation : stakeholder management and organizational wealth /
James E. Post, Lee E. Preston, Sybille Sachs.
     p.   cm.
  Includes bibliographical references and index.
  ISBN 0-8047-4304-5 (alk. paper — ISBN 0-8047-4301-X (pbk. : alk. paper)
  1. Corporate governance.   2. Corporations—Investor relations.   3. International business
enterprises.   4. International trade.   5. Globalization—Economic aspects.   6. Corporations.
I. Preston, Lee E.   II. Sachs, Sybille.   III. Title.

  HD2741 .P67   2002
  658.4—dc21   2001049813

Original Printing 2002

Last figure below indicates year of this printing:
11   10   09   08   07   06   05   04   03   02

Designed by James P. Brommer
Typeset by Interactive Composition Corporation in 10.5/15 Minion

IN MEMORIAM

MAX B. E. CLARKSON, 1922–1998

Business Leader, Philanthropist, Scholar, Friend

CONTENTS

CASE STUDIES

EXHIBITS, FIGURES, AND TABLES

Exhibits

Figures

Tables

ACKNOWLEDGMENTS

A work of this type necessarily involves the cooperation and support of many people and organizations. We appreciate the cooperation of the firms involved in the field studies, and of many other colleagues and contacts as well. Many individuals assisted the field research at each company, and these individuals are acknowledged in the "source notes" that accompany the company case studies presented at the end of the book.

We acknowledge here the roles of three major contributors to the overall manuscript, as well as many others who have assisted us in various ways.

Professor Edwin Ruhli, University of Zurich, has had a major influence on this project from its very beginnings, and has reviewed and commented upon many of our ideas and drafts as the work has proceeded. His interest and support for the project has been invaluable. Professor David B. Sicilia was able to follow up his earlier work at Cummins with additional interviews and material collected for our use, and has reviewed all portions of the manuscript dealing with Cummins for accuracy. Daniel H. Rosen prepared an extensive research memorandum based on his work on foreign multinationals in China, including additional interviews conducted at our request; this material is utilized in Chapter 7.

Throughout the entire project, we have also enjoyed and benefited from the support of the Jesse Ausubel and Gail Pesyna of the Sloan Foundation. Many colleagues, friends, and associates have reviewed parts of this work and offered valuable suggestions. They bear no responsibility for errors or omissions, but have earned our appreciation and respect for selfless contribution to this effort. We thank Joe Bailey, Manuel Becerrra, Shawn Berman, Leonard Brooks, Candida Brush, Archie Carroll, Stephen J. Carroll, Tom Donaldson, Martin Gannon, Jennifer Griffin, Kirk Hanson, Andrew Hoffman, Allen Kaufman, Jay Kim, Jeanne Logsdon, John Mahon, Frans Ryckebosch, Melissa Schilling, Susan Schwab, Brian Shaffer, Ken Smith, Sushil Vachani, Sandra Waddock, and Donna Wood.

We owe a debt of gratitude as well to a small army of research assistants, editors, and colleagues who have helped us resolve research questions, editorial issues, and administrative challenges throughout the several years of this project. We are especially grateful for the assistance of Lee Benson, Sarah Cruz, Dante DiGregorio, Bob Dudley, Rangamohan Eunni, Almundena Grau, Michael Johnson-Cramer, Susanna Khavul, Yun Jung Lee, Jennifer Meyers, Danielle Mihalko, Debbie Menor, Daniel Peter, Kristin Sacca, Ruth Schmitt, Janelle Walthour, and Guorong Zhu.

At the Stanford University Press, we have enjoyed the support and collaboration of Bill Hicks, Sumathi Raghavan, Kate Wahl, and Judith Hibbard. We appreciate the artistic and graphic design work of Bill Nelson. Thanks also to Rick Reser and Anita Wagner of R&W Productions, our copy and art editors, respectively, and to Interactive Composition Corporation.

Finally, we note with appreciation the effort of a group of anonymous reviewers who, over several years, have read numerous iterations of these materials. Their thoughtful comments have been quite valuable and we appreciate the perspectives and suggestions they have shared for our benefit.

James E. Post
Lee E. Preston
Sybille Sachs

REDEFINING

THE CORPORATION

INTRODUCTION

For more than a century the business corporation has been a successful and widely adopted institutional arrangement for creating and distributing wealth. But the power and purpose of corporations and of the entire corporate system has been continuously questioned and debated. The interaction between global economic growth and global social challenge has led to changes in the character and behavior of corporations and in public expectations about the role and responsibility of corporations within society. We believe these evolutionary developments have gone so far that a redefinition of the corporation is required, along with a reexamination of the means by which the benefits of corporate activity should be generated and distributed in the 21st century.

In this book we present the corporation as a collaboration of multiple and diverse constituencies and interests, referred to as *stakeholders*. Our *stakeholder view* of the corporation integrates stakeholder relationships within the firm's resource base, industry setting, and sociopolitical arena into a single analytical framework. Our central proposition is that *organizational wealth* can be created (or destroyed) through relationships with stakeholders of all kind—resource providers, customers and suppliers, social and political actors. Therefore, effective *stakeholder management*—that is, managing relationships with stakeholders for mutual benefit—is a critical requirement for corporate success. Progressive corporate leaders have long understood the value of listening and responding to the concerns of their constituents and of the general public in order to take advantage of new opportunities and to anticipate and deal with problems before they become critical. Such activities are often described in terms of "enlightened self-interest." Our analysis goes beyond this, however, to argue that specific stakeholder relationships are central to the creation (or destruction) of organizational wealth, and hence to the core purposes and operations of the corporation. Indeed, much of the focus among professional managers on "customer relationship management," "supply chain management," "intangible assets," "balanced scorecards," and so on rests explicitly on the proposition that the corporation is a network of interdependent people, organizations, and interests.

Our redefinition of the corporation rests on the maxim that "Corporations ARE what they DO." In this book, we discuss three major companies that apparently developed a stakeholder perspective through their strategies, structures, and policies over the long term. Our aim is not to generalize from these field studies, but to examine the concept of stakeholder management through these particular experiences. We use the studies to show how some firms have evolved and implemented the stakeholder view to achieve financial and market success. The experiences of Cummins, Motorola, and Shell, considered over several decades, enable us to show where and how stakeholder management (or its absence) makes a difference in the business and institutional evolution of these firms.

This book is intended for scholars, students concerned with the role of business in society, and executives and management professionals concerned with the larger questions of corporate purpose and its contribution to society. We recognize that various readers will differ in their level of interest in parts of the text. But we believe the combination of theoretical analysis and empirical evidence is mutually reinforcing. We describe the three companies *only* as particular examples of the kinds of stakeholder relationships that arise in the actual practice of management. We believe that these examples substantiate our general conception of the stakeholder view.

In Chapter 1, we frame the debate about the definition of the corporation in its historical and current context. The modern case for redefinition of the corporation rests, in part, on the inadequacy of the conventional "ownership" concept of the corporation, and the complexity—as well as the generality—of the relationships between corporations and their stakeholders. Chapter 2 analyzes the sources of organizational wealth, especially intangible assets and stakeholder relationships, and the critical role of trust in modern organizations. In addition, the "stakeholder view" is formally compared with the conventional resource-based and industry structure theoretical explanations for the relative success or failure of the firm. Chapter 3 introduces the three companies to which we have applied these conceptual lenses and describes the critical stakeholder relationships and issues that evolved in each of them over the past quarter century. The deeper analysis of these companies begins in Chapter 4 with a focus on the strategic role of values at Motorola and Cummins. The importance of developing and engaging stakeholders in response to competitive challenges is examined in Chapter 5. Chapter 6 focuses on Shell's responses to societal challenges, particularly its experiences with the disposal of the Brent Spar oil storage facility and with political conflict in Nigeria. Chapter 7 examines how companies address stakeholder issues within the process of globalization through an analysis of corporate activity in China, currently one of the world's most complex, challenging, and important business environments.

In Chapter 8, we examine the adaptive and transformational learning processes of the focal companies as they addressed stakeholder relationships and issues. Chapter 9 draws the analysis to conclusion, highlighting the "stakeholder journeys" of each company over several decades, and summarizing our conceptual and empirical conclusions. The book ends with our speculations about the relevance of the stakeholder view to the evolution of the so-called "new economy."

We stress that this book is *not* about the political concept of a "stakeholder society" that has been the focus of discussion in the United Kingdom for some years, nor about the wealth redistribution proposal of the same name that has appeared in the United States (Ackerman and Alstott, 1999). These macro-level political and social analyses lie far beyond the scope of our work. Our analysis focuses exclusively on the characteristics and management of business enterprises, particularly the large multinational firms that play a dominant role in the global economy. We believe that the ideas presented here are appropriate to firms operating in any democratic political system and under a wide range of ownership and taxation arrangements. Examples of the disastrous disregard of stakeholder interests by state-owned enterprises around the world (often within undemocratic political settings) suggests that new approaches to management are as necessary there as in investor-owned corporations.

The concept we present here is also different than the so-called "Asian management model" that attracted considerable attention in Western countries in the 1980s and 1990s. After much discussion in the management literature, it now appears that there is no single, generally accepted Asian management model. The turmoil in Asian economies during the late 1990s put an end to any notion that the practices of Asian corporations might insulate individual firms and entire economies from the instabilities and pressures of global competition. The idea that all corporations—especially global corporations—are converging toward common "best practices" in response to competitive and cyclical pressures, irrespective of their cultural heritage, is under active study and debate. We believe that practices that serve to enhance wealth *and* preserve legitimacy are likely to be adopted by corporations in the twenty-first century. In this context, the concept of *kyosei*— "working together for the common good"—developed by Ryuzabura Kaku, president and chairman of Canon, is broadly consistent with a stakeholder view of the corporation (Kaku, 1997). The *kyosei* concept does not appear to have been widely adopted by many other firms, Asian or otherwise, but it points to broadly consistent premises about stakeholder management.

SLOAN FOUNDATION PROJECT

This book is part of a larger project involving several hundred scholars from all over the world over a five-year period (1995–2000). The "Redefining the Corporation Project," supported by a grant from the Alfred P. Sloan Foundation, focused on the stakeholder model of the corporation and its implications for management theory and teaching, empirical research, and business practice. The present volume is the final publication to emerge from this project.

The Clarkson Centre for Business Ethics, part of the Rotman School of Management at the University of Toronto, maintained the project's website and electronic communications network and served as its center of operations. The project conducted several invitational conferences and seminars, both in Toronto and elsewhere, and arranged and presented several programs at annual meetings of the Academy of Management, International Association for Business and Society, and Society for Business Ethics. The project also made a series of small research grants to individual researchers and small teams to encourage empirical work related to stakeholder analysis and management issues; many of these people were invited to make presentations relating to their work. The overall guideline for the project was the idea that the nature of the corporation should be discovered through observation of its characteristics and behaviors, rather than through abstract legal, economic, or philosophical reasoning.

The late Max B. E. Clarkson, founder and director of the Clarkson Centre, was one of the original partners in this project, along with Lee E. Preston and Thomas Donaldson. His rich experience as a highly successful entrepreneur and business leader, along with his keen intellect and broad academic background, shaped the project from the beginning and had a powerful influence on our research plan and on the present book. This book is dedicated to Max in recognition of his profound impact on the development of stakeholder research in both theory and practice, and on our own evolving views.

In addition to the current book, the project has produced four other publications:

Max B. E. Clarkson, ed. 1998. *The Corporation and Its Stakeholders*, University of Toronto Press. A collection of the most important previously published articles dealing with the stakeholder concept, as selected by the participating scholars.

Principles of Stakeholder Management. 1999. Clarkson Centre for Business Ethics, University of Toronto. This document includes a formal statement of seven key stakeholder management principles, with rationale and discussion, accompanied by two supporting essays.

Jeanne M. Logsdon, Donna J. Wood, and Lee E. Benson, eds., 2000. *Research in Stakeholder Theory 1997–1998.* This publication contains a collection of reports on studies sponsored by minigrants from the project.

Business Ethics Quarterly, Vol. 12, No. 2, April 2002. A special issue devoted to Principles of Stakeholder Management and the Sloan Foundation project, edited by Thomas Donaldson.

1

WHAT *IS* THE CORPORATION?

From the time of Adam Smith, through the age of industrialization, the Great Depression, and the recent half-century of globalization and prosperity, the purpose and role of the business enterprise, and particularly of the large corporation, has been the focus of debate. Some governments have attempted to tame the corporation through regulation. Others have taken major spheres of economic activity into the public sector, often with unsatisfactory results and subsequent privatization. Whatever the terms of debate, the fundamental questions remain the same: *What is the corporation, and to whom and for what are it and its managers responsible?*

The persistence of these questions is a tribute to the success of the corporation, which, for more than two centuries, has evolved into a highly adaptable and successful form of human enterprise. As a result, its structures and processes have been emulated throughout the private sector all over the world, and in public and nonprofit institutions as well. The global scope of the private sector—and therefore of corporate activity—has also gradually been enlarged, even in those parts of the world where it was once severely restricted. But even as the global corporate system evolves, questions about its nature and purpose become more complex and challenging, and the public debate about the corporation in society grows more intense.

The corporate form originated in medieval times, when it was used by governments to grant special institutional status to cities, religious institutions, and universities. During the 18th and 19th centuries, business corporations were increasingly chartered in North America and Europe, typically in order to pursue narrow purposes—financing ocean voyages and building canals, turnpikes, or railroads, for example. By the 20th century governments in many countries were granting corporate charters with broad and general purposes—such as "to carry on business for a profit." As a result, corporations operating within market-oriented environments became free to pursue almost any legal business activity and to change their purposes, activities, and organizational structures almost at will. Freedom of action is, of course, more limited for corporations operating within authoritarian settings. However, the scope of market processes has been widening globally—and the extent of government control over business correspondingly declining—for a couple of decades, and this trend is expected to continue.

This book presents a view of the corporation quite different from its medieval origins—in which social purpose was the dominant consideration—and also different from both the model of comprehensive social control by government and the currently prominent "ownership" model that places primary emphasis on the private interests of investors. Our analysis is based on the empirical proposition that "Corporations ARE what they DO." The modern corporation is the center of a network of interdependent interests and constituents, each contributing (voluntarily or involuntarily) to its performance, and each anticipating benefits (or at least no uncompensated harms) as a result of the corporation's activities. Our proposed redefinition of the corporation, and our ideas about the ways in which corporations can and should be managed, are based on this observation.

The purpose of the business enterprise is to create wealth. Corporations create wealth in many different forms—earnings for investors, compensation for employees, benefits in excess of costs for customers and others. The attraction of the corporate form of enterprise, as it has emerged in advanced industrial countries, lies in its capacity to amass capital from multiple sources and to spread financial risks, always for the purpose of creating wealth. The diverse and flexible variants of the corporation that emerged during the 20th century proved uniquely appropriate, and highly successful, in accomplishing this objective. Recent improvements in global wealth, welfare, and opportunity are most likely to be sustained in the 21st century by an economic system that operates on market principles and provides ample opportunity for creation of new enterprises, as well as the growth of established firms. And the long-term success of the corporate system requires greater and systematic managerial attention to the interests and concerns of the diverse individuals and groups who are voluntarily or involuntarily affected by corporate activity.

The reasons for the corporation's extraordinary success in creating new wealth for its constituents are well known. One is that most of the corporation's primary constituents—investors, employees, customers, and suppliers—voluntarily contribute resources to the corporation in pursuit of their own interests. And, as Adam Smith long ago recognized, the pursuit of individual benefits through such arrangements often generates benefits for all. A second reason for the success of the corporate system is its general openness to competition and innovation. Businesses compete not only for customers in the marketplace, but also for investors, employees, locations, ideas, and every other resource needed to pursue their productive purposes. Resource providers—including host communities and sometimes customers—compete for the benefits provided by the firm. When competition is absent or weak, the corporation is no more immune from corruption and inefficiency than any other form of bureaucracy. But when the competitive environment is open and active, the pursuit of individual gain through market processes— including the introduction of innovative technologies and the creation of new enterprises and industries—has usually produced widespread economic and social benefits.

Although the ultimate justification for the existence of the corporation is its ability to create wealth, the legitimacy of the contemporary corporation as an institution within society—its social charter, or "license to operate"—depends on its ability to meet the expectations of an increasingly numerous and diverse array of constituents. The modern, large, professionally managed corporation is expected to create wealth for its constituents in a responsible manner (that is, not by theft or deception). The connection between wealth and responsibility has been stressed by both business leaders and critics for more than a century, and if the corporation can continue to survive and succeed today it must continue to adapt to social change. United Nations Secretary-General Kofi Annan recently challenged leading multinational corporations to subscribe to a new "Global Compact" expressing their responsibility for labor practices, human rights, and environmental protection throughout the world.

This chapter explains why the corporation needs to be redefined in the minds of its managers and constituents, and ultimately in law and public policy. Done correctly, this redefinition will clarify the role and purpose of the corporation within the evolving global social and economic system. This chapter introduces the *stakeholder model* of the firm, already established in the literature, and in chapter 2 it is extended to develop the *stakeholder view* of the corporation as a distinctive perspective on strategic management. The stakeholder view shows how stakeholder linkages can contribute to organizational wealth and to the overall well-being and success of the corporation.

Subsequent chapters explore and illustrate the value of a broad constituent-oriented approach to management as reflected in the experience of three firms that have made serious efforts to establish and incorporate stakeholder principles and procedures into their operations.

Of course, some of these initiatives have not been successful, even when well intentioned, and various mistakes have been made. But the companies profiled in this study have redefined themselves in ways that take overt and explicit account of the value derived from their linkages with multiple and diverse constituencies. In line with this broader and more accurate organizational identity, these firms have expanded their criteria of success—and therefore the goals of their operations—to include a wide range of performance criteria that are consistent with the stakeholder view of the corporation presented here.

THE CASE FOR REDEFINITION

In spite of the overall success of the corporation as an agent of beneficial long-term economic and social change, there is a need to reassess and redefine the large, well-established corporation, for two principal reasons:

- *Size and socioeconomic power.* Leading global corporations have access to vast resources (including specialized knowledge), overwhelming bargaining power with respect to most of their constituents, and extraordinary ability to influence their environments. They are not microscopic economic actors at the mercy of market forces and omnipotent governments.

- *Inaccuracy of the "ownership" model and its implications:* Shareowners hold securities, but they do not own the corporation in any meaningful sense, nor are they the only constituents vital to its existence and success. The notion that shareowner interests should dominate those of all other corporate constituents is inconsistent with the observed behavior of successful firms. Therefore, the conventional shareowner-dominant model of the corporation is unrealistic, as well as normatively unacceptable.

Size and Power

The size, bargaining power, and impact of major multinational firms, both individually and collectively, strongly suggest the need for a redefinition of their political and legal status, and for the scope of their managerial responsibilities. Far from being independent actors on the global playing field, these firms by their very presence alter the environments—social and political, as well as physical—in which they operate. Many of these impacts are welcomed by some or all of their constituents, but the point is that these broad impacts—favorable or unfavorable to others—have to be considered as part of the output of the firm, and therefore within the scope of responsibility of its managers. Moreover, there is an extraordinary imbalance of knowledge, resources, and power between the corporation and most of its constituents, sometimes even including the governments that ostensibly provide the legal framework for its operations. Some of the voluntary constituents of the firm (such as employees and customers) may have little access to or knowledge about competitive alternatives, and therefore become subject to inequitable treatment. Some employees have limited bargaining power because firm-specific competencies are of little value in alternative settings. In addition, some members of society, outside the network of expressed and implied contracts that frames the corporation, may be involuntarily affected by corporate activity; some of these involuntary and noncontractual impacts, both physical (pollution, for example) and cultural, may be unwanted or even harmful.

Government regulation has been the usual means of addressing such issues and providing protection for potentially disadvantaged corporate constituents (including shareowners), both internal and external. However, regulatory protections have often proved to be costly, controversial, and less than fully effective, even in advanced industrial countries. In less-advanced countries the ability of governments to bargain effectively and to control the activities of large multinational firms is often inadequate. Furthermore, influencing public policy and regulatory activity on behalf of corporate interests (in the form of lobbying) has now evolved into a highly skilled—and highly paid—profession. Hence, the notion that corporations are generally dominated by constituent-oriented governments is fallacious. Nor is the redress of grievances through the courts a realistic alternative in many jurisdictions. Even where such redress is available, legal actions are costly, time-consuming, and highly problematic—and always *ex post*, hence incapable of heading off undesirable outcomes in advance (except when a large penalty serves as an object lesson for others).

Many inequitable or harmful impacts of corporate activity could more cheaply, and probably more effectively, be reduced through adaptive behavior by managers, *if* (and this is a big "if") they were motivated to do so. Hence, one goal of redefining the corporation is to bring the legitimate concerns of both voluntary corporate constituents and involuntary, noncontractual parties—as well as those of the larger community as a whole—more clearly within the purview of managers.

The Ownership Model

The second stimulus for redefinition is that, at least in the Anglo-American tradition, the legal framework of the corporation and the great bulk of legal and managerial rhetoric are cast in terms of an ownership model in which the corporation is seen as an extension of a basic human right to own property. If individual citizens possess such a right and voluntarily collaborate to own property in common, then the corporation is simply another form of personal property ownership. Some societies severely limit citizens' rights of property ownership, and even the most property-oriented European and Asian traditions emphasize that critical features of the corporate form—legal status, unlimited life, and limited liability—are *not* natural attributes of the individual, but extraordinary privileges granted by the state on behalf of the larger host society.

As early as 1946 Peter Drucker dismissed the argument that the corporation is "nothing but the sum of the property rights of the individual shareholders" as a "crude old legal fiction" (p. 30). In spite of the relative ease with which corporations are formed, dissolved, and reorganized in many countries, the core image of the corporation has to include the fact that the corporate form is *socially created* and thus not a natural phenomenon. Therefore, conformance with broad social norms and values is an inherent requirement for the corporate system as a whole.

Uncritical acceptance of the ownership model of the corporation is often accompanied by ignorance of the societal privilege, and associated responsibilities, that the corporate form involves. Analysts and critics have attempted to instruct managers about the extent and importance of these responsibilities for many decades (Clark, 1916; Dodd, 1932; Bowen, 1956) and stressed the "interconnectedness" of owners with other constituents (Follett, 1918). More recently, both commercial and nonprofit organizations have begun to offer training programs and practical assistance for firms that wish to address these issues. For example, Business for Social Responsibility (BSR), an organization established in 1994 that now has more than 1,400 member firms, offers programs and information intended to "help companies be commercially successful in ways that demonstrate respect for ethical values, people, communities and the environment" (www.BSR.org).

Adherence to the ownership model is also often associated with imprecise reference to a managerial goal of "maximization," whether of profit, value, or some other measure. The concept of profit maximization originally entered the literature of economics as an *assumption*, intended to explain the behavior of firms as viewed by outside observers. More recently, in the context of a highly oversimplified legal-economic model of the firm, it has evolved into a normative goal, underlying the notion that the overriding objective of corporate management should be to generate wealth for shareowners (Boatright, 1996).

Sophisticated observers realize that no mathematical functions exist than can quickly and with detail describe the income- or wealth-producing possibilities of any real organization. Nor can an overall maximum for any significant performance variable be readily computed. This means that, despite the rhetoric, comprehensive "maximization" practices are rarely observed. As Michael Jensen has written (2000, pp. 49–50):

> Value maximization tells the participants in an organization how they will assess their success in achieving a vision or implementing a strategy. But value maximization says nothing about how to create a superior vision or strategy. . . . It only tells us how we will measure success in the activity. . . . Defining what it means to score to a goal in football or soccer, for example, tells the players nothing about how to win the game. It just tells them how the score will be kept.

Jensen correctly states that a better description of what corporations do, and what they can and should do, is to "seek value." That is, within the limitations of their knowledge and skills, and within limited and often ill-defined time horizons, they attempt to make and implement decisions that will increase their value over the long run.

Are shareowners entitled to returns on their investments? Of course. They are significant stakeholders, contributing to the success of the corporation and therefore fully deserving of rewards. In particular, individuals who contribute funds to start or expand businesses, often at considerable risk, should expect to reap significant benefits. However, new, innovative, and high-risk ventures, though vital for the maintenance of a dynamic economy over the long term, account for only a small part of total shareowner investment. The great bulk of investment is in established companies of substantial size, and much of this investment is channeled through fiduciary institutions that greatly attenuate the relationship between the individual saver-investor and the firm. Even then shareowners properly expect to receive returns on their capital, but the distinction between shareowners and bondholders (that is, between owners and lenders) under these circumstances becomes very weak. Both are concerned with the level and stability of their earnings and are also concerned with possibilities for capital appreciation and protection against loss. In spite of the spectacular investment gains and losses that some people experience, the actual returns that owners and lenders receive on their capital depend primarily on the composition of their portfolios and on systemic and macroeconomic factors.

Shareowners, of course, are not all alike. Those of family-owned and employee-owned enterprises may be intimately involved in corporate affairs, and some very large shareowners and fiduciary interests occasionally attempt to have direct influence on the operations of larger firms. These situations are, however, exceptions to the norm for large investor-owned corporations and their passive, and often indirect, investors. Hence the ownership status of individual shareowners and their agents in large, ongoing corporations—and therefore in the corporate system as a whole—is largely an artifact. The shareowner cannot actually *do* anything with any part of the corporation, nor does he or she ordinarily have any expectation or desire to do so. In fact, even the ability of individual shareowners to gain information about a company, or to raise questions about its operations, is severely limited.

What the shareowner owns is really a piece of paper—or an entry in a computer database—that grants two significant entitlements:[1]

1. To receive fractional distributions of income from the corporate source—if, in fact, there is any income available for distribution, and only to the extent that the officers and directors of the corporation choose to authorize such distributions.

2. To sell this token of ownership to someone else on any terms that the two trading parties may voluntarily establish.

These entitlements are not trivial, but obviously most large corporations need not (and do not) manage themselves primarily for the benefit of individuals who are in this passive and often indirect ownership role. Charles Handy (1997), in a paper marking the 75th anniversary of the *Harvard Business Review*, said: "The idea of a corporation as the property of the current holders of its shares is confusing because it does not make clear where the power lies. . . . A public corporation should now be regarded not as a piece of property but as a community . . . created by a common purpose." As Jensen (2000, p. 50)

---

[1]To emphasize exactly what ownership of a share of stock involves—and to correct the common misconception that shareholders and stakeholders have opposing interests even though the former are part of the latter—we use the term "shareowner" throughout this book. In addition to the two entitlements mentioned, shareowners are also entitled to vote in the election of directors and occasionally for other, usually minor, purposes.

clearly states: Although the long-term value of a firm's securities is an important indicator of its overall economic value, "stockholders are not some special constituency that ranks above all others."[2]

Rejection of the conventional ownership model of the corporation does not, however, mean "the death of property rights," as one commentator on the 1992 American Law Institute *Principles of Corporate Governance* declared (Carney, 1993), nor does it presage "the end of shareholder value" as suggested by Allan Kennedy (2000). On the contrary, the stakeholder perspective emphasizes the similarity and mutuality of interests among the diverse constituents of the corporation, and the many forms that ownership may take. In the modern theory of the firm, ownership is seen in cognitive and behavioral, as well as physical and legal, terms. An individual owns his or her own knowledge and capabilities, and groups of people own the common understandings and routines that they have learned to rely on over time. Commitment to working within and among specific organizations, and development of situation-specific capabilities that serve organizational purposes, involves investments comparable to—and possibly rarer and more valuable than—the financial investments of shareowners (Blair, 1995). The implications of these realities are included within the redefinition of the corporation proposed in this book, and will be further discussed in connection with the concept of *organizational wealth* in the next chapter.

A New Definition

The conventional concept of the corporation is descriptively inaccurate and ethically unacceptable. The corporation requires and receives inputs, some of them involuntary, from multiple sources, and has an impact on many constituents, favorable or otherwise. The corporation cannot—and should not—survive if it does not take responsibility for the welfare of all of its constituents,

---

[2]Evidence that investors will respond to promises of value, as reflected in dividends and/or stock prices and divorced from the fiction of property rights, is provided by the current popularity of "tracking stocks." Owners of these tradable securities anticipate gains or dividends related to the performance of a particular subsidiary or line of business within a company, but have no control over the underlying assets.

and for the well-being of the larger society within which it operates. The contractual agreements and government regulations it must follow are not always enough.

Fortunately, in spite of "shareholder value" rhetoric, many large corporations are managed (as all of them *should* be) such that they serve the interests of a broad range of constituents, both internal and external. We refer to these constituents as *stakeholders*, and we believe that a new concept of the corporation is needed to recognize their relationship with the firm. This new concept should be based on the obvious fact that corporate activity involves the collaboration, both voluntary and involuntary, active and passive, of numerous and diverse constituents; and it should acknowledge that these constituents have good reason to expect benefits, not harm, from their association with the corporation. Hence, we express the *stakeholder* view of the corporation in the following definition:

> *The corporation is an organization engaged in mobilizing resources for productive uses in order to create wealth and other benefits (and not to intentionally destroy wealth, increase risk, or cause harm) for its multiple constituents, or stakeholders.*

This definition provides a more accurate description of reality and offers better guidance for managers and directors in the discharge of their responsibilities. Its most important implication is that corporate performance should be appraised from multiple perspectives. The interests of shareowners are, of course, among these, but they are not always primary and never exclusive. A further implication is that corporate managers should attempt to identify their significant and legitimate stakeholders (particularly those who are noncontractual and involuntary, and hence easily overlooked), and to listen and respond to their interests and concerns.

Our definition of the corporation is congruent with the ideas presented in a publication by the Organization for Economic Cooperation and Development (1999, p. 18), which includes the following statement:

> The corporate governance framework should recognize the rights of stakeholders as established by law and encourage active co-operation between corporations and

stakeholders in creating wealth, jobs and the sustainability of financially sound enterprises.

This document offers no formal definition of the term "corporate governance," and formal definitions are hard to find in the voluminous literature that has recently appeared on this subject. Williamson (1998, p. 76), writing about transactions-cost economics that recognizes the dual principles of conflict and mutuality in every transaction, defines governance as "the means by which order is accomplished," so that conflict can be reduced and mutual gains realized. Preston (2002) suggests a broad concept of "governance," defined as "the set of institutional arrangements that legitimates and directs the corporation in the performance of its functions." He describes the diverse ways in which various classes of stakeholders actually participate in governance in this broad sense, and in both collaborative and adversarial ways, in the varied types of corporate structures that are currently operating all over the world.

The OECD document also offers no formal definition of the term "stakeholders"; in fact, a definition congruent with the most frequent use of this term in the management literature has proved elusive. Schilling recently discovered that Mary Parker Follett fully developed the stakeholder concept, although without using the term, in her 1918 book *The New State*. She foreshadowed the concept of "interpenetrating systems" and saw stakeholder networks as a subset of these more general phenomena. She pointed out that the purpose, structure, and management of business organizations could be redefined in terms of "interconnectedness," and that the role of managers is to *integrate* diverse efforts and interests for mutual benefit (Schilling, 2000). The term "stakeholder" was first popularized in the strategic management literature by Freeman in 1984; he subsequently emphasized that a stakeholder perspective required a redefinition of the firm itself, emphasizing that its purpose is "to serve as a vehicle for coordinating stakeholder interests" (Evan and Freeman, 1993, pp. 102–3).

Most subsequent analysts have paraphrased Freeman's loose statement that a "stakeholder in an organization is (by definition) any group or individual who can affect or is affected by the achievement of the activities of an organization" (1984, p. 46). However, this broad definition would include entities, such as competitors, whose interests are directly *opposed* to those of the focal corporation (but who nevertheless can affect or be affected by it). This inclusiveness would make the usual use of the term in the management literature, as presaged by Follett's analysis, inappropriate; it would turn into an absurdity the OECD statement that corporations and their stakeholders should "cooperate in creating wealth, jobs," etc. Thus the notion that corporations should aim for mutually beneficial (and certainly not harmful) relationships with their stakeholders requires a definition with narrower scope. Here is the definition used in this book:

> *The stakeholders in a corporation are the individuals and constituencies that contribute, either voluntarily or involuntarily, to its wealth-creating capacity and activities, and that are therefore its potential beneficiaries and/or risk bearers.*

The fundamental idea is that stakeholders have a *stake* in the operation of the firm, in the same sense that business partners have a common stake in their venture or players on a team a common stake in the outcome of a game. Stakeholders share a common risk, a possibility of gaining benefits or experiencing losses or harms, as a result of corporate operations. Their common desire is that the corporation should be run in such a way as to make them better off, or at least no worse off, than they would be otherwise. Our definition of the term "stakeholders" emphasizes both benefits and risks, and is congruent with the most frequent use of the term in the management literature, including the OECD document. Our definition is also consistent with the recent work of Kochan and Rubenstein (2000, p. 373), who suggest three criteria for identifying significant stakeholders:

1. They supply resources that are critical to the success of the enterprise.
2. They place something of value "at risk"; that is, their own welfare is directly "affected by the fate of the enterprise."
3. They have "sufficient power" to affect the performance of the enterprise, either favorably or unfavorably.

The resources provided by stakeholders can include social acceptance, the "license to operate," as well as more obvious contributions such as capital, labor, and revenue. The risks include not only financial exposure but employment and career opportunities, the quality of products and services, environmental and community impacts, and so forth. The power of stakeholders may arise from their ability to mobilize social and political forces as well as their ability to withdraw resources from the firm.

Investors, employees, and customers associate themselves voluntarily with the corporation in the hope of obtaining benefits. Other stakeholder individuals and groups adversely affected by pollution or congestion may be involuntarily involved with the firm, and may seek to minimize its negative impact on their welfare. However, their tacit acceptance of the firm's license to operate is nevertheless a significant contribution to its welfare. The status and interests of some classes of stakeholders (shareowners and employees, for example) are at least partially protected by law in most advanced countries, and most stakeholders have recourse to the courts to resolve any serious conflicts between themselves and the corporation. However, the possibility of receiving greater or lesser harms or benefits applies to all stakeholders; some, perhaps many, may receive both benefits and harms at the same time. From the perspective of any class of stakeholder, the term "corporate performance" properly includes the impact of corporate activity on themselves.

Freeman points out that "management theory is inherently prescriptive" (p. 47). The prescriptive implication of the stakeholder concept is that corporate managers should take into account the interests of those stakeholders that may be impacted, either favorably or unfavorably, by their decisions and actions. Hence, the term *stakeholder management* refers to management practices that reflect awareness of and response to the legitimate concerns of the multiple constituencies of the corporation. Note that the term does *not* refer, in this book, to the manipulation of stakeholders for narrow organizational purposes—that is, the management *of* stakeholders. We believe that effective stakeholder management is a critical requirement for sustaining and enhancing the wealth-creating capacity of the corporation.

Comprehensive stakeholder management requires recognition of stakeholders who *voluntarily* associate themselves with the corporation in pursuit of their own interests, and other persons and entities that are *involuntarily* impacted by corporate activity. With respect to voluntary constituents, the key managerial concept is obviously *mutual benefit*. Constituents such as investors, employees, and customers stand to gain from the success of the firm in creating new wealth through productivity improvements, innovations, and increasing customer acceptance (an indicator of increasing—or at least increasingly recognized—customer benefits). Their continued voluntary involvement with the firm—including their cooperation as it adapts to change—rests on their perception that they do, in fact, benefit as a result. With respect to individuals and groups involuntarily impacted by corporate activity, in particular those subject to pollution, congestion, unwelcome cultural influences, or the like, the critical management goals have to be *avoidance of harm, reduction of risk, and/or creation of offsetting benefits,* so that the continued operation of the individual enterprise—its "license to operate"—remains acceptable to all parties. In democratic political systems, which are uniquely hospitable to market-oriented economic arrangements, no business activity that causes substantial negative impact on any significant group of people or interests can be expected to survive, unless it offers conspicuous and broadly distributed offsetting benefits.

These points may seem obvious—and they are certainly well-understood by many sophisticated corporate managers and analysts—but they are entirely at odds with much contemporary corporate rhetoric, which places almost exclusive emphasis on the primacy of investor interests and short-term, bottom-line results. In fact, companies in Europe, Asia, and other places where a broader social role for the firm has been traditionally recognized are now being urged by management consultants and pressed by financial analysts to adopt more Western—that is, shareowner oriented—strategies. The influence of Western management modes is also increased, of course, by the long-term globalization trend, in which U.S.-based companies with conventional shareowner-focused management practices have played a pattern-setting role. These international pressures are well documented from a European perspective by Mills and Weinstein (2000, p. 89), who nevertheless argue that current shareholder value imperatives and constituency interests can be reconciled because "stakeholders play a key role in the value creation process."

THE STAKEHOLDER MODEL

A conventional diagram of the stakeholder model, intended to describe the multiple linkages between the corporation and its diverse stakeholders, is presented in Figure 1.1. Several points about this conception should be noted.

Benefit Flows

The flows between the firm and its stakeholders run in both directions; each stakeholder is perceived as contributing something and receiving something from the corporation. (Even involuntary and essentially passive stakeholders contribute by tolerating the existence and operation of the firm, and receive some combination of benefits and harms as a result.)

Multiple Linkages

All of the linkages may be operational at once; hence, contact with the firm creates indirect linkages or networks among the various stakeholders themselves—who may also, of course, be linked in other ways (as members of the same

Figure 1.1 The Corporation and Its Stakeholders.

community, for example). The frequently encountered statement that "the corporation is a nexus of contracts" sometimes suggests that the firm is engaged in a series of unrelated bilateral arrangements with various parties that have no relationship with each other. This is *not* an accurate description of stakeholder relationships for two reasons.

First, it omits the interests of involuntary and passive stakeholders, who may lack even an implied contractual relationship to the firm. Second, it fails to recognize the fact that, because of their mutual connection with the firm, all stakeholders are linked—at least indirectly, and often quite importantly—with each other. As the OECD notes: "Corporate governance is affected by the *relationships among participants* in the governance system." In addition to shareowners, the text lists creditors, employees, and governments among those playing important roles (OECD, 1999, p. 10).

Simultaneous Roles

Particular individuals and groups may simultaneously occupy several roles—employee, customer, shareowner, neighbor, and the like. Recognition of these overlaps should lead both managers and constituents to acknowledge the varied impacts of corporate activity, and to think of corporate performance in multidimensional and comprehensive terms, rather than from the perspective of any single interest. It should also be noted that *competitors* do not appear among the classes of stakeholders shown in Figure 1.1. The competitors of a particular firm contribute no stake to its operation and are more likely to benefit from its failure than from its success; they are therefore not *stakeholders* in it, as that term is used here. Of course, firms in the same or related industries, competitive or not, may develop a common stake in some industry-wide concern, such as support of R&D efforts or specific public policy issues.

Issue Variance

Finally, relationships between corporations and their stakeholders vary from issue to issue and from time to time. Some issues are more important to one class of stakeholders than to another. Concerns and priorities change over time; new classes and configurations of stakeholders appear in response to changing circumstances. Long-term relations, favorable or unfavorable, with various categories of stakeholders are path-dependent; trust builds over time, and so does distrust and opposition. Hence, the stakeholder map for any particular firm is not a permanent chart in which each recognized interest has a fixed weight or priority, but rather a flexible vision of a dynamic situation, akin to a hologram.

The stakeholder model contrasts sharply with the ownership model of the firm in both its Adam Smith and Karl Marx versions. The Adam Smith version presents the firm as an input-output system through which various resources are brought together in order to generate products and services for the benefit of customers. Those contributing inputs to this process receive benefits because they have provided goods and services that others want; customer demand both directs the flow of activity and determines its success. The Karl Marx version presents the ownership model in its most extreme form, with all involved parties, including the customers, contributing resources, effort, and money in order to generate benefits for owner-investors. This view of ownership may be morally repugnant, but is not too different from some commonly held conceptions. As a practical matter, even the simplest forms of corporate law and regulation protect at least some interests other than shareowners (for example, lenders and employees); and most stakeholders can take their claims to the courts if necessary. Some legal provisions even protect the corporate entity from the shareowners themselves.

Descriptive Evidence

There is ample case and anecdotal evidence of the descriptive accuracy of the stakeholder model from corporate sources. The widely cited Caux Roundtable *Principles for Business* (1994) recognizes a conventional list of stakeholder interests. The Hitachi Foundation's 1997 *Global Corporate Citizenship—Rationale and Strategies* presents a strong case for the strategic importance of corporate citizenship, and focuses attention on the challenges of working with specific stakeholder groups.

Individual corporations often state their commitment to stakeholders. For example, Novartis, a global pharmaceutical firm, published the following statement on its web site (1999): "We aspire to capture and hold a leadership position in all of our businesses with a strong, sustainable performance based on continuous innovation. Our long-term success is founded on meeting the expectations of all our stakeholders—our customers, our people, our shareholders and the communities in which we live." The purpose of such codes, statements, and policies is to codify the importance and role of stakeholders to the corporation. This idea was expressed by Bell Atlantic CEO Ivan Seidenberg, who stated (1998, p. 11) that his firm (now called Verizon) was developing "new ways of behavior that give people—our customers, the government, our stakeholders and suppliers—confidence that we know how to act (to do what is right). . . . That marketplace confidence becomes our competitive edge." The prevalence of these expressions is reported among major corporations in Europe (Wheeler and Sillanpaa, 1997) and Australia (Suggett, 2000) as well as the United States.

In a particularly interesting case, Tom Chappell, founder and president of Tom's of Maine, a consumer health products firm, recounts his own discovery of the philosophical notion of "being as relation" in a course at the Harvard Divinity School, and tells how this idea caused him to reinterpret the status of his own firm "not only as a private entity but in relation to many other entities" (1993, pp. 15–19). His book gives a short sketch of his beliefs, which are essentially the same as the stakeholder model pictured in Figure 1.1.

Formal survey studies over a span of several decades show that many managers describe their operations in similar "relational" terms (Baumhart, 1968; Brenner and Molander, 1977; Posner and Schmidt, 1984; Wang and Dewhirst, 1992). Three recent studies confirm and strengthen these results. Steger (1998) gathered responses from about 300 European managers through questionnaires, interviews, and focus groups; and a similar study by Agle, Mitchell, and Sonnenfeld (1999) analyzed questionnaires returned by 80 CEOs of major U.S. firms. The main conclusion of both of these studies is that senior managers recognize both business-sector and external stakeholders, and that they view the former—shareowners, employees, customers—as more important than the latter. Similar results were obtained from a smaller sample of firms, plus selective interviews, by Logsdon and Lewellyn (2000), who found that stakeholder-performance measures concentrated on shareowners, customers, and employees.

These findings are not surprising. Stakeholders functionally linked to the firm through the value chain have obvious roles in organizational stability, growth, and wealth creation. Moreover, managers have many more numerous and frequent contacts—and therefore more possibilities for favorable or unfavorable outcomes—with shareowners, employees, and customers than with other stakeholders. However, all of these studies also found that there is considerable variation in the perceived importance of particular types of stakeholders among firms and industries. For example, external stakeholders such as governments and regulatory agencies are highly salient for corporations operating in regulated industries, as Robert Miles's classic study of the insurance industry (1987) clearly demonstrates.

Common experience, as well as our own research, reveals that the relative importance of different kinds of stakeholders varies greatly among firms, as well as among various critical management issues. Customers are probably more important for product quality issues, employees for workplace safety issues, communities and governments for environmental issues, and so forth. The importance of particular issues to particular stakeholders also varies over time, and different groups have different time horizons. The important point for management is that stakeholder concerns and priorities are varied and dynamic; hence, stakeholder management is necessarily an ongoing process, flexible and situation specific. Every class of stakeholders could probably identify some specific category of potential benefit or harm as being of top priority; each could probably identify implicit or explicit cutoff points at which they would cease to cooperate with the firm if minimum expectations are not met.

Instrumental Implications

The descriptive accuracy of the stakeholder model as a picture of the modern corporation implies that management policies and practices that take account of multiple stakeholder interests will prove advantageous. If corporate performance depends upon favorable interactions with multiple stakeholders, then strengthening linkages with critical stakeholders should result in firmwide benefits. Thus, stakeholder management should contribute to stability, growth, profitability, and other commonly recognized indicators of business success.

Wheeler and Sillanpaa (1997) demonstrate this, and the philosophy is reflected in many corporate documents and reports (such as Hitachi Foundation, 1997) and academic analyses (Jones, 1995).

The strategic connection between stakeholder management and the overall performance of the corporation is, in fact, the principal focus of this research. That the relationship between the two is strong is enshrined in a long tradition of corporate rhetoric. As early as 1950, General Robert E. Wood, then CEO of Sears, identified customers, employees, community, and stockholders as the "four parties to any business," adding, "I have named them in what I regard as the order of their importance." He believed that "if the other three parties . . . are properly taken care of, the stockholder will benefit in the long pull" (quoted in Worthy, 1984, p. 64). More recently, John Kay (1995, p. 8), an experienced U.K.-based analyst and consultant, stated: "A firm adds value through the distinctive character of the relationships it establishes with its stakeholders—its employees, customers, shareholders, and suppliers." And Jensen's concept of "enlightened stakeholder theory" arises from the observation (2000, p. 50) that "it is obvious that we cannot maximize the long-term market value of an organization if we ignore or mistreat any important constituency."

Over the past few decades, the possibility that there might be some association between conventional indicators of corporate performance and the presence or absence of stakeholder-oriented policies and practices has been extensively explored in the academic literature. The most comprehensive survey lists 83 published studies on this topic during 1972–2000 (Margolis and Walsh, 2001). Some of these studies utilize data purporting to reflect corporate attention to particular stakeholder interests (employees or communities, for example), whereas others are based on broader indicators of general social performance and reputation. Some of the individual studies report diverse (and sometimes inconsistent) results.

Margolis and Walsh conclude that 48 of 83 studies reveal positive relationships between indicators of social and financial performance; 17 show mixed results; and 19 show no relationships at all. Only three studies conclude that social and financial performance are negatively associated (poor social performance accompanied by good financial performance). An earlier study of 50 published studies produced similar results (Roman, Hayibor, and Agle, 1999).

One of the most recent studies focusing on the 500 largest public corporations found that those that mentioned their commitment to stakeholder interests and codes of conduct in their annual reports (more than 100 firms) reported superior financial performance to those that did not (Verschoor, 1998). Another study, based on new data and methodology, indicates that managerial attention to employee and customer stakeholders is associated with favorable financial performance, but no other stakeholder-related effects are observed (Berman, Wicks, Kotha, and Jones, 1999).

All of these studies are subject to serious criticisms about data reliability and completeness, time period of coverage, statistical methodology, and interpretation of results. The safest generalization from them is that the empirical evidence on this matter is somewhat unreliable and the results mixed. However, it is important to note that there is very little evidence of a *negative* association between social and financial performance—that is, that undesirable social performance is profitable. To put it another way, the empirical studies do not prove that corporations can "do well by doing good," but neither do they disprove that view, and there is no substantial evidence that corporations can "do well by doing harm" (Frooman, 1997).

Even a relatively weak "doing well *and* doing good" interpretation of the statistical results raises a significant cause-effect issue. Do companies do well financially because they recognize and respond to the concerns of diverse stakeholders, or do they adopt broad and socially responsive practices because they are financially secure and able to do so? Some studies have attempted to address this question through lead-lag analysis (Preston and O'Bannon, 1997), but the statistical problems are so great that the results cannot be taken too seriously. Burke and Logsdon (1996) have developed a plausible theoretical argument that various types of socially responsible behavior can be favorably linked to various dimensions of corporate strategy. We extend their analysis in our discussion of stakeholder relations and organizational wealth in the next chapter.

Normative Implications

The accuracy of the stakeholder model also carries normative implications; that is, it suggests guidelines for the behavior of all parties involved, particularly managers. If the corporation is a network of linkages with and among stakeholders and requires their support for its existence and operation, then it follows that this network should be managed, if possible, to provide the stakeholders collectively with benefits. When viewed this way, one tends to wonder how else it would be managed. Indeed, it might be argued that basic stakeholder-corporation relationships are essentially "natural" phenomena, arising from the inherent characteristics of the corporate system. The American Law Institute commentary on Principles of Corporate Governance (1992, p. 72, italics added) affirms this position:

> The modern corporation *by its nature* creates interdependencies with a variety of groups with whom the corporation has a legitimate concern, such as employees, customers, suppliers, and members of the communities in which the corporation operates.

Following this line of thought, Donaldson and Preston (1995) assert two fundamental propositions:

1. Stakeholders identify themselves because of their interest in the corporation (regardless of the corporation's functional interest or lack of interest in them).

2. The interests of all stakeholders have intrinsic value and merit consideration (although not all of the desires of every group of stakeholders can or should be satisfied.)

Acceptance of these two propositions defines a kind of *organizational morality* that forms the normative "core" of the stakeholder model: legitimate stakeholder interests require managerial recognition and attention as a matter of moral right. (An analogy to the two-way moral relationship between child and parent is too strong, but suggests the idea. It is morally unacceptable for either party to say "I don't care" about the other, but not inevitable that either will accede willingly to all of the other's demands.)

A recent article by Jones and Wicks (1999) argues that neither the instrumental view (stakeholder management is economically sound management) nor the normative view (stakeholder management is ethically "good" management) is complete in itself. They believe that the two perspectives can be integrated through a focus on relationships emphasizing trust and coopera-tion rather than contracts and transactions. Their presentation has touched off an ongoing round of controversy and comment, and it is not certain that a theoretical perspective fully integrating the two themes will emerge. This book conforms to Jones and Wicks' position insofar as the instrumental and normative implications of the stakeholder model are entirely compatible with each other. The two perspectives are often mixed—and sometimes fully integrated—in the company practices revealed in our own field studies.

Problems with the Model

The stakeholder model of the corporation appears to be plausible and rele-vant. However, when utilizing the model as a framework for management decision making, some important issues have to be addressed.

Identifying Stakeholders and Balancing Interests

Who are the stakeholders, and how can their interests be taken into account? Although the conventional classes of stakeholders—employees, customers, and so on—are universally recognized, their desires and levels of concern in many areas of management decision making are difficult to ascertain and may conflict. Establishing priorities and making choices among trade-offs are not easy, leading some managers to believe that comprehensive stakeholder man-agement is impossible. Jensen strongly criticizes conventional stakeholder analysis for refusing to specify appropriate trade-offs among competing inter-ests, so as to define a single-valued function suitable for maximizing (or at least increasing). He writes (2000, p. 52): "The absence of a scorecard makes it easier for people to engage in intense value claiming activities at the expense of value creation." This is certainly true, but trade-offs among stakeholder inter-ests vary from case to case; there is no universal way to generate a single-valued "corporate performance" function. Hence, identifying critical stakeholders and properly evaluating their concerns are always part of managers' role, whether or not they officially accept the stakeholder management approach. It seems likely that such situations can be dealt with more effectively and fairly—and possibilities for mutually satisfactory solutions more clearly examined—if they are identified and examined through managerial procedures, rather than addressed *ex post* and under crisis conditions. (For specific suggestions about stakeholder identification and prioritizing, see Mitchell, Agle, and Wood, 1997; Cummins and Doh, 2000.)

Shareowners as Stakeholders

The passive, attenuated, and frequently transient character of most shareowners' ownership relationship to the corporation has already been pointed out. But note, in addition, that shareowners are unique among *contractual* stakeholders in that the specific benefits they gain from association with the firm are *residual*—in other words, they come only after all other claims have been settled. This applies not only to the distribution of net income after the discharge of all costs, but also to the appreciation or depreciation of capital values as well. As a result, the situation of shareowners, who appear to be the stakeholders most closely linked to the firm because of their ownership and formal (but largely irrelevant) role in corporate governance, is much like that of noncontractual involuntary third parties, such as communities. Each is affected by whatever the firm intentionally or inadvertently produces, but has very little effect on the firm itself except through quasi-political and *ex post* processes. (Shareowners can, of course, easily withdraw from their corporate relationships; many involuntary stakeholders cannot.)

The representation of shareowner interests through third-party fiduciaries, the largest of which often pursue their own agendas, further complicates the shareowners-as-stakeholders situation. Some of the largest fiduciaries— CalPERS and NYCERS, TIAA-CREF, and church-related funds—have actively advocated broader and more long-term management perspectives, closely akin to stakeholder management principles. Many have chosen to limit their range of investment choices through "screens" and decision criteria that support their policy positions (Kinder, Lydenberg, and Domini, 1993) Thus, whether shares are owned directly or through third parties, it is difficult for corporate managers to know what goals the shareowners of the firm would like to pursue. Similarly, it can be difficult for the shareowners to make their views known, or even to know whether desired goals have actually been achieved.

Managers as Stakeholders

The normative implications of the stakeholder model give rise to a serious dilemma about the role of managers within the corporate system. (Throughout this book, "manager" refers to a person or group vested with decision-making authority and consequent responsibility, regardless of level or title.) On one hand, managers are stakeholders in their own right and can reasonably be expected to try to advance their own interests. But they are also arbiters and mediators of all stakeholder interests, and are responsible for the success and viability of the enterprise as a whole (Jones and Hill, 1992). There is often a conflict between these two roles. Both survey and anecdotal evidence, to say nothing of current news stories, provide ample evidence of the tendency of top-level managers to treat their own wealth and well-being as the primary goal of the firm.

Complex compensation schemes have been designed to overcome the so-called "principal-agent" problem, and to motivate managers to pursue objectives that are consistent with those of shareowners. Arrangements to assure managerial attention to the concerns of employees, customers, or others are still rare, but even minimum recognition of the stakeholder network probably exerts some influence on the actions of managers. The possibility of strikes, law suits, lost markets, and regulatory proceedings precipitated by nonowner stakeholders doubtless creates pressure for managers to attend to their interests. This is true even though most of these actions, like those of dissatisfied shareowners, occur after the fact and have uncertain outcomes.

The loyalty managers owe to the firm is a matter of law, and managers who place their firm in jeopardy are often sacked, and sometimes fined or even jailed. But beyond these formal constraints, managers have an obligation to all stakeholders, even when it requires balancing their own stakeholder interests against those of others. The reason for attracting more explicit attention and commitment to the concept is to increase managerial attention to the diversity of stakeholder interests and to the possibility of mutual gains and unavoidable tradeoffs in the distribution of benefits among stakeholders, including themselves (see Jones, 1995).

CONCLUSION

The conventional notion that the corporation should create wealth only for its shareowners is incorrect. The corporation should be redefined to emphasize its relationships with and responsibilities toward *all* stakeholders, both voluntary and involuntary. This broader definition is consistent with widely held views about the nature of the corporation, and also with some empirical studies of corporate performance. The stakeholder model of the corporation fits in with broadly accepted normative and ethical considerations.

Chapter 2 integrates the stakeholder model with a broad conception of organizational wealth to develop an original "stakeholder view" of the corporation.

2

ORGANIZATIONAL WEALTH
AND THE STAKEHOLDER VIEW

The purpose of the corporation is to create wealth. At their best, firms create wealth for their employees in the form of compensation, working conditions, and career opportunities; for their customers in the form of product and service benefits that are worth more than they pay for them; for investors, whether as shareholders or lenders; and for suppliers, communities, and governments.

Fundamentally, a corporation creates wealth by increasing its capacity to generate such benefits over time. The success of the corporation in creating and distributing wealth accounts for its current global prominence and popularity as an economic and social institution. The sustainability and growth of this system depends, in large measure, upon the continued demonstration that the benefits obtained are worth more than the resources, time, effort, and inconvenience involved in the wealth-creation process; that is, that the positives of corporate activity outweigh the negatives.

The stakeholder concept of the corporation implies that favorable relationships and linkages with stakeholders, both internal and external, are important assets of the firm. Indeed, they are part of its current wealth and its capacity to generate more wealth in the future. Chapter 1 summarized some statistical analyses of associations between measures of financial performance and various indicators of stakeholder orientation and ethical management practices. None of those prove that companies can "do well by doing good," but they do suggest that stakeholder-oriented business practices are not inconsistent with conventional financial and market success.

This chapter presents a broad concept of *organizational wealth*, including but extending beyond conventional accounting and financial measures. It also introduces the core concept of this study, the *stakeholder view (SHV)*, which states that mutually beneficial stakeholder relationships can enhance the wealth-creating capacity of the corporation. This view is then compared and integrated with the "industry-structure" and "resource-based" views already established in the strategic management literature.

ORGANIZATIONAL WEALTH

Organizational wealth is the cumulative result of corporate performance over time, including all of the assets, competencies, and revenue-generating capacities developed by the firm. Compared to less successful companies, wealthier firms can pay higher wages and offer better career opportunities, take greater risks, provide greater customer benefits, respond better to adversity, provide more value for shareowners, and maintain better relationships with other stakeholders. They can also increase their capacity to generate wealth in the future by reinvesting in their businesses, launching new and innovative ventures, buying other companies, and building their own internal enterprises. This chapter describes the contributions of intangible and relational assets to organizational wealth and explains some of the ways corporate managers can enhance long-term wealth creation by taking into account the interests of all stakeholders, not just shareowners.

Intangible Assets

Knowledgeable people are aware that there are sources of corporate value other than physical and financial assets. Managers, financial analysts, and accountants realize that know-how, core competencies, tacit knowledge, information bases, operating routines, well-known brand names, market contacts, and other intangibles can increase the value of an already successful company, as compared to a start-up or less experienced firm whose other resources are the same.

Until the bubble burst in mid-2000, the intangible assets that led to the late-1990s high market valuations of many technology and knowledge-based companies seemed to confirm this. So did the mergers and acquisitions in which the purchaser paid premiums far in excess of the value of the physical and financial assets of the companies being bought. Companies being reorganized also were able to take great advantage of their intangibles. (For details on the worldwide situation at that time, see *Economist*, 1999; Condon, 1999; and Rindova and Fombrun, 1999). Regardless of the recent fluctuations in the values of high-tech stocks, which were greatly inflated in comparison to their physical and financial assets, it is still true that a firm's intangibles are valuable. Fombrun (1996), for example, refers to the "reputational capital" of the firm.

Intangible assets can be represented by the accounting concept of *goodwill,* a catchall category for going-concern values not recorded elsewhere on the balance sheet. The value of goodwill is rarely made explicit except in connection with corporate acquisitions, when the "goodwill premium" is simply any amount paid by acquirers greater than the total value that can be attributed to other identified assets of the acquired firm. American accounting practice requires that goodwill premiums be made explicit in purchase acquisitions and then written off through depreciation in future years. However, goodwill premiums need not be made explicit when mergers occur through "pooling of interests," which for this and other reasons has become the preferred transaction mode. The Financial Accounting Standards Board recently considered restrictions on the use of pooling and other proposals to bring intangible assets onto conventional balance sheets (Lev and Zarowin, 1998; Jennings and Thompson, 1996; Lev, 2001).

The "balanced scorecard" concept developed by Kaplan and Norton (1996) was inspired by a belief that the ability of a company to mobilize and exploit its intangible or invisible assets has become a decisive factor in competitive success. These authors think it highly desirable to expand financial accounting systems to include intangibles, but they acknowledge the difficulties of doing so. They mention, for example, a client who insisted that "outstanding environmental and community performance" was a critical part of the company's value. The client said that, in the face of changing circumstances, "we expect to have earned the right to continue operations." Kaplan and Norton believe that "all stakeholder interests, when they are vital for the success of the business unit's strategy," can—and should—be incorporated into their flexible "balanced scorecard" analysis (p. 35). The importance of a firm's broad "license to operate" is further discussed in Chapter 4.

These ideas have yet to be reflected in financial reporting requirements, but a number of companies have included intangibles in their regular financial and operating reports. For example, since 1994 the Swedish insurance company Skandia has distinguished between "structural capital," such as business partnerships and customer loyalty, and "human capital," such as the specific capabilities of employees. Skandia chief executive Leif Edvinsson argues that the values of both can be measured and related to conventional corporate performance indicators (Edvinsson and Malone, 1997). The fact that distinctive but intangible assets such as widely recognized brand names, superior supply chain and distribution linkages, talented and creative personnel, good employee relations, and so forth, may be sources of long-term corporate value is understood by investors. Although accounting practice lags such developments, it is likely to eventually develop measures and methods for incorporating this value into the organizational wealth equation.

Market Valuation of Intangible Assets

The value of intangible assets is closely related to, and often mixed with, the role of more general trends and expectations in the market valuation of firms. A commonly used indicator of changing investor preferences for particular stocks is the price-earnings ratio (P/E), the ratio of the stock price to annual earnings per share. If ownership interests in all companies were equally attractive to investors, then the current market value of a given flow of income would be the same, regardless of its source, and therefore P/E ratios for all stocks would be identical. It is often said that a dollar of income from a high P/E firm is worth more, but this is untrue; a dollar of current income is worth a dollar regardless of its source. However, the current market value of ownership interests in different firms, relative to their respective current earnings per share, varies because of anticipated differences in their future earnings and/or capital values. And it is common knowledge that investors use nonfinancial information, including information on stakeholder relations, to assess prospects for future business success and investment value.

Other indicators of differences between "going-concern" values and conventional accounting data can be computed from the balance sheet. The market-to-book ratio, defined as the ratio of the stock market value of the firm (stock price times number of shares outstanding) to the equity value of the firm (assets, including retained earnings, minus liabilities) is widely used for this purpose. Lev's research shows that market-to-book ratios have, on average, increased considerably in recent years, particularly in R&D-intensive industries, and he interprets this as indicating the value of "knowledge assets" (Lev and Zarowin, 1999). However, the general relevance of this statistic is questionable because nonfinancial assets are usually carried on the balance sheet on the basis of their historical costs, less subsequent depreciation. This practice creates significant (but unknowable) distortions in the computation of equity values, and therefore in the comparability of this statistical artifact among firms.

Nobel Laureate James Tobin has suggested a different statistic to provide a more accurate estimate of the distinctive contribution of a business organization to the value of the economic resources under its control. This statistic, referred to as "Tobin's q," is defined as the ratio of the market value of assets (as indicated by the value of a firm's equity and debt securities) to the estimated replacement cost of these assets. If the market places a higher value on the collection of resources under the firm's control than these resources alone would command in the marketplace, then this additional value must be attributable to its "going-concern" status, including its intangible attributes and its market position. (Note that the effects of broad external trends are, in principle, removed from this indicator, because their impact should be reflected in the replacement cost of the assets.) Hence, "Tobin's q," if it could be readily calculated, might be an effective indicator of the value of the intangible assets of the firm. The data necessary to calculate this ratio are hard to obtain, but there is some evidence that firms with intangibles such as strong brand images, reputations, and "know-how" do, indeed, have higher q values (Lindberg and Ross, 1981, cited in Brearly and Myers, 1996, pp. 774–6). The most extensive large-scale study based on Tobin's q is Smithers and Wright (2000).

Relational Assets

Because it is hard to estimate the value of intangibles directly, some analysts today emphasize the ways that the value-creating capacity of a firm can be increased. These factors include developing "human capital" through training, job assignment, and other individual-focused programs; others emphasize accumulated knowledge, know-how, and intellectual property. Perhaps the most original current approach, however, is based on relationships, both among individuals and units within an organization and between any focal entity or organization, on one hand, and other entities, groups, and organizations, on the other.

Leana and Rousseau begin their analysis of "relational wealth" as follows (2000, p. 3):

> Work—and how it is carried out in organizations—is fundamentally about relationships: relationships between a firm and its employees; relationships of employees with one another; relationships between a firm and its investors, suppliers, partners, regulators and customers.

Blair and Stout (1999) describe the purpose of corporate law as an attempt to deal with the relationships involved in "team production"; that is, to provide a vehicle by which shareowners, creditors, executives, employees, and other stakeholders can gain individual benefits for themselves by jointly producing a "nonseparable output." Dyer and Singh (1998) stress the value of interfirm relationships, focusing particularly on the supply chain as viewed from the perspective of a particular "nodal" firm. A similar analysis, from a marketing perspective, is presented by Keep, Hollander, and Dickinson (1999). Donaldson and Dunfee (1999) argue that implicit normative agreements ("microsocial contracts") reduce opportunism and shirking among stakeholders, thus decreasing rise and enhancing a firm's economic performance. All these writers view the firm as operating within a network of relationships, both internal and external, that can have positive or negative impact on its overall performance and value depending on the way in which they are structured, managed, and mediated.

Interest in relational assets and their impact on corporate performance has been stimulated by their importance in new, knowledge-based industries and by the prominence of strategic alliances and other forms of interfirm collaboration in the global economy. The importance of some critical stakeholder relationships has also been revealed by "negative evidence," that is, unfavorable consequences apparently associated with their absence or neglect. In their analysis of "what went wrong at IBM," for example, Mills and Friesen (1996, pp. 180–1) declare that "Any business runs on two relationships: with its customers and with its employees. . . . IBM broke its contracts with both . . . ; the whole story of its decline can be told in these terms." They found that transformations and changes underway in an effort to correct this situation included an emphasis on team contributions and employees as assets, and a recognition that quality is ultimately defined by customers, not by IBM's technical standards and cost structures. They believe that IBM has partially succeeded in modifying its social contract with the two key stakeholder groups, but that its ultimate success, in the face of strong relationship-oriented competitors and rapid technological change that it can no longer control, is still uncertain.

The story of General Motors during the 1980s is much the same. Maryann Keller (1989, p. 30) describes GM's traditional posture toward stakeholders as "contemptuous paternalism." Employees, for example, were assured of good wages, job security, and little pressure for performance, but their own concerns and goals received little attention. The views of customers were similarly disregarded; GM knew best. According to Keller (p. 114), the GM-Toyota NUMMI joint venture of 1983 was a revelation:

> The Toyota secret was, finally, no secret at all, and it was as old as history. Treat both white- and blue-collar workers with respect. . . . Combine that culture with a good car and quality parts, and the results were obvious. . . . At NUMMI, Toyota would demonstrate a business strategy based on trust, respect and teamwork.

By 1985, when GM was ready to launch its own Saturn venture based on the NUMMI learning experience, it followed the example of the Japanese auto companies and chose an entirely new operating environment in which it could create a new set of stakeholders. It also attempted to create new kinds of relationships with key stakeholders, both customers (no price negotiation) and employees (participative representation throughout the operating structure). CEO Roger Smith's intention was that ideas from the Saturn venture would spread "like a virus" throughout the company (Keller, 1989, p. 96). By the end of the much-discussed GM management conference held at Traverse City, Michigan, in October 1988, GM executives found themselves committed to a "philosophy founded on the beliefs and values of trust in our people, teamwork, continual improvement and customer satisfaction" (p. 242).[1]

Anecdotal evidence supports the view that relationships with internal and external stakeholders may be of critical importance for the success of the corporation. This argument is developed in detail, with numerous examples, by Coff and Rousseau (2000, p. 29):

> By its very nature, relational wealth *mediates* among the attributes and capacities of people, groups, and firms (including firms' human and financial capital) and affects successful work coordination, task performance, and goal achievement. For inimitable benefits to accrue from inputs, they must be bound together in an inimitable way.

As for the role of relationships as sources of competitive advantage, they note that even if competitors know that a firm's strategic capability is built on stakeholder linkages, "such ties are so complex and idiosyncratic that they cannot be readily copied" (p. 27).

The Role of Trust

The role of trust in personal and social life has recently become an important focus of analysis and discussion throughout the social sciences (Bercerra and Gupta, 1999). Fukuyama (1995) emphasizes that trust is a kind of "social glue" that enables people to work together without reducing every interaction to explicit bargaining and formal contracting. Putnam (2000) stresses the importance of "social capital," based upon trust, that both facilitates and results

---

[1] Although apparently successful within its own scope, Saturn has not become a model for other GM units or other companies. Indeed, Saturn continues to be viewed as a controversial anomaly by both business and labor (Kochan and Rubinstein, 2000).

from collaborative activities among individuals. Ring and Van de Ven (1992) and Jeffries and Reed (2000) view trust in the business world as a feature of "relational contracting," a middle ground between the conventional alternatives of fully negotiated market exchange and complete integration within an organizational hierarchy (Williamson, 1975). The terms of relational contracts are intentionally incomplete; "the intent of the contracting parties is to work together, [but] the potential for opportunistic behavior does exist" (Jeffries and Reed, 2000, p. 874). Ring and Van de Ven (p. 488) conclude that "some element of trust will be required for any transaction in which simultaneous exchange is unavailable to the parties," a situation that is almost universal in modern business.

Contemporary analysis of trust focuses on the characteristics of the trustor (the party who trusts), the trustee (the party who is trusted), and the role of risk (Mayer, Davis, and Schoorman, 1995). A critical aspect of trust relationships within and between managerial organizations is that they are typically reciprocal. Each party is both a trustor, dependent upon the behavior of the other, and a trustee, expected to perform in accordance with the other party's intentions. (For example, managers expect employees to come to work, and employees expect managers to pay them for their efforts.) There is some debate about the role of risk in trust relationships, but there is no doubt that actions based on trust leave the trustor vulnerable to the behavior of the trustee, and are therefore inherently risky. Trust does not reduce (and may actually increase) risks, but it is also expected to reduce transactions costs (Nooteboom, 1999). There may, of course, be other costs associated with the development of long-term trust relationships.

The presence or absence of trust within and between organizations presents a serious challenge to economic analysis and to conventional contractual-transactional approaches to management (Ghoshal and Moran, 1996). These analytical traditions tend to treat trust as an aspect of the "principal-agent problem," which focuses on the development of explicit or implicit contractual relationships to insure that the trustee (agent) behaves in a fashion consistent with the goals and intentions of the trustor (principal). By contrast, according to Mayer and others (1995), trustworthiness depends upon three characteristics of the trustee:

Ability—The trustee is believed to possess the resources and competence to perform in the desired manner.

Benevolence—The trustee is believed to *want* to behave in ways that will benefit (or at least not harm) the trustor.

Integrity—The trustee is believed to adhere to a set of principles that are acceptable to the trustor.

Again, the fact that intra- and interorganizational trust relationships tend to be reciprocal, each party trusting and being trusted by the other, implies that these characteristics must be displayed by both sides. Some attempts to develop empirical measures of the levels of trust between business organizations are beginning to appear in the literature (Nooteboom, 1999; Dyer and Chu, 2000).

It is easy to see that mutual trust is a desirable attribute of stakeholder relationships. The more reliance can be placed upon common understandings and shared benefits—as opposed to detailed negotiations and formal contracting—the less costly, time-consuming, and restrictive the interactions between a corporation and its stakeholders will be. Hence, the development of social capital through trustworthy behavior—both vis-à-vis individual stakeholder groups and in relation to all actual and potential stakeholders, and to society at large—is an obvious way of enhancing organizational wealth over the long term. Some authors, however, believe that there is an upper limit to the benefits of trust, and that there is an optimal balance between cost-reducing trust and cautionary distrust (Wicks, Berman, and Jones, 1999). Jeffries and Reed state that "too much trust is as bad as too little" (2000, p. 873). It is nevertheless clear than an understanding that individuals and organizations will act in predictable and mutually supportive ways is a critical feature of stakeholder-oriented policies, and is both a requirement and a result of proactive stakeholder management practices.

Organizational Wealth

Sveiby (1997) has developed a conception of organizational wealth that combines the value of tangible assets (less liabilities) and intangible elements to determine the total value of an organization. He classifies intangibles into three categories:

- Competence of personnel, reflected, for example, in skill levels, job satisfaction, and retention.
- Internal structure, such as arrangements for information handling and decision making.
- External structure, such as customer and supplier relations.

Both of Sveiby's structure categories are essentially relational, and there is also a clear connection between the competence of individuals and their ability to function within organizational units and teams. He analyzes how each set of intangible factors might explain the overall value of the organization in terms of three criteria: stability, growth/renewal, and efficiency. He proposes specific measures and indicators for each, and illustrates his approach in a case study of WM-Data, the largest publicly owned computer software and consulting company in Sweden. Based on the considerable current literature dealing with the importance and valuation of intangible and relational assets, and specifically on Sveiby's applied work, here is a definition of organizational wealth:

Organizational wealth is the summary measure of the capacity of an organization to create benefits for any and all of its stakeholders over the long term.

The principal components of organizational wealth are these:

- The market value of physical and financial assets (less liabilities).
- The value of individually separable intangible assets, such as specific human capital, patents, and licenses.
- The value of relational assets, both internal and external, involving stakeholder linkages, collaborations, processes and reputational factors (relational assets may combine both tangible and intangible elements, as in the case of collaborative R&D projects).

Organizational wealth is enhanced whenever the value of output from operations is increased without comparable increases in resources or risks, or when resource use and/or risks are reduced without comparable reductions in the value of the output. In its relationships with stakeholders, the corporation may achieve these results directly—as when favorable customer relations increase brand loyalty (reducing market risk)—or indirectly, as when improved collaboration and trust within the operating environment increases productivity. It appears that both specific and general effects can be achieved when the firm bases its relationships with stakeholders on mutually supportive contributions and benefits.

Of course, a harmonious operating environment is of value in itself, easing the tasks of individuals charged with managerial responsibilities and facilitating adaptation to change. The development of a culture of learning within an organization requires having in place a network of reciprocal trusting and trustworthy relationships based on mutual understanding and widely distributed benefits. In addition, favorable stakeholder relations can generate favorable response cycles; good community relations may help attract superior employees, strengthen customer loyalty, and so forth. Moreover, it is obvious that unfavorable relations with stakeholders can *reduce* organizational wealth, and that *negative* impacts often spread from one stakeholder group to another—as when threats of strikes or consumer boycotts have repercussions in the stock market, increasing the costs and risks of a firm's financing arrangements.

STAKEHOLDER RELATIONS AND ORGANIZATIONAL WEALTH

The sources of organizational wealth arising from relationships with each major stakeholder group are summarized in Table 2.1 and described in more detail below.

- *Investors: Shareowners and Lenders.* Investors, whether equity or debt holders, provide the capital necessary to finance the corporation. However, capital flows directly from the investor to the firm only in new stock offerings and bond issues. Nevertheless, it is the willingness (or unwillingness) of investors to hold the securities of a firm that determines the ease with which (and cost at which) additional capital can be raised. Although many corporate investors hold their interests through fiduciary institutions (mutual funds, pension funds, and the like),

Table 2.1
Stakeholder Contributions to Organizational Wealth

Stakeholders	Contributions
Investors: shareowners/lenders	Provision of capital, equity, and/or debt Financial market recognition and status (reducing borrowing costs and risks)
Employees	Development of specific human capital Team production and routines based on understanding and trust Collaborative relations in the workplace
Unions	Workforce stability and conflict resolution
Customers/users	Brand loyalty and reputation Repeated/related purchases Collaborative design, development, and problem solving
Supply chain associates	Network and value chain efficiencies Collaborative cost-reducing routines and technologies
Joint venture partners and alliances	Strategic resources and capabilities Options for future development (R&D, technology, etc.)
Local communities and citizens	Mutual support and accommodation Planning, municipal services "License to operate"
Governments	Macroeconomic and social policies Supportive relationships with policymakers
Regulatory authorities	Validation of specific product/service characteristics and quality levels Reputation for compliance, integrity, and best practice
Private organizations	Constructive collaboration with individual organizations and groups Favorable public opinion environment Voluntary normative standards (e.g., ISO 9000, UN Global Compact)

whether investor relationships are direct or indirect, favorable investor relations tend to stabilize corporate financial structures and plans. The term "patient capital" (Smith, Pfeffer, and Rousseau, 2000) has been applied to investors who are willing to hold stocks over the long term, without regard to temporary fluctuations in earnings or values, even when greater short-run returns appear to be available elsewhere. Reductions in financing costs and risks—and in the costs and media concerns associated with poor investor relations—contribute directly to the wealth and security of the organization. The belief that a firm attracts patient capital may also give employees and other stakeholders some assurance that their own commitments to the firm will not be jeopardized because of short-run financial pressures.

- *Employees.* Employees include everybody who works in an organization, including managers, staff, and line workers, whether union or nonunion workers. In most large organizations, employees comprise a large, diverse group of males and females of many nationalities, ethnic backgrounds, and ages. Favorable employee relations help reduce employee turnover and encourage long-term and cooperative commitment to the organization. Committed employees understand and accept the goals of the organization, and seek to enhance them through personal skill development, teamwork, constructive suggestions, and a willingness to walk the extra mile. As Prusak and Cohen (2001) have observed, employee communication is the unique asset that flows from such social capital. A reputation for good employee relations and personal development opportunities is, of course, a major advantage in recruiting and retaining a talented workforce.

- *Unions.* Where labor unions are present, mutually respectful and cooperative relationships with them are essential for business success. Unfavorable relationships virtually guarantee conflicts, negative publicity, financial market pressures, and other wealth-reducing developments. Collaborative relations with unions can reduce labor turnover, increase the stability and productivity of the workforce, and help to resolve the conflicts that inevitably arise in large, complex organizations. Kochan and Rubinstein (2000) argue that local unions contribute to firm performance by organizing workers into a "dense social network" that contributes to problem solving, conflict resolution, and quality improvement.

- *Customers/Users.* Customers and users also come in many forms and sizes, and there are substantial differences between a firm's relationships with large industrial and OEM (original equipment manufacturer) customers on one hand and household consumers on the other. Yet, in all cases, a reputation for product quality, reliable and competent service, and fair pricing tends to pay off in customer loyalty. And, as the literature on relationship marketing emphasizes, customer loyalty to brand and firm reduces marketing costs, and stabilizes production and sales volume (Webster, 1992). Favorable customer relations also can lead to active collaboration in product and service design, further attracting and holding customers to the firm.

- *Supply Chain Associates.* The potential benefits of favorable relationships with members of the firm's entire "value chain," including suppliers, contractors, and subcontractors (and market-channel relationships with wholesalers, distributors, and franchisees) are vital to firm success. Combined with favorable investor, employee, and customer contacts, these value chain relationships form the core of the organization's capacity to generate wealth over time. Familiarity and mutual trust can lead to new cost savings, operating procedures, design collaborations, redistribution of tasks among organizations for greater efficiency, and reductions of risks and costs associated with potential unreliability (such as large "just-in-case" inventory holdings).

- *Joint Venture Partners and Alliances.* Formal joint venture partners and contractual allies can give rise to the same wealth-enhancing benefits as supply chain associates. They also add to the diversity of physical and intangible resources (knowledge, reputation) available to the firm. Such alliances can also reduce financial and nonfinancial risk through closer, more knowledgeable managerial control.

- *Local Communities and Citizens.* The wealth-enhancing advantages of good relations with local communities and citizens can scarcely be overstressed. The phrase "social license to operate," widely used in the chemical, mining, and petroleum industries, means more than just good citizenship. It implies that the firm is accepted as an integral and valuable entity within the immediate political and institutional setting, and enjoys the support (or at least does not attract the hostility) of members of the general public. A firm that enjoys favorable community relationships can be a regular participant in local community planning and problem solving, and can have a chance to present its own side of the story when problems or opportunities arise. Reasonable treatment with respect to local tax and service fees can also have direct impact on operating costs and risks.

- *Governments.* Any firm of substantial size operates in many political jurisdictions and has critical relationships with government at every level—local, state, regional, national—and with intergovernmental and international bodies. National governments and international organizations affect the conditions under which all firms do business, including international trade and investment arrangements, taxation structures, macroeconomic policies, and social concerns such as human rights and environmental protection. Subnational governments may have critical influence on operating conditions, land use issues, and other matters critical to the corporation. The influence of government goes far beyond the scope of industry-specific regulatory authority. For example, during recent decades some of the most technologically advanced companies in the United States have been accused of antitrust violations—IBM and AT&T during the 1970–80s, Microsoft in the 1990s. Their experiences highlight the importance of corporate-government relations and the effective management of the public affairs function. Regardless of the technical issues involved, it was apparent that these firms received generally favorable public acceptance for their side of the story. By contrast, increasing public hostility toward the tobacco industry and toward producers and distributors of firearms during the 1990s resulted in extraordinary litigation costs, fines, and damages, with substantial negative impact on the wealth of the firms involved.

- *Regulatory Authorities.* Relations with industry-specific or function-specific government regulatory bodies are of critical importance to the firm. Regulations may be costly and have direct, negative effects on organizational wealth. Government regulatory systems (such as agricultural product grading by the FDA) may serve as an indicator of product quality more valuable than the debatable claims of advertising, and a corporate reputation for regulatory compliance, integrity, and the use of "best practice" technologies may have favorable impacts on other stakeholders.

- *Private Organizations.* Private organizations such as trade associations, voluntary standards-setting groups, and cause-oriented activists may both support and challenge the wealth-creating activities of corporations. Organizations related to the firm's own industry and interests (such as trade associations and research centers) provide benefits by pooling resources and knowledge from many firms in order to advance common goals. At the same time, industry-level organizations based in *other* industries may generate challenges and problems unless some basis for mutual benefit can be found. Similarly, the activities of critics and activists can require the firm to incur public relations and other expenses, including the "opportunity cost" associated with management's time and attention. But activist groups can also be helpful, enabling the firm to identify legitimate issues and respond to them in ways that improve its performance and reputation for openness, social concern, and citizenship. For example, the Environmental Defense Fund brought together a coalition of firms to collaborate on reducing greenhouse gas emissions (*New York Times*, October 18, 2000). In dealing with these diverse interests, the stakeholder-oriented firm seeks ways in which the concerns and activities of such organizations can generate wealth-enhancing effects.

THE STAKEHOLDER VIEW

The *stakeholder view (SHV)* of the corporation holds that the capacity of a business enterprise to generate sustainable wealth, and hence long-term value, is determined by its relationships with critical stakeholders. The SHV is based on the fact that every firm has critical stakeholders in every dimension of its strategic environment—resource base, industry structure, and social and political setting. Favorable and mutually beneficial relationships with these stakeholders enable the firm to create wealth, whereas conflict limits or destroys wealth. The stakeholder view stands in theoretical and practical contrast to other views. We argue that organizational wealth, including both the tangible and intangible assets of the corporation and the value of its reputation and network of external relationships, is increased by favorable relations (and reduced by unfavorable relations) with its significant stakeholders. Empirical observation and logical analysis reveal limitations of the contemporary resource-based view (RBV) and industry-structure view (ISV) of the corporation, both of which are derived from economic analysis. The stakeholder view (SHV) presented here integrates and supplements the RBV and ISV into a broader framework of considerations.

There is an ongoing and vigorous debate between adherents of the resource-based and industry structure views. Penrose (1959) is generally credited with formalizing the RBV in the management literature, although the idea that the unique resources and capabilities of the firm determine its market success has long been familiar. Porter (1980) introduced the ISV as a challenge to this perspective, arguing that the firm's ability to generate wealth depends upon its position within its industry, including relations with competitors, suppliers, and customers and the impact of government regulation. Wernerfelt (1984) responded that a resource-based analysis including access to capital, labor, locations, and technologies would lead to different insights than an analysis focused on industry structure. Barney (1991) concluded that a firm's success is ultimately determined by the value, rarity, inimitability, and substitutability of its resources—in other words, by economic scarcity. The validity of the RBV as a theory of the firm has recently been seriously challenged by Priem and Butler (2001), drawing an equally forceful response from Barney (2001).

Some scholars have sought to synthesize these views. Peteraf (1993), for example, offered a partial integration of RBV and ISV perspectives, combining resource characteristics and competitive conditions. Henderson and Mitchell (1997), editors of a special issue of *Strategic Management Journal* that focused on this topic, concluded that attempts to choose one explanation over the other would prove fruitless because there are continuous "reciprocal interactions" between the firm and its environment, with competition shaping capabilities, and capabilities in turn shaping competitive positions. Teece, Pisano, and Shuen (1997) moved the analysis into a dynamic framework, emphasizing that the *processes* of developing and utilizing the firm's resources were probably more important to its long-term success than *strategizing* about competitive activities and entry barriers. Hatten and Rosenthal (1999, 2001) argued that a firm's capacities and capabilities—rooted in knowledge acquired through its business processes—are central to long-term success. These recent contributions suggest some ways to overcome Schendel's earlier criticism that most strategic management research has been "static rather than dynamic, cross-sectional rather than longitudinal" and has paid inadequate attention to "path dependence" and "complex contingencies" (1997, pp. 1–2).

The stakeholder view (SHV) embraces elements of both the RBV and ISV within a framework that is both dynamic and longitudinal, with an emphasis on path dependencies. All of the firm's resources are represented in some way by various stakeholders, and it is the firm's relationships with stakeholders that make resources available to the organization. Similarly, customers, suppliers, regulators, and other players will be more (or less) collaborative, supportive, and reliable in their dealings with the firm depending on the kind of stakeholder relations the firm has developed with them. (Remember: the firm's competitors, although important elements of its industry structure, are not stakeholders in the firm as that term is used here because they hold no "stake" in the firm's successful performance.) It is not simply the firm's stock of resources nor its static position in the industry structure that determines its long-term success. Rather it is the dynamic interaction with customers, employees, suppliers, investors, and other stakeholders that generates the organizational capacity to generate wealth over time. That is the central implication of the stakeholder view for strategic management. The failure to establish and maintain productive relationships with all of the firm's stakeholders is a failure to effectively manage the organization's capacity to generate future wealth.

The distinctive features of the three views are summarized in Table 2.2, which broadens the "relational view" of the firm presented by Dyer and Singh (1999) to include all relevant stakeholders. Dyer and Singh stress that relational values are created by mutually beneficial collaboration among firms, and cannot be achieved by an individual firm acting alone (as implied by the RBV) or by one firm attempting to gain at the expense of others (as implied by

Table 2.2
Comparing Three Views of the Sources of Organization Wealth

Dimensions	Resource-Based View (RBV)	Industry Structure View (ISV)	Stakeholder View (SHV)
Unit of analysis	Firm	Industry	Network of a firm's stakeholders
Primary sources of organizational wealth	Physical assets Human resources Knowledge Technology Financial resources Intangibles	Bargaining power vis-à-vis suppliers and customers Market power vis-à-vis competitors Collusion	Relationships leading to increased revenues and/or reduced costs and risks Relational benefits leading to increased capacity to generate wealth
Means to preserve organizational wealth	Firm-level barriers to imitation	Industry-level barriers to entry: • Production economies/sunk costs • Government regulations	Firm-specific stakeholder linkages and implicit agreements leading to increased revenues and/or reduced costs and risks

the ISV). For example, relational benefits can be generated by collaboration between a firm and its suppliers, whereas the other views would suggest that such benefits should be captured through integration (RBV) or by playing off one supplier against another through aggressive bargaining (ISV). Dyer and Singh also note that both the RBV and ISV suggest that a firm should attempt to protect, rather than share, information and know-how. By contrast, firms linked in supply-chain and alliance relationships often gain by collaborative product and process development and by continuous and interactive exchange of data. Note also that the SHV (like the analyses of Teece, Pisano, and Shuen, 1997, and Hatten and Rosenthal, 1999, 2001) places much greater emphasis on managerial skills and processes than either of the other perspectives.

The relationship among the three views is further illustrated in Figure 2.1. To become operational, the firm must acquire resources (financial resources, labor, knowledge, technology) that are critical to its success. These factors are part of its resource base as emphasized by the RBV. Once in existence, the firm becomes embedded within its industry structure—including its competitors,

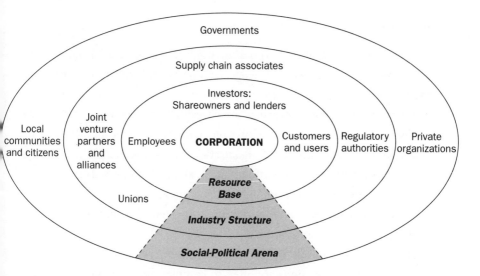

Figure 2.1 The Stakeholder View of the Corporation.

suppliers, and regulatory authorities. These structural characteristics are emphasized by the ISV. But in addition to being located within a resource field and an industry structure, the firm is also located within a social and political environment that includes individuals, groups, and interests that contribute to, and/or bear the risk of, its wealth-generating activities. It can no more ignore these stakeholders than it can operate without resources or ignore the features of its industry structure.

In Figure 2.1, the important groups of stakeholders identified in the conventional stakeholder map (Figure 1.1) are shown to be distributed at all three levels of the stakeholder view diagram. Investors and employees are sources of critical inputs for the firm's operations, and the customer base of the firm may also be considered a "resource." Supply chain associates, JV partners and alliances, unions, and regulators are elements of its industry structure. Governments, local communities and citizens, and relevant private and voluntary organizations operate in the social and political arena. Note that relative closeness to the center of the diagram does not indicate anything about the level of importance of any group of stakeholders; the "license to operate" from the firm's host environment is as important as its financial resources.

CONCLUSION

The stakeholder view of the corporation holds that collaborative linkages and behaviors based on shared knowledge, familiarity, and trust can increase revenues, reduce risks, and improve the operating efficiencies of the firm in ways that preserve and enhance organizational wealth. Organizational wealth in the modern corporation is *the capacity of an organization to create value over the long term*. The broad concept of organizational wealth presented in this chapter includes intangibles and relational assets, along with physical and financial resources. Managers have a responsibility to conserve and increase organizational wealth in ways that take into account the interests of all the firm's stakeholders, both internal and external.

Our analysis recognizes the central role of trust in business success. Both internal and external relations are often so complex and dynamic that formal bargaining and contracting is infeasible. Individuals working within organizations need to trust each other, and to trust the organization itself to live up to its responsibilities. And corporations need to trust one another as well to carry out collaborative activities for mutual benefit. Trust is the glue that holds together relationships that can not be fully defined in contractual terms. For the modern corporation, the trust of its stakeholders is an important component of its capacity to create value over the long term.

This chapter compared and contrasted the stakeholder view of the firm with the resource-based and industry-structure views already established in the strategic management literature. The stakeholder view is integrative, embracing elements of the firm's resource base and of its industry setting, but also recognizing actors in the social and political arena who are impacted by, and may have an impact upon, the operations of the firm.

Contemporary corporations encounter challenges and make decisions that can be understood and evaluated only within an interactive, multiple-stakeholder context. How relationships with stakeholders can contribute to overall corporate performance will be illustrated in greater detail in the following chapters.

3

RESEARCH DESIGN AND CRITICAL

ISSUES: THREE COMPANIES

Contemporary strategic management analysis recognizes that the essential core of a corporation consists of three interrelated elements—strategy, structure, and culture. The stakeholder view of the corporation, discussed in Chapters 1 and 2, involves all three and emphasizes the importance of their appropriate alignment, both internal and external, to the successful performance of the firm. This book demonstrates through case studies that corporations can achieve both competitive advantage and public legitimacy through stakeholder management that is derived from, and supported by, the key elements of the corporate core.

This chapter is a bridge between the theoretical analysis presented in Chapters 1 and 2 and the empirical research studies that follow. Here we explain the design of our research and state the major research questions that have guided our work. We also introduce Cummins, Motorola, and Royal Dutch/Shell, where we did much of our research, and identify the stakeholder relationships and issues that have been critical for each of them over the past quarter century. More detailed historical and statistical information on each of the companies is presented in the case studies at the end of the book. At the end of this chapter we introduce the problem of going beyond a single stakeholder environment, whether seen in "home" country or "host" country perspective, in order to globalize stakeholder management policies and practices.

The three companies described here are not perfect models; each has sometimes made operational and strategic mistakes with serious effects on their reputation and economic performance. But each has also experienced significant organizational learning about their stakeholder relationships and has made a serious long-term commitment to stakeholder management practices. Their overall corporate performance illustrates the validity of the stakeholder view as an explanation of the sources of organizational wealth.

RESEARCH METHODS AND QUESTIONS

In their introductory essay to a recent "Special Research Forum" in the *Academy of Management Journal,* Harrison and Freeman (1999, p. 482) draw a distinction between case studies "designed with a purpose" and those that "just happened," in the sense that the researcher chanced to observe an interesting situation and decided to write it up. They believe that the former type of study is most likely to contribute new knowledge, and cite Eisenhardt (1989) and Yin (1994) as providing guidelines for conducting "case research with a purpose." These guidelines include "entering the case study process with specific research questions and a deliberate case study design."

Most of the research for this project was carried out before the Harrison and Freeman essay was published, but we believe that we have met the criteria they endorse. Our central proposition is this: *The stakeholder view of the corporation is a distinct and significant addition to the strategic management literature; it integrates and builds upon other views and offers insight into important, and heretofore often neglected, sources of organizational wealth.* This proposition was developed on the basis of theory and the prior literature cited in Chapters 1 and 2. The remaining chapters in this book redefine the corporation in stakeholder terms and analyze the experience of three important, and very different, multinational firms over the past quarter century from this perspective.

The need for depth and comprehensiveness in this kind of research necessarily implies that only a small number of empirical cases can be examined. We began by identifying a number of firms that appeared to reflect a stakeholder orientation in their operations, and to which we could gain sufficient access for research purposes. Motorola and Shell were selected as research sites with a purpose. Although quite different from one another, both Motorola and

Shell presented unique windows into management thinking about stakeholder issues and relationships. While engaged in the process of site selection, we studied the history of Cummins Engine Company, which is well known for its distinctive approach to issues of business responsibility. The official company history, written by Jeffrey Cruikshank and David Sicilia (1997), documents the spontaneous and gradual evolution of stakeholder management within that firm. With the active collaboration of Sicilia, Cummins was added as a third research site. We were thus able to examine the evolution and impact of actual stakeholder management policies and practices in three distinctive corporate settings, supplemented by relevant examples from other firms.

Throughout this project, we focused on the following research questions:

- What is the essential character of the stakeholder commitment in each of these companies, and how has it evolved over time?
- How and why did each of them make and adapt this commitment?
- How is this commitment reflected in their strategy-structure-culture mix?
- What is the content of their stakeholder-oriented policies and practices?
- How are these policies and practices implemented, and with what results?
- What has been the impact of their stakeholder commitment on the overall performance of these firms over the long run, and on their ability to generate organization wealth?

Our study examines how the three companies were affected by fundamental social, economic, and technological trends over roughly a quarter century, and how they responded to major challenges and opportunities that arose during this period.

A longitudinal study of this type necessarily involves the analysis of *path dependencies*, the way in which developments during any time period depend upon events and situations that happened earlier. This concept, drawn from evolutionary theory, describes the cumulative adaptation of an organism to changes that occur over time. As applied to the study of the corporation, path dependencies become important when the prior experience of the organization strongly influences its response to new stimuli, both internal and external (Nelson and Winter, 1982; Nelson, 1995). Some path dependencies are conspicuous, overt, and deliberate; others appear to have occurred without being noticed by key actors and organizational units. For example, Cummins' responses to external developments appear to have emerged gradually from its corporate values and prior modes of operation. By contrast, Shell's responses to external challenges over the past decade involved a sharp break with the past and involved a major redirection of the firm. We also noted that responses are not equally enduring. Shell's responses to major external challenges during the 1990s were somewhat similar to the actions of Nestlé during the 1980s, following a controversy about that company's marketing practices in developing countries. Nestlé appears to have abandoned many of its innovative efforts (see Post in Williams, 2000), thereby raising questions about what is required to institutionalize change in large, global companies. Thus, the assessment of Shell's responses must be made with this experience in mind.

STRATEGY, STRUCTURE, AND CULTURE

Since the publication of Chandler's *Strategy and Structure* (1962), a classic study of a small number of major companies (DuPont, General Motors, Sears, and Standard Oil of New Jersey) that designed their strategy and structure to achieve high levels of performance, management scholars have understood the importance of alignment as a critical requirement for business success. Chandler's key finding was that strategy is the fundamental element in this mix. Strategic objectives should be established, and structural arrangements developed to support them, rather than the other way around. Both the resource-based view (RBV) and industry-structure view (ISV) of the firm are extensions of this conception. As noted in the preceding chapter, the RBV argues that the success or failure of the specific strategy-structure combination adopted by the firm depends upon its ability to acquire and develop unique combinations of resources. The ISV argues that the firm's success, given a well-conceived strategy and structure, is determined by its market position in relation to other actors, including suppliers, customers, competitors, and by government regulation.

During the 1980s, a third significant element—organizational culture—was added to the strategy and structure mix (Deal and Kennedy, 1982). Culture includes the values and policies of the corporation, and the normal ways in which it functions both internally and externally. According to Davis (1984, p. 1), the basis of a corporate culture is the pattern of shared beliefs and values that give the members of an institution meaning and provide them with the rules for behavior in the organization. Schein states that culture involves a multidimensional learning process: "Culture is what a group learns over a period of time as that group solves its problems of survival in an external environment and its problems of internal integration. Such learning is simultaneously a behavioral, cognitive, and emotional process." Schein stresses that it is the "pattern of basic assumptions . . . that has worked well enough to be considered valid" in its dealings with both internal and external forces that becomes part of the firm's culture (1990, p. 23; see also Detert and others, 2000, and Ogbonne and Harris, 2000). Thus, how stakeholder relations are managed is an important aspect of the culture of the firm, as well as a feature of its structure and strategy.

Increasing emphasis on the importance of culture, as well as the evolution and analysis of specific firms, has called into question the primacy of strategy within the corporate core. To illustrate: The strategy of many new high-technology companies is to achieve market success through frontier-shifting innovations. Such innovations are most likely to be developed by highly skilled and creative individuals, working alone or in very flexible groups. These companies also tend to adopt very flat and open organizational structures rather than elaborate hierarchies. The culture of such companies encourages informal and cross-functional contact, a collegial atmosphere with ample scope for individual and collaborative initiatives, and a corresponding system of recognition and rewards. It can be argued that a rational flow of decision making would lead from strategy (innovation) to structure (flat, flexible) and culture (open, informal) in such situations. The actual history of such companies strongly suggests, however, that a culture of creative independence, personal freedom, and entrepreneurial spirit is often the starting point, leading to the development of compatible (and often highly successful) strategies and structures. Highly creative individuals often have little taste for formal, authoritarian structures, and they are not energized by conventional strategies of "making it cheaper" or "selling it harder." Hence, a new model of the high-tech or

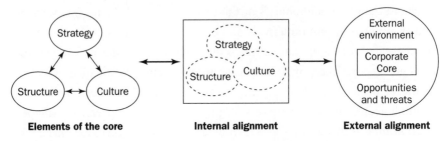

Figure 3.1 Aligning the Corporate Core: Strategy, Structure, Culture.

new-economy firm has emerged, and its attributes and effectiveness have become increasingly recognized. As a result, older and more established firms—challenged by competitive pressures and stimulated by awareness of these organizational innovations—have found it necessary to realign their own strategic options, becoming more entrepreneurial, flexible, and open (Khavul, 2000).

Whether or not one element of the corporate core takes primacy over the others, the *alignment* of the elements with each other within the firm, and with the external environment, is clearly critical for organizational success (see Figure 3.1). *Internal alignment* involves the relationship among the three core elements and their common contribution to the business operations of the enterprise. The firm's strategy, structure, and culture must be mutually supportive, enabling the firm to address its business tasks with an appropriate design of authority, tasks, and responsibilities and with a shared understanding of behavioral norms. Internal alignment is achieved through cross-functional processes such as planning, budgeting, communication, evaluation, and rewards. The challenge of *external alignment* involves the development of supportive, or at least acceptable, relationships with forces and actors outside the firm, particularly those in the social and political environment. *Boundary-spanning* processes, including listening and responding to stakeholders and engaging in effective issues management practices, are critical for achieving effective external alignment. As discussed in the chapters that follow, Cummins, Motorola, and Shell have enjoyed varying success in achieving internal and external alignment over the course of several decades. And, as the Shell experience shows, appropriate internal alignment does not guarantee—and may even jeopardize—external alignment.

The stakeholder view of the corporation (SHV) argues that both internal and external alignment are essential because every firm has relationships with numerous and diverse stakeholders—some of whom contribute to the resource base, whereas others form part of the industry structure or operate in the social and political arenas. The SHV encompasses *all* stakeholders. A genuine commitment to stakeholder management penetrates an entire organization—affecting its strategy, structure, and culture, its policies and processes—and evolving over time as a result of experience and in response to both internal and external developments. As our empirical studies make clear, firms that find particular policies and practices useful (or harmful) in dealing with one stakeholder group often extend and adapt (or learn to avoid) those same approaches to dealing with others. In addition, experience with any class of stakeholders in one situation or time period leads to organizational learning, influencing managerial decisions and behavior in the next similar case. Moreover, in a true stakeholder orientation, managers learn from stakeholders, gaining new and productive ideas as well as understanding stakeholder concerns and goals. Robert Galvin, long-time CEO of Motorola, remarked (1999) that "every company is a stakeholder company" today because of the importance of relationships with multiple stakeholders to long-term success.

The stakeholder view of the corporation becomes useful to managers and important to society when it is translated into the language of business practice and behavior. Corporations become redefined in stakeholder terms when they adopt and implement stakeholder-oriented policies and practices. This means, at minimum, recognition of the firm's stakeholders, their issues, interests, and concerns; commitment to responsible policies; and institutionalization of appropriate processes and practices. Although public communication is an essential element of practice, rhetoric alone is not sufficient.[1] Reinforced by the results of our detailed company studies, we think an approach that recognizes and responds to the importance and potential value of collaborative stakeholder relationships will prove more successful than one that does not.

---

[1]The differences between corporate rhetoric and actual behavior in two companies, Ball Corporation and Eli Lilly, were examined by Llewelyn (1998).

This implies that a stakeholder-oriented corporate culture, aligned with an appropriate strategy and structure, will enable the firm to create value for all of its constituencies, and enhance this aggregate wealth over the long run.

THE COMPANIES UNDER STUDY

In order of their size and complexity, these are the companies considered here:

Cummins Engine Company. A midsize industrial company, Cummins is one of the world's foremost manufacturers of diesel engines for motor vehicles. Its engines are synonymous with advanced technology in diesel engine design and operation. Cummins had revenues of about $6 billion in 1999. The company has manufacturing operations in only a few locations, but has built a network of international alliances that enable it to sell its products in the global market.

Motorola. Motorola develops, manufactures, and markets telecommunications technologies and components, including semiconductor chips, for industrial and consumer applications around the world. The company has grown from modest beginnings to become a global leader in electronics and telecommunications technology in just a few decades, with 1999 revenues of more than $30 billion. The company has an international network of production and software operations, and is the largest U.S. investor in China.

Royal Dutch/Shell Group. Enormous and complex, Shell is one of the largest energy resource companies in the world and a technological leader in its field. The company's business includes exploration and extraction, refining, transportation, distribution, and marketing of petroleum products and the development of new sources of energy. Shell has been a leader in the oil industry for nearly a century, and is one of the world's largest companies with 1999 revenues of $150 billion. It is also extraordinarily diverse, both geographically and functionally, and highly decentralized.

The companies differ greatly in nearly every respect, but their combined experience in dealing with a wide variety of constituencies and issues makes it easier to examine a wide range of critical corporation-stakeholder relationships. Each company has had significant problems and changes in critical stakeholder relationships over the past couple of decades, and each has revised and renewed its fundamental strategy-structure-culture alignment to adapt to new circumstances. Many of these developments, and the individual corporate responses to them, are analyzed in succeeding chapters. The companies were clearly at different starting points when they encountered these new management challenges, and their learning and adaptation processes were different as a result—all examples of path dependencies. Following is an introduction to each company.

Cummins Engine[2]

Cummins is the world's leading independent manufacturer of diesel engines and equipment. It is based in Columbus, Indiana, a small city in a rural area; from there, Cummins conducts business with partners and customers all over the globe. Founded in 1919, Cummins has been one of America's most progressive industrial manufacturing companies for more than 80 years; one CEO described it as an "improbable company" (Cruikshank and Sicilia, 1997, p. 1). Throughout its history, Cummins has managed complicated stakeholder relations with customers, some of whom are also jealous and vigorous competitors. It has developed extensive and innovative programs of corporate philanthropy and has made an enduring commitment to team-based work practices. These features, seemingly at odds with the self-discipline required for survival in such a highly cyclical and ferociously competitive industry, have helped the company survive and prosper.

Cummins' strategy has been both remarkably consistent and quite adaptable throughout its history. The company has consistently sought to develop, build, and sell the best diesel engines in the world. To create its engines, it invested heavily in the advancement of diesel technology. To produce its engines, it pioneered creative workplace designs and innovative work practices that emphasized the importance of the knowledge and attitude of the workforce in maintaining manufacturing quality. To sell its engines, Cummins built creative

---

[2]For additional detail and background information, see the Cummins Case Study at the end of the book.

marketing and distribution channels, both at home and abroad. Incentives and commitment have been intimately linked throughout its history.

Cummins' organizational structure has necessarily adapted to changing times and circumstances. After operating essentially as a family business for decades, the company recognized the need to expand and professionalize its management during the rapid postwar expansion. By the early 1960s Cummins was recruiting new MBAs for management careers.

The company's geographic reach expanded during this same period. Although the company's headquarters have remained in southern Indiana, plants were opened at other locations in the United States (Jamestown, New York, and Rocky Mount, North Carolina) and other countries. In all locations where it exercises complete control, the company has invested in local communities and in the development of people and workplace practices that make its facilities and products world class.

Cummins was an early entrant into diesel engine production and marketing on a global scale, and pursued international operations in creative and innovative ways. The company's first international manufacturing operation was established in Scotland, followed by the establishment of "beachheads" in Europe and India. The beachhead strategy involved selecting a desirable location and exporting engines to other countries in the region. Cummins also created joint ventures and alliances with other companies long before these concepts were fashionable, and worked with them to build successful businesses. (See Chapter 4 for discussion of Cummins' experience in developing countries.) By the late 1990s, international sales from major markets in Europe, Asia, and Latin America comprised more than 40 percent of Cummins' total revenues.

The culture of Cummins derived from the beliefs and attitudes of its leading executives, particularly J. Irwin Miller and Henry Schacht. Miller held deep religious convictions, and Cummins recognized the interests of multiple stakeholders—particularly employees and the local community—at an early date. The company has also played a leadership role in the development of corporate philanthropy in the United States for many decades. Throughout its history, Cummins' culture has blended a spirit of progressive humanitarianism with bottom-line thinking that has emphasized clear objectives and accountability for results. The language of "stakeholders," "doing the right thing," and "ethical standards" has never been foreign at Cummins. Leaders at every level of the company have understood that such ideas were the sources of strength and creativity that would enable the company to face the future with confidence.

Despite its long history of stakeholder-oriented policies and practices, Cummins has been challenged in recent times to rethink and realign its relations with certain stakeholders. The company has faced ownership and governance challenges from hostile shareowners, conflicts with government agencies and advocacy organizations about the environmental impact of its diesel technology, and the need to rethink relations with its global business partners. As discussed in later chapters, Cummins' experience underscores the continuous and evolving character of genuine stakeholder management. Stakeholder relationships are never static and the job of managing them is never finished.

Motorola[3]

Motorola is one of the world's leading providers of wireless communication products, semiconductors, and advanced electronic systems, components, and services. Major businesses include cellular telephones; two-way radios; paging, data, and personal communications equipment; networking peripherals; and automotive, defense, and space electronics products. Since the 1930s the company has been responsible for major technological innovations in microelectronics and communications technology. After World War II, Motorola added to its core strategy of technological leadership the goal of global market presence. Its brand name and reputation for high-quality products are now recognized throughout the world.

Technological innovation has been Motorola's defining characteristic from its earliest days of building radios for automobiles. Building on its wartime and postwar business successes, Motorola anticipated the explosion of telecommunications and consumer electronics markets in the 1970s and 1980s, and became the premier global supplier of cellular telephones. As a result of the

---

[3]For additional detail and background information, see the Motorola Case Study at the end of the book.

wireless communications revolution, Motorola's sales rose from $3 billion in 1980 to more than $10 billion in 1990. Between 1990 and 1999, Motorola's worldwide employment grew to more than 140,000, and sales reached $30 billion, 59% of which came from outside the United States. Throughout these decades of rapid growth, Motorola's commitment to leading-edge technology, product development, quality, and customer satisfaction have marked it as an exceptionally progressive, visionary firm. On several occasions it has been named one of America's most admired companies.

Motorola operates in more than 120 countries, and its operations are highly decentralized. However, two staff areas—human resources and technology—report directly to the Chief Executive Officer. These reporting arrangements reflect the company's core commitment to technological leadership and its stress on human values and skills. These values have been maintained while the company's product mix has evolved and its global scope and public policy activities have increased dramatically.

Motorola executives traditionally focused on three principal groups of stakeholders—customers, employees, and investors. Apart from experience during World War II, and the continuing importance of government customers, Motorola executives did not view public officials and political actors as primary stakeholders or important strategic actors. However, the development of aggressive Japanese competition in the new electronics marketplace brought a new awareness of the impact of public policy on the strategic environment, and Motorola sought federal government help in responding to the challenge of "Japan, Inc." Subsequently, because of its major expansion into China, Motorola became a leading advocate of normal trade relations with that country. In the course of these activities, Robert Galvin and his successors became frequent visitors to Washington and important spokesmen for "fair and free trade."

Motorola has been a leader among multinational corporations in articulating its cultural norms and behavioral codes. The commitments to uncompromising integrity and respect for the individual have been reaffirmed as key beliefs and core values at Motorola throughout its history. These values have influenced the way Motorola does business and adapts to changing circumstances over many decades. The orientation toward values encountered new challenges during the 1980s and 1990s, when the company's global workforce grew rapidly—often in new social and cultural settings—and when domestic restructuring and downsizing presented new problems as well. "Renewal" is a recurring theme among the three generations of Galvins who have led the company; each has affirmed the company's core values—respect for the individual and uncompromising integrity—as he dealt with periodic crises and challenges. This commitment to continuous renewal, based on core values, is at the heart of Motorola's culture.

A specific implication of Motorola's commitment to integrity and individual values is its emphasis on "total customer satisfaction," which includes high quality standards as well as reliable service, open communication, and fair dealing. The success of Motorola's quality commitment was recognized when the company received the first Malcolm Baldrige National Quality Award, the U.S. government's highest award for quality achievement, in 1988. A second important emphasis within Motorola's culture is employee training. Motorola believes that its employees must be well educated and continuously trained if they are to achieve the company's ambitious innovation and quality goals. To ensure that the skill level of all employees is high, the company makes large investments in training, much of which is done through Motorola University (MU). MU is highly regarded by training experts; by 1990 its programs reached all major Motorola locations in the United States and the principal operating sites in Europe, Latin America, and Asia (see further discussion in Chapter 4).

Open communication and a participatory atmosphere where management and employees can deal directly with each other are other features of the Motorola culture, but an intense spirit of internal competition is also fostered. Employees are rewarded for results, and major technological disagreements have led some observers to describe the company as a culture of "warring tribes." Such conflicts contributed to serious losses in the cellular telephone business during the 1990s, when the company resisted the move from analog to digital technology.

At the same time, strong international competitors emerged and interacted with other financial issues to form critical management challenges. As a result, the company underwent major reorganizations beginning in 1998 and refocused its diverse technologies and far-flung operations on wireless communications and "embedded-solutions" businesses. At the beginning of the 21st century, Motorola is a leader in its field and a major contributor to the global telecommunications revolution now in progress.

Shell[4]

The Royal Dutch/Shell Group of Companies has been among the 10 largest companies in the world for nearly a century. It is one of the leading integrated producers of energy, operating in every region of the globe. Shell is currently engaged in petroleum and natural gas exploration and production in more than 45 countries, and produces about 6% of the world's total supply of these commodities. It operates refineries, individually or through joint ventures, in more than 50 countries, producing a full range of petroleum-based products. Its products are distributed through more than 50,000 retail outlets, and it operates an extensive international fueling service for both aircraft and ships. During the 1970s and 1980s, Shell expanded into a series of unrelated businesses, all of which have now been divested. The company's current activities include lines of business in exploration and production, chemicals, gas and coal, and Shell International Renewables (SIR—which focuses on new and renewable sources of energy), as well as the major oil products business.

Shell was one of the first truly international corporations, and despite its foray into unrelated businesses during the 1980s, its fundamental strategy has always been finding, extracting, transporting, processing, and distributing oil. The company has been known as one of the most technologically advanced of the integrated oil majors and has been responsible for important advances in both drilling and refining. Recent innovations in transportation, such as the "multiphase pipeline" and improvements in tanker design, have yielded sustainable strategic advantages for Shell.

From the very beginning, Shell's two headquarters locations were assigned distinct tasks; London was the administrative center, and The Hague the center of technical operations. During its century-long evolution, Shell founded national companies in various countries. The result was essentially a commonwealth of

---

[4]For additional detail and background information, see the Shell Case Study at the end of the book.

firms with common brand identification and numerous unit-to-unit links, but with each operating independently and little control from the weak dual-location central headquarters. By the late 1950s this set of arrangements was found to be too weak for effective results, and in 1957 McKinsey consultants were invited to develop a new organizational structure. The following year a committee of managing directors (CMD) was established to manage the entire portfolio of Shell businesses, its external representation, and the development of the group's resources. However, in spite of the formal leadership provided by the CMD, Shell remained a highly decentralized company and local Shell managers, whatever their formal titles, were referred to internally as "barons." The Shell Oil Co., with headquarters in Houston, remained essentially outside this structure and did not even use the otherwise global "golden shell" logo.

Shell employees often use the metaphor "Planet Shell" to describe the size and insularity of their organization. With a dominant technical orientation in top management, and relatively few senior executives recruited from outside, Shell long functioned as an essentially closed system. Its culture was stable, homogeneous, and shaped by male executives. Insular and inward looking in many ways, management decision making tended to be consensus oriented, according to experienced Shell executives. Decisions are reached by discussing a problem until a consensus is found, and there is no formal voting within the top management group. In modern times, most of Shell's employees have enjoyed life-time job security, predetermined careers, and the satisfaction of being identified with a leading multinational corporation.

The "global village" created by instantaneous worldwide communication made international public opinion a more important consideration in the Shell Group's long-term policy decisions. Media attention during the 1970s, including accusations that Shell had violated international sanctions imposed on the white minority government of Rhodesia, suggested the need for more formal company-wide policies relating to business conduct. Recognition of this led to the creation of Shell's first "Statement of General Business Principles," distributed internally in 1976 and externally published in 1984. This document, which explicitly recognized "honesty, integrity and respect for people" as core values, gradually became the cornerstone of Shell's global management culture.

By the early 1990s, Shell believed that its corporate identity and reputation were at stake in both the marketplace and the policy arena. Oil prices were at all-time lows, its rate of return on capital was unsatisfactory, and its weak organizational structure was inadequate for the effective control of a global enterprise. After divesting itself of the last of its unrelated acquisitions in the early 1990s, Shell began to develop a new organizational structure that would permit greater global management oversight and control. By 1995, when the evolution of the "New Shell" model was well under way, problems with the disposal of the Brent Spar facility in the North Sea and Shell's relationship with Nigeria's repressive military regime revealed new levels of international public concern with the company's activities.

Recognition of the need for global analysis and response to such external concerns led to a major extension of the New Shell model to include a comprehensive alteration in Shell's global management culture. As the detailed analyses in Chapters 6 and 8 make clear, few observers inside or outside the company understood—or would have predicted—how powerfully these issues would ultimately shape the New Shell.

CRITICAL RELATIONSHIPS AND ISSUES

The evolution of every company is marked by a series of critical relationships with various groups of stakeholders—investors in one period, employees in another, supply chain partners, government regulators, and so on. Sometimes the relationships are highly positive, as when investors flock to the IPOs of new high-tech enterprises; at other times the relationships are challenging, as when unions threaten to strike, customer needs and tastes turn in a different direction, or regulators question business practices or product quality. Well-managed companies try to develop and maintain continuous and stable relationships with key stakeholder groups so that new opportunities can be met advantageously and potential crises anticipated and avoided. For example: Long-standing and close supply chain relationships have characterized the motor vehicle industry from its inception; efforts to establish strong brand identity and loyalty characterize consumer goods firms like Coca-Cola and McDonald's; and financial stability and service reliability are the key concerns of public utilities.

Each of the three dimensions encompassed by the stakeholder view of the firm—the resource base, industry structure, and the social and political arena—presents its own special challenges for the development and maintenance of favorable stakeholder relationship. With respect to the resource base, the challenge is to acquire, maintain, and enhance the firm's ability to secure critical physical, financial, human, intellectual, and social assets. In the industry structure, the challenge is to establish and maintain relationships with customers, suppliers, and partners in ways that enable the firm to enhance its position in the marketplace and within the value chain while conforming to relevant regulatory guidelines and industry standards. In the social and political arenas the challenge is to identify the key actors and issues and to anticipate and respond to new developments in ways that bring long-term benefits (or at least no harm) to the organization and its key stakeholders.

Figure 3.2 shows the stakeholder relationships that have been most critical for Cummins in each dimension of the stakeholder view during the past

igure 3.2   Critical Stakeholder Relationships and Issues at Cummins.

couple of decades. The company's strategy, structure, and culture created unique patterns of stakeholder interaction and raised different critical issues for management. At Cummins, development and maintenance of a highly trained, stable workforce, along with reliable financial support, were critical to the company's success in a specialized, intensely competitive niche within a highly cyclical industry. When diesel technology was criticized for its environmental effects, however, Cummins needed to address both the competitive viability of its technology and the management of its relationship with regulators and environmental activists. A culture of shared values provided a platform on which responsibility to community and employees stood equally with responsibility to investors and customers. Culture and strategy together have driven the company to emphasize technologically sophisticated diesel engines for a world market and to be a good corporate citizen wherever it is located. Feedback from business partners was consistently used to improve both product and processes, enabling Cummins to enhance value (Jensen, 2000) for all of its stakeholders.

At Motorola, the corporate culture that originated in the firm's traditional values became the primary driver of both strategy and structure. A commitment to uncompromising integrity became the basis for company-wide policies reflecting respect for the individual, whether inside or outside the firm, and for an unwavering emphasis on technological leadership. The result was a long-term willingness to invest in and adopt new ideas, both managerial and technological, and to strive for global excellence in product quality. Throughout the company's battles with Japanese competitors regarding market practices, and with both domestic and foreign competitors over technical standards for products, Motorola has sought to create value by improving quality and challenging barriers to competition. Beyond its technological and competitive challenges, Motorola's greatest concern has been the translation of its fundamental commitments to new operating environments, particularly the company's "second home" in China. See Figure 3.3.

At Shell, organization structure has been a dominant factor in influencing the way the company has conducted its business. Within the Shell Group of affiliated companies and their various joint ventures and alliances, primary managerial responsibility rested with local and regional executives, and technical

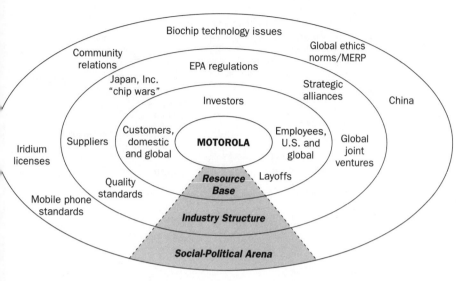

igure 3.3   Critical Stakeholder Relationships and Issues at Motorola.

expertise and operational expediency usually governed decision making. As the company became involved in activities that raised issues in multiple jurisdictions, sometimes in connection with governments and state-owned enterprises that it could neither control nor defend, the need for greater company-wide analysis and leadership became apparent. The result was a transformation in the company's self-image, with broad implications for its culture and strategy, and ultimately for its structure as well. See Figure 3.4.

As these comments suggest, issues arising from the social and political arenas have had substantial and pervasive impact on the operations and competitive positions of all three of these companies in recent years. Issues and trends that seem to be external can still penetrate the corporate core, alter the resource base and industry position, and influence the path of corporate development. This reality is inadequately appreciated within the management literature. Similarly, the potential impact of sociopolitical developments on the firm is often neglected in managerial practice—at least until the demonstrators arrive at the gate and the lawyers appear in the boardroom, events usually followed by a rapid loss of investor confidence in the company. This analysis of how Cummins, Motorola, and Shell dealt with their diverse stakeholders,

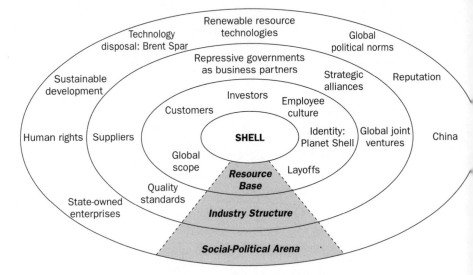

Figure 3.4 Critical Stakeholder Relationships and Issues at Shell.

both internal and external, over the course of recent decades highlights the interaction among stakeholder issues and their impact on the core strategy, structure, and culture of these corporations.

THE CHALLENGE OF GLOBALIZATION

One of the most significant developments of the past half century has been the export of management skills and practices from advanced countries—first from North America, and later from Western Europe and Japan—to other parts of the world. The spread of managerial knowledge and skills during this period has coincided with advances in communications and transportation technology, and with a vast increase in the volume and speed of international financial flows. The result is a process of globalization, in which economies and societies all over the world are becoming increasingly interdependent, both because of the volume of contacts of all kinds among them and because of their increasing sensitivity to each other and to common worldwide trends and developments. The role of the corporation in this process has been addressed through the development of a number of international codes of conduct (see Preston and Mihalko, 1999, for a comparative analysis; and Kolk, van Tulder, and Welters, 1999, and Williams (ed.), 2000, for recent surveys and evaluations of these initiatives). The United Nations Global Compact, announced by Secretary-General Kofi Annan in 2000 and with initial support from more than 50 leading multinational corporations, is the latest development in this area (U.N., 2000).

The globalization process confronts managers with complex combinations of competitive and societal challenges in many different cultural settings. The management task is not only to deal with diverse competitive and societal operating conditions, but also to adapt company-wide policies so that they will be flexible enough to fit diverse situations and yet maintain sufficient consistency that fundamental principles and operating efficiencies are not compromised. This is particularly difficult when firms expand their operations to countries and regions that have not been integrated into current international economic and political systems. The challenge for corporations, then, is to globalize stakeholder management policies and practices while retaining their fundamental principles even as they are implemented in dissimilar and unfamiliar settings.

In their pursuit of profits, companies enter foreign countries for two very different purposes: to extract and/or produce goods for export to home or third countries, or to produce and/or distribute goods and services for local markets. Product characteristics, quality standards, and business practices may vary substantially between the two, and the evolution of an enterprise from one emphasis to the other is often problematic. The most common form of Western business organization in many foreign settings has been the joint venture, often in collaboration with a government-controlled entity, although wholly foreign-owned subsidiaries have also been permitted in most places. In addition, many kinds of supply chain relationships (such as contract production and distributorships) link foreign firms into developing economies. The impact of Western management ideas on local operations in new environments is heavily dependent on the purpose and structure of the project, as well as on its size.

Foreign multinationals confront similar opportunities and problems in many developing and transitional countries, but every country and culture presents challenges in one form or another. The three companies described in this chapter have encountered a variety of challenges as they entered and expanded in different operating environments. Several examples of their experiences are discussed in the next three chapters, and Chapter 7 gives an extensive analysis of the challenges encountered by foreign multinationals in their attempts to adapt stakeholder management practices to operations in China.

CONCLUSION

The three firms profiled in this chapter—Shell, Cummins, and Motorola—are drawn from the broad spectrum of contemporary industries. Each has faced many complicated and diverse challenges, and each has developed a different core strategy, structure, and culture to deal with them. Consideration of the concerns and contributions of diverse stakeholders has played a major role in the strategic policies and decisions of all three firms in recent decades. Many, though not all, of their strategies have been highly successful. But all three have learned from experience and are successful multinationally, and they have kept their stakeholder orientation wherever they operated. The chapters that follow analyze the evolution and impact of stakeholder-oriented ideas in these companies over recent decades and assess the role stakeholder management played in their development and in their ability to increase organizational wealth over the long term.

4

THE STRATEGIC ROLE OF VALUES

The stakeholder view of the firm (SHV) presented in the preceding chapters argues that organizational wealth can be increased by the development of productive relationships with various stakeholders, as well as by the accumulation of resources (RBV) and the establishment of strong industry positions (ISV). The instrumental impact of stakeholder management on corporate performance does not, however, appear to provide a complete explanation of corporate stakeholder orientation. On the contrary, stakeholder-oriented firms often seem to be motivated by normative considerations that underlie a pervasive organizational commitment to humanistic values for their own sake. Both the rhetoric and the actual practices of these firms reflect recognition and respect for the integrity and intrinsic merit of the individuals and groups with which they come into contact. In effect, management recognition of the corporation's involvement with various stakeholders leads to the development of an "organizational morality," a recognition of responsibility and duty that ultimately supports a company-wide system of humanistic policies and practices. When a humanistic commitment has been made and shown to be effective with one group of stakeholders, it appears to be relatively easy to extend it to others. Collins and Porras (1995) note, for example, that companies that manifest concern for the welfare of employees seem to have little trouble in implementing the same principles in their contacts with customers, suppliers, and communities.

A commitment to humanistic values is explicit in the rhetoric of our three focal companies. Motorola formally declares "uncompromising integrity" and "constant respect for people" to be its key beliefs (Code of Business Conduct, 1999). Shell earlier defined its core values as "integrity, honesty, and respect for people" (Statement of General Business Principles, 1997), and now states its core purpose as "Helping People Build a Better World" (1999). Cummins declares an organizational commitment to "quality, innovation and integrity," made possible because "each member of Cummins follows the highest standards of ethical conduct" (Cummins Code of Business Conduct, 1996).

This chapter examines corporate commitments to humanistic values and shows how they were implemented in human resource management at Motorola and in community relations at Cummins. (Shell's response to broad social concerns is discussed in Chapter 6.) The validity of the stakeholder view—that stakeholder management can contribute to corporate success—depends on how rhetoric is translated into business practice. The Cummins code's strongest guarantees are that high principles will become embodied in corporate practices in the form of "individual integrity" and "strong corporate culture." This chapter, therefore, emphasizes corporate culture and its implications for strategies and structures that implement a strong commitment to humanistic values. Evidence suggests that the social capital created by constructive interactions between the firm and its stakeholders, evolving over time and compounding on the basis of favorable experience, becomes the source of increased organizational wealth.

VALUES, ETHICS, POLICIES, AND PRACTICES

Stakeholder management evolves within a network of values, ethics, policies, and practices that are difficult to disentangle but are fundamental to the organizational culture.

The fundamental elements are values, ideas, or concepts that are viewed as ends in themselves without requiring further justification. *Ethics* are a system of moral principles and behavioral norms intended to express and support an underlying set of values (or, alternatively, a set of precepts that both identifies "good" objectives and prescribes means of achieving them). Thus, if the dignity and integrity of the individual is a basic value, then respect for individual concerns and differences, and attention to the needs and wants with whom one comes into contact, are ethical guidelines intended to serve that value.

In a corporate setting, values and ethics become the basis for policies and practices that define how the company will achieve its goals. But what if a policy and a practice seem to conflict? Indeed, there is often two-way interaction among these conceptually distinct elements. Experience with actual practice results in reexamination of policies, which in turn leads to refinement of ethical guidelines; and fundamental values commitments, although rarely abandoned, are reviewed, renewed, or revised as a result. Rawls characterizes the result of this Socratic process as "reflective equilibrium," noting that "we may want to change our [initial] considered judgements once their regulative principles are brought to light" (1971, pp. 48–49).

The interplay of basic values and specific objectives and policies is well illustrated by Hewlett-Packard's statement of "Corporate Objectives and the H-P Way," available on the company's web site (www.hp.com). Starting with the slogan "Building Trust in an Internet Economy," this statement stresses the importance of "trust and respect for individuals," "achievement and contribution," "uncompromising integrity," "teamwork," and "flexibility and innovation." The financial objective is to generate "sufficient profit" to finance company growth and provide the resources needed to achieve the company's *other* objectives, which include customer satisfaction, technological development, helping employees to "share in the company's success which they make possible," and "citizenship"—the obligation to be an "economic, intellectual and social asset to each nation and each community in which we operate."

Reichheld (1996) has examined the ways in which an emphasis on humanistic values can create a "loyalty effect," a strong bond between the corporation and its employees, customers and other stakeholders. He cites the efforts of diverse companies such as State Farm and Northwestern Mutual (insurance), Olive Garden and Chick-Fil-A (restaurants), Toyota (automobiles), Leo Burnett (advertising), A. G. Edwards (brokerage services), and MBNA (banking) as success stories in this regard. A similar analysis, which stresses the *negative* impact of the absence of humanistic practices in companies, is presented in Pfeffer (1998). The consistent theme of these and many similar studies is that corporate policies and practices demonstrating respect for the individual build relationships that lead to stakeholder collaboration and productivity (Leana and Rousseau, 2000).

Obstacles

Although many corporate codes of conduct and other statements of general policy declare commitments to humanistic values and other admirable philosophical and social goals, organizational size and complexity often seem to be insuperable barriers to the implementation of these commitments. Boards of directors and management committees may be quite sincere when they declare "respect for the individual." But when that message is filtered and translated through many layers of a decentralized global company that operates in more than one hundred countries and employs tens of thousands of people, actual practice may fall far short of the ideal. Indeed, it often seems to be the case that field managers—to say nothing of line employees, customers, and other affected parties—are entirely unaware that any official commitments to humanistic principles have been made. Pervasive and meaningful internal communication about corporate values and goals—workshops and operating guidelines, not simply memoranda—are critical elements of effective stakeholder management.

The efforts of large, multinational firms such as Mattel and Nestlé to build company-wide awareness of stakeholder issues, and to institutionalize humanistic policies and practices around supply chain and market channel issues respectively, are examples of the difficulty encountered and the resolve needed to institutionalize humanistic principles in complex industry settings (see Sethi re: Mattel, in Clarkson Principles report, 1998; and Post re: Nestlé, in Williams (ed.), 2000).

Broad humanistic commitments can be overwhelmed by the pressures on managers to meet short-term performance goals. Making the current sales or production quota, reducing costs to a target level, acquiring a minimum number of new customers, and other immediate objectives may take precedence over the long-term welfare of employees, customers, and other stakeholders.[1] Mid-level managers have extraordinary responsibility for bridging the gap between top management commitments and field operations. Hence, an understanding of, and commitment to, long-term organizational objectives and ethical standards is a requirement for effective stakeholder management over the long term. Once again, corporations *are* what they *do*.

IMPLEMENTING THE HUMANISTIC COMMITMENT

Corporations interact every day with vast numbers of stakeholders of many different kinds, and new stakeholder issues—and even new stakeholders— emerge regularly. In spite of their best efforts to anticipate developments and establish comprehensive and equitable policy guidelines, managers know that they cannot specify in advance which issues will arise, or when or where, much less the priorities for consideration and action that may be appropriate. Routine collaboration and problem solving within large and complex organizations depends upon cultural norms that go beyond formal guidelines and bureaucratic procedures. Organizations require some kind of "social glue" to hold their parts together, and some kind of "social grease" to keep the parts working smoothly. The cultural norms that serve these purposes can be described as *shared values*. Shared values enable the members and units of an organization to trust each other and to collaborate without depending on prescriptive directives or detailed negotiations. Shared values are a strategic asset that can be a distinctive strength because, in the words of Reebok CEO Paul Fireman, they enable a company to move from a "culture of compliance" to a "culture of commitment" (Fireman, 1999).

Bollier (1996) documented the experiences of two dozen diverse companies that have achieved business success by adhering to core values. The examples

---

[1]This conflict is dramatically illustrated by an incident involving the pharmaceutical firm Novartis. The company's Purpose and Aspirations document states, "Our long term success is founded on meeting the expectations of all our stakeholders." Its Human Resource Principles declare, "We seek to maintain high ethical standards in everything we do." But the head of the pharmaceutical division, under pressure for better performance, stated at a meeting of the division's sales staff, "Do whatever it takes. Kill to win. No prisoners!" This statement was subsequently published in Switzerland's largest newspaper, to the embarrassment of the company and the executive involved (www.SontagsZeitung.ch, August 8, 2000).

include large, well-known companies such as GE Plastics, Starbucks, Prudential Insurance, Merck, and Ben & Jerry's Homemade, as well as small- and medium-sized firms in manufacturing and service industries. The common theme in these companies, according to Bollier, is "creative, socially committed business managers (who) have enhanced their long-term profitability by instilling the best of their humanity into the nitty-gritty operations of their organizations." These businesses "do not just demonstrate the compatibility of business success and socially motivated action. They also suggest the constructive *synergies* that can emerge when such a convergence takes place. Values define organizations and empower people within them to "aim high" and create both business success and human value (1996, pp. 1–2).

The importance of a values orientation is often most clearly revealed in times of crisis. Companies responded immediately to the needs of survivors and families of victims of terrorism in the attacks on the World Trade Center and the Pentagon on September 11, 2001. Within hours, businesses had mobilized relief efforts to assist employees, customers, and others in need. These responses were spontaneous, not calculated, and flowed from the human values that ultimately shape organizations and guide behavior.

Johnson & Johnson's decision to recall Tylenol from the market after a series of deaths that resulted from tampering with the product was hailed as an act of corporate responsibility in 1982 and remains a landmark example of business decision making based on stakeholder values. The decision reflected J&J management's understanding of the company's "Credo," which committed the company do whatever necessary when the interests of consumers, health care providers, and other critical stakeholders were at risk. The Credo begins with these words: "*We believe our first responsibility is to the doctors, nurses, and patients, to mothers and all others, who use our products and services. In meeting their needs, everything we do must be of high quality.*" (Johnson & Johnson, *Credo*, n.d.) James Burke, J&J's chief executive at the time, wrote of the decision in these terms: "To this day we do not know who poisoned the Tylenol capsules. But our response was to put the customer first—to serve the public interest—regardless of the cost. *The critical difference was the social and ethical commitment we shared with our customers*" (quoted in Bollier, 1996, p. 6; italics added).

Corporations that commit to recognizing the integrity of the individual as an integral part of their culture are challenged to implement it in many different ways and on a wide range of issues as they deal with individuals, groups, communities, and society at large. Companies are often involved with the same person in different roles (employee, customer, neighbor), and with persons in each role at several different levels—as individuals, as constituents of various groups, and as members of larger communities and society. For example, companies interact with employees as individuals in hiring, compensation, and advancement decisions; as members of groups in the establishment of staffing patterns and wage levels, and in collective bargaining; and as members of an even bigger group in connection with broad social issues such as minimum wages and benefits, equal employment opportunity, and workplace safety. Examples of issues involving the implementation of humanistic commitments to employees, their families, customers and communities at the *micro* (individual unit), *meso* (group), and *macro* (societal) levels are shown in Table 4.1. Some aspects of implementation at each of these levels are discussed

Table 4.1
Humanistic Commitment Levels and Implementation Issues

Stakeholders	Micro Level	Intermediate (Meso) Level	Macro Level
Investors	Security Share price Dividend policy	ESOPs Dividend reinvestment programs	Governance and disclosure Accounting standards
Employees (and employee families)	Compensation Participative relationships Flexible hours Consideration of personal situations	Wage patterns/ gender equity Workplace diversity On-site child care Family leave policies	Minimum living wage Support for "family-friendly" programs and legislation
Customers	Quality and service Collaborative design and problem solving	Warranty policies/ practices	Consumer protection programs and laws
Communities and society	Local impacts and practices Community projects	Community relations policies Philanthropy	Environmental practices Human rights standards

briefly before examining humanistic practices at Motorola and Cummins in more detail.

Micro-Level Issues

Respect for the individual—and for each individual's diverse roles in families, groups, communities, and society—is the basis for all normative commitments to stakeholders. Respect for the individual implies that people are viewed as unique persons, not simply as units within some abstract classification or pieces of numerical data. Individuals have basic needs, such as food, shelter, and security, and complex higher-level needs such as self-esteem, personal growth, and the fulfillment that psychologist Abraham Maslow called "self-actualization." As economic development permits the basic needs of most people to be satisfied, higher-level needs become more important, and these have to be taken into account in stakeholder-related corporate policies.

Respect for the individual also requires that the corporation treat all individuals equally, without discrimination based on characteristics irrelevant to their relationship to the firm. Race, gender, age, physical characteristics, sexual orientation, and marital status are normal dimensions of human diversity, but they should not become the basis for differential treatment of stakeholders unless they have a direct connection with the stakeholder relationship itself, and hence require some kind of special consideration. Implementation of this idea is often obvious, but sometimes difficult. For example, controversy has surrounded the issue of employment opportunities and safeguards for women of childbearing age in jobs that might have some impact on their ability to have children or on the health of their offspring. Some reproductive hazards involve male employees as well (see Kenan, 1996).

In addition, social change affects the ways corporations respond to traditional individual concerns. For example, when divorce and marital separation become commonplace, these lifestyles have to be taken into account in policies governing wages, health insurance, pensions, and other matters. This means that employers must design benefit plans that do not favor or penalize beneficiaries on the basis of their marital status, and that recognize long-term dependency relationships among unmarried persons as well. Many of these issues have been, or will be, addressed by various levels of government, but the responsibility of the corporation toward its stakeholders precedes and goes beyond specific legal requirements. Micro-level issues for financial stakeholders include investment security, share price, bond rating, dividend policy, and the impartial disclosure of material information.

Stakeholder-oriented policies extend beyond the individual employee or customer to include family members and others that might be affected, both directly and indirectly. Such considerations are most obvious with respect to spouses and children, and to the conditions affecting an employee's ability to fulfill familial responsibilities (such as working hours and leave time). These practices (daycare, elder care, flexible hours) extend the principle of respect for the individual, and also benefit the firm by making it an "employer of choice," a guideline to corporate human resource management policies now in widespread use.

Similar considerations also arise with respect to customers and communities. Customers should reasonably expect that no hazards or harms—to themselves or to third parties (family members or others)—result from normal use of the firm's products and services. Significant issues arise here in connection with packaging and with the disposal of unwanted merchandise (such as the safety of old refrigerators or damage from products with ozone-depleting chemicals), as well as with the possession and safe use of desired products. Communities are correspondingly concerned with specific local impacts—pollution, congestion, beautification, and the like. The "neighbor of choice" concept has evolved as a guide to corporate practices in local settings.

Intermediate- (Meso-) Level Issues

Although respect for the individual is the cornerstone of stakeholder management, corporations necessarily develop policies and deal with people in groups, either specified for convenience by the company (hourly employees, female customers, and others) or created voluntarily by the stakeholders themselves (unions, community organizations, religious groups). Respect for the individual necessarily extends to respect for collections of individuals and for the voluntary organizations that individuals may form. Indeed, development and implementation of stakeholder-oriented policies *requires* identification of appropriate groups with common interests and concerns. The equitable treatment of individuals in organizations is ordinarily achieved by the establishment of policies that apply to all employees with similar workplace-relevant characteristics (such as hourly or exempt workers) or levels of responsibility, but *not* to personal characteristics (such as age, color, or gender).

Voluntarily formed groups of stakeholders often present a challenge to corporate managers. Some such groups—customers with particular needs or concerns, for example—may be supportive of the corporation and contribute to advancing its interests. Others—dissatisfied customers or critics—may question the firm's purposes and practices. Labor unions and community organizations may play both supportive and critical roles. Whatever the orientation of the group, or the basis for its formation, respect for the individual necessarily requires a willingness to engage in dialogue with persons, or representatives of persons, with whom the firm has (at least in *their* eyes) some kind of relationship. Although *all* claims to stakeholder status may not merit significant response, recognition that stakeholders may identify themselves, whether or not they have been initially identified by the corporation, is a critical aspect of stakeholder management.

Widespread corporate downsizing and the increased use of temporary workers, overseas workers, and outsourcing in recent years raised serious issues for many U.S. companies about their long-term domestic employees and home communities. Whether unionized or not, long-term employees clearly constitute a group of people with which a corporation is linked in a close stakeholder relationship. When members are expelled from this group through downsizing, or the status of its members is seriously altered (through the loss of pension benefits, for example), issues of stakeholder equity arise and trust may be seriously undermined. And, taking an opposite perspective, failure to extend normal employee benefits to temporary workers (some of whom may be "permanent temps") or workers in "contract" facilities may also violate the principle that persons similarly situated with respect to the firm should be similarly treated.

Starbucks has attracted considerable media attention for voluntarily extending health benefits to part-time as well as full-time employees, whereas other firms (Microsoft, for one) have been cited for utilizing a cadre of "permanent temps" who do not receive regular employee benefits. Recognition of relevant groups of employees and customers, whether self-identified or not, and careful attention to equity issues that may arise among them, is a critical requirement for successful stakeholder management.

A meso-level policy issue of special interest involves the development of an ownership culture through Employee Stock Ownership Plans (ESOPs) and similar devices. ESOPs bring employees into the complementary stakeholder role of shareowners, and dividend reinvestment makes it possible for all shareowners to increase their investments in the company at rates convenient with their own cash flow (regardless of share price levels) and without payment of brokerage fees. There is extensive documentation of the strengthening impact of these programs on stakeholder linkages (Brohawn, 1997). The trend toward expanded use of stock options to reward employees, especially among small, entrepreneurial start-up firms, is a further extension of the multiple stakeholder phenomenon in the modern economy.

Macro-Level Issues

Employee, customer, and investor-related implementation issues cluster heavily at the micro- and meso-levels. Macro-level issues for employees include general working conditions and compensation policies; customer issues consumer protection programs, guarantees and warranties, and others. Macrolevel investor issues include corporate governance mechanisms and disclosure, and maintenance of accounting standards.

Respect for Communities

Implementation of genuine respect for the communities in which the corporation operates primarily involves macro-level policies and responsibilities. The community stakeholders of a large, multinational corporation are numerous and diverse. The local site of each of its facilities clearly defines a micro-level community, but larger metropolitan areas, regions, and nations may also be relevant communities for certain types of decisions. Respect for community, at every level, implies an intention to minimize and mitigate negative effects of corporate activity, and to work with governments, community groups, and other stakeholders to enhance the community and protect it from harm. It also implies a willingness to respond to community needs following disasters, such as natural disasters or terrorist attacks.

At the local level, most firms attempt to establish some sort of "citizenship" status, often with a view to obtaining favorable treatment or minimizing negative community impact (such as tax burdens) on their own operations. Extending this idea, many companies have established general community relations and philanthropy policies that can be applied to all locations in which they operate and to multiple jurisdictions (states, regions, and nations, as well as localities). As Burke (1999) notes, the practical purpose of corporate citizenship is to create a relationship with the community that makes the corporation a "neighbor of choice," much as it seeks to become an "employer of choice," "supplier of choice," or "investment of choice" for other kinds of stakeholders. The tendency to target philanthropy and community relations programs to create favorable community impacts at headquarters locations, while neglecting other sites where employees and customers are located, has gradually come to be seen as inequitable and not reflecting a genuine stakeholder commitment. The commitment to respect communities also becomes more complicated when companies operate in diverse cultural and ethnic settings, with differing social, economic, and political conditions. Respecting stakeholders involves striking a principled balance between local cultural norms and traditions and more universal humanistic standards and norms.

In citizenship, as in all other areas, corporations are what they do, and actual practices vary greatly depending on industry, firm size and complexity, and corporate strategy (see Post, 2000a, 2000b). The characteristics of the community itself, and its general relationship to the firm—such as metropolitan center rather than company town—also are significant. In the Internet age, the relevant community of a company is likely to be defined in terms of type and frequency of interaction (one-way versus two-way communication, formal registration or membership, purchase or sale through a web site, and the like). Companies such as iVillage and eBay, for example, have created "communities" that go beyond their commercial activities. As Hagel and Armstrong (1997) have written, the underlying proposition is that "communities precede customers."

Whatever the particular circumstances, corporate citizenship policies depend fundamentally on an understanding of voluntary and involuntary stakeholder relationships, with special concern for any negative impacts the firm may have on the involuntary community stakeholders. Even when a community is willing to accept greater risks in order to secure the benefits of economic activity, corporations with a humanistic commitment will not allow their operations to fall below "best practice" safety or environmental standards. Normatively, the precautionary principle leads firms to avoid imposing such risks. Instrumentally, concern for stakeholder communities is a necessary aspect of corporate stewardship that is essential to preserving reputation and the license to operate in industries such as mining and petrochemicals.

There are many positive reasons to exercise corporate citizenship as well. Merck, for example, has for many years provided one of its pharmaceutical products free of charge to ministries of health in developing nations. The drug is able to prevent river blindness, a dreaded and debilitating disease. Merck's rationale is both altruistic and commercial. It provides a unique formula that can prevent a terrible disease, and it also develops positive relationships with governments and populations that may purchase its other products. Merck's chairman and CEO Raymond Gilmartin states it this way:

> [B]asing relationships on trust and respect leads to more lasting and constructive interactions with the vital forces of society. . . . Trust, however, is not granted to us just because we pay our share of taxes or hire residents to work in our company. While that may have been the case at one time, that is not the only criterion today. People expect us to become partners in solving community problems. They want the private sector to support programs and institutions that improve the quality of community life (Gilmartin, foreword to Burke, 1999; see also Logan and others, 1998).

Respect for Society: Environment and Human Rights

The corporation receives both its legal charter and its functional justification and legitimacy from the society in which it operates. Some countries (such as

Germany and Japan) recognize a social purpose in their incorporation procedures, whereas others (such as the United States and United Kingdom) require only a general statement of intent to engage in business. In all cases, governments impose a wide array of regulations, tax obligations, and protections of public health and safety on business activities. But the corporation's true license to operate does not come from governmental sources but from the needs and expectations of the individuals and groups within its social and political environment (local, national, and global). As many of its important social impacts cannot be fully and specifically anticipated or spelled out in advance, the corporation's license to operate ultimately rests on a belief that the firm and its managers will respect, and serve the interests, of the larger society within which it exists.

Respect for the environment is a critical aspect of respect for society in general, because it involves maintenance of the setting within which human and social life is possible. Corporations are increasingly realizing that they are stakeholders in society and the environment, and that they need to preserve the integrity of physical and social systems as a basis for their own continued existence. These relationships are most obvious at a local level, but are receiving increasing attention at national and international levels. The concept of sustainable development, promoted by the United Nations Development Program (UNDP), has drawn support from such business groups as the World Business Council for Sustainable Development and Business in the Community, a U.K. business leaders' group formed by the Prince of Wales Business Leaders Forum (1996, Pt. 3, Ch. 3, esp. section 3.7, in Logan and others, p. 109). Individual firms have taken the initiative to address these issues as well. Home Depot, one of the world's largest retailers of building supplies, for example, has announced that it will stop selling products containing wood from ancient forests by 2003. This action is intended to protect redwoods, rain forests, and other ecologically sensitive tracts. In making this announcement, CEO Arthur Blank stated: "Frankly, given the size of the company today, we have the ability to make a change in the world" (*Boston Globe*, 1999).

Respect for human rights involves respect for diverse individual and collective rights, including those of persons and groups with whom one may have no direct contact—indeed, of whom one may be totally unaware. The United

Nations' Declaration of Universal Human Rights—the basic document on which most contemporary human rights discussions are based—includes free association, expression, and education among the basic rights of all human beings. Most of these rights are recognized and protected in advanced industrial countries, but some receive only limited support or are denied altogether in some parts of the world. Exploitation of natural resources by both corporations and governments on the lands of aboriginal (native) peoples in both economically advanced (Canada, Australia) and developing nations has raised important new human rights issues and has aroused activism all over the world. Some of these campaigns have led corporations to develop significant new approaches to stakeholder relations, as the discussion of Shell's Camisea project in Chapter 6 clearly illustrates (also, see Chapter 8).

The trend toward expanding individual freedom all over the world, irrespective of political regime, requires that corporations grant comparable respect to every individual with whom they come in contact. Where this is made impossible because repressive governments deprive individuals of basic freedoms, the corporation may be unable to operate. At a minimum, the corporation should avoid complicity in repressive acts, and should challenge such governmental policies through legitimate means wherever possible. The ultimate success of the long campaign to recover damages from corporations that used workers from Nazi slave labor camps during World War II provides an instructive example. More than 50 years after the fact, an international agreement was reached whereby damages amounting to more than $5 billion are to be paid by the corporations whose executives authorized such practices. Respect for human rights also involves issues such as income distribution and the payment of a living wage; sale of weapons and other questionable merchandise to repressive regimes; and imposition of health and safety risks on unsuspecting populations.

These macro-level responsibilities will inevitably change and increase as corporations expand their global scope and develop stakeholder relationships with more numerous and more diverse societies and cultures. Goran Lindahl, chairman of ABB, a multinational firm that operates in more than 120 countries, called for global companies to become "co-guarantors of human rights" everywhere they operate (2000). In July 2000, more than fifty global companies, including ABB, entered into the U.N. Global Compact (2000) with the Secretary-General of the United Nations and leaders of labor unions and prominent international NGOs (such as the Human Rights Watch) to adopt a set of global principles to protect the environment and human rights, to alleviate poverty, and to advance the U.N.'s Declaration of Universal Human Rights (see Kell and Ruggie, 1999). The modern corporation is challenged to implement its commitment to humanistic values at every level of its operation, from its contacts with specific individuals to its role in the global arena of economics and policy. Shared values are an important asset of the corporation; they form the common ground on which cooperation, collaboration, and conflict resolution can be based and mutual benefits realized.

SHARED VALUES AT MOTOROLA

At Motorola, two core values are cited as being at the heart of the enterprise— "respect for the individual" and "uncompromising integrity in all we do." These values are deeply rooted in the company's history and date back to periods of economic hardship that are now long in the past. During the Great Depression of the 1930s, Motorola founder Paul Galvin provided loans that helped his consumer product distributors stay afloat until times improved. Galvin felt that "his close friendship with these men, . . . [and] the fine organization they had welded together, were his *real wealth*" (Petrakis, pp. 161–2, italics added). During World War II, when his distributors had few products to sell to civilians, Galvin found a way to convert surplus car radios into home radios that would work on regular house current. This enabled the distributors to stay in business and strengthened the network of downstream stakeholders that formed the foundation of Motorola's postwar distribution system.

These early, and very ad hoc, examples of actions reflecting respect for the individual evolved into an elaborate system of cultural norms and policy guidelines as Motorola has grown into a vast, global enterprise. Ethical behavior, reflecting the commitment to uncompromising integrity, has been equally important throughout company history. During the 1960s, for example, Motorola had an opportunity to make substantial sales in a Latin American nation. The company's contract proposal was to be reviewed by a high-ranking government official. Motorola representatives were informed that a significant payment would be required to close the deal. Despite the economic loss involved, the company turned down the contract and did no business in that nation for several decades (Galvin, interview, 1999). This story of principled decision making became part of the lore and culture of Motorola.

Motorola's clear and oft-stated commitments reflect the personal characteristics of its founders and the midwestern values that were part of their upbringing and home environment. The challenge to Motorola has been the preservation and implementation of these commitments as the company has grown over time, expanded into global operations, entered very different and more complicated industries, and experienced competitive challenges and reversals within its long period of successful evolution.

As described in the previous chapter and in Case Study B, rapid global growth increased the number of Motorola employees to 140,000 (1998), nearly half of whom live and work outside the United States. Motorola employees speak more than 50 home languages and represent hundreds of cultures, subcultures, and ethnic groups. Much of this growth took place in Asia during in the 1990s, and involved new communications technologies and products such as cellular phones and advanced telecommunications systems. This rate and pattern of growth challenged Motorola to find ways to preserve the company's historic commitment to human values—originally developed among people who knew each other and shared a common culture—under totally new circumstances.

According to Moorthy (1996, p. 3), three specific challenges were identified:

1. How to translate Motorola's ethical values into consistent, reliable business practices around the world?

2. How to convey the key ethical values of the company's culture so that new employees would embrace and be guided by these values in their day-to-day business activities?

3. How to understand and learn from host cultures with which Motorola engages, and to make Motorola's values more meaningful in these settings?

Motorola responded by using its education and change processes. The company developed an ethics component within the core education programs offered through Motorola University, supplemented by a global process of local consultation and training (see Chapter 7). The principle guiding this activity was that Motorola's humanistic commitment—respect for the individual and ethical behavior (uncompromising integrity)—was central to the culture and strategy of the company everywhere, and that it should be implemented throughout the company, regardless of particular local conditions or situations that might be encountered. By recognizing and responding to these issues early in the growth era of the 1990s, Motorola's leaders demonstrated their commitment to a shared-values approach and encouraged learning, experimentation, and risk taking throughout the entire company. As discussed in Chapter 8, the leadership commitments promoted continuous learning and adaptation, including stakeholder management throughout the company.

Policies and Practices

The specific policies and practices required to implement the broad humanistic commitment of a corporation naturally vary with time and circumstances. As Motorola became an increasingly global enterprise in the 1990s, for example, cultural differences became prominent and the need to articulate specific policy guidelines increased. R S Moorthy, the executive charged with implementing Motorola's Ethics Renewal Program from 1995 to 1998, stated (p. 4): "The decisions we make as a business to create more wealth must hinge on our core values." He cited three concrete examples:

1. *Bribe-free business.* "We will not pay or accept bribes."

2. *Environmental protection.* "Doing environmental harm is unethical and might have negative results that would emerge clearly only 10 or 20 years down the road. The cost of a clean-up then, and the damage done to people and the environment in the interim, would be far too high a price to pay for short-term profits or environmental ignorance."

3. *Gender and ethnic equity.* "We believe in treating all people with constant respect, regardless of their gender (or race or national origin). We would be inconsistent in living our ethical values if we treated female employees differently because that is the way they are treated in a particular host culture."

Motorola also recognized the need for rules of engagement for dealing with suppliers, distributors, contractors, and joint venture partners. Although business practices vary widely throughout the world, serious breaches of ethics such as bribery (either giving or receiving) are not tolerated in any supplier, agent, distributor, or customer relationship. The core value of "uncompromising integrity" is viewed as absolute with respect to bribery, and within Motorola's own direct activities. However, Moorthy noted (p. 5): "In other situations, though, since we do not own or control these businesses, it will sometimes be difficult to expect them to meet our ethical standards in every respect. . . . In such cases, we might not be able to hold ourselves responsible for their actions in the same way that we are for our own." As the line between overt bribery and the giving and receiving of "gifts" is often difficult to draw, Motorola prohibits most gift exchanges beyond token promotional items bearing the corporate logo. However, this strict rule conflicts with the strong Japanese tradition of gift exchange as a part of close business working relationships. For this reason, Motorola's company-wide policy has been modified with respect to a number of countries, including Japan. At the same time, a strict gift reporting system has been established, and reciprocation through gifts to charity in the name of the involved party (rather than gifts to firms or individual) is strongly recommended (Moorthy and others, 1998, pp. 232–6).

Human Resource Management

A corporation's commitment to humanistic values is often most conspicuously demonstrated—and most seriously challenged—in its treatment of employees. Motorola employees are portrayed, and often see themselves, as part of a family with a rich history, traditions, and customs. This philosophy is traceable to the Galvin family members who have led the organization as chief executive officer and/or chairman since the 1920s—founder Paul Galvin (1928–1959), Robert Galvin (1960–1990s), and Christopher Galvin (1996–present). For more than seventy years, Motorola has retained a strong commitment to the founders' values: people, technology, innovation. Robert Galvin has remarked: "From the very beginning, human resources has reported directly to the Chief Executive Officer" because people are critical to every facet of the company's activity and success (Galvin interview, 1999).

Education and Training

Motorola is strongly committed to the personal and professional development of employees, and reflects this commitment in education and training programs that reach every level of the organization. Senior management commitment to these activities is substantive as well as symbolic. For example, all new vice presidents participate in a program in which the company's CEO and chairman are members of the faculty.

The company's training programs place great emphasis on leadership development and on innovation, as well as on job-specific objectives. The slogan "be a change agent" is commonplace. According to the company's current senior human resources executives, the tone was set long ago when Paul Galvin told employees to "bring to work a healthy spirit of discontent." Today, according to Glenn Gienko (1995), executive vice president of human resources, "brutal honesty is still part of our culture. We give people the freedom to express divergent opinions."

In the early 1990s, Motorola recognized that its global growth depended in large measure on its ability to succeed in what came to be known in the popular press as the "war for talent." Throughout the decade, the company developed and relied upon an elaborate organizational management development plan to guide its global human resources planning and training. The stated goal, according to Glenn Gienko, has been to manage the global talent pool in a way that will eventually move the center of power from the United States to key operations and markets in other countries. To cultivate this pool of global business leaders, Motorola annually brings a group of global managers to company headquarters in Schaumburg, Illinois, for a two- to three-year work assignment; they later rotate back to other regions, functions, and businesses. Through an elaborate program of courses and work assignments, these elite (high potential) executives apply the company's strategy and values to the company's most challenging problems. It is a cultural experience that fuses practical skills with a deep personal understanding of the power of shared values to guide business decision making.

All Motorola business units have training and education teams, including designers, facilitators, developers, and instructors. They are members of what the company calls its "league of innovators." Business units provide about 50% of the company's total training and education program; 5–10% comes from the central human resources office (diversity, leadership development, stress management); and the remaining 40–45% from Motorola University (MU), established as a separate institute with extensive responsibilities for materials, publications, and actual training activities. Most importantly, every business unit leader must ensure that each employee in that unit receives approximately 40 hours of training per year. It is a way of ensuring that Motorola employees are effectively "competing against their one-person counterparts . . . in any other company in the same business" (Galvin, 1995).

Many companies have created education programs to set the stage for change. Motorola designed its education and training to *be* the change process itself. This is especially evident in the work of Motorola University. Motorola University's specific role has been to serve as an agent for change within the company. Former CEO Robert Galvin is said to continuously press the staff: "Are you pushing change? Are you pushing tomorrow? I don't want you to push yesterday or necessarily today. I need for you to push concepts for tomorrow." Thus, Motorola University is supposed to identify and emphasize the skills and knowledge the company will need 5–10 years into the future, not just what it needs today. All MU courses are evaluated at three levels. Level 1 assesses materials and content. Level 2 assesses the trainees' mastery of principles, facts, techniques, and skills. Level 3 involves how well the skills and behaviors have been transferred to the job at intervals of 30, 60, 90, and 365 days. As one training director said, "Every Level 3 (review) is individually designed and serves as an organizational intervention." In this way, Motorola's education investments are actually investments in the continuous process of learning and change. As further discussed in Chapter 8, this process focuses on concepts and implementation techniques that promote learning, renewal, and stakeholder management.

Transmitting the Culture

By the mid-1990s, Motorola's rapid growth had raised a serious challenge: the need to find, hire, train, and integrate large numbers of new people into a deep and humanistic corporate culture that affected every aspect of the company's operations. In an effort to focus attention on this matter, Robert Galvin described a set of principles that should be the bases for company-wide policies and practices (Galvin interview, 1995):

- *The Importance of Values.* Galvin stated that every organization must have an underpinning of values that are essential to organizational success and activate its purpose. Speaking of Motorola's commitment to uncompromising integrity and respect for the dignity of the individual, he declared: "These are both our inner spirit and our outward manifestation."

- *Trust.* Motorola should strive to become a "trusting institution of trusting people." "When we trust each other," said Galvin, "we can devote our entire being to the institution and our loyalty to each other." The importance of trust to team building is recurrent in conversations with Motorola personnel.

- *Competitiveness.* Galvin urged his colleagues to "be competitive, one at a time." "The way we will be competitive," he explained, "will be as one-person counterparts to the best [people] in any other company in the same business." Galvin subsequently called this having a "Super Bowl mentality," with an emphasis on teamwork and team spirit.

- *Leadership.* According to Galvin, successful teams need leaders who are "anticipators" of change. When leaders anticipate change well, cycle time will drop and the company's ability to "turn on a dime" will provide competitive advantage. "Trusted leaders who make sound commitments will drive our company to the newest opportunities." To Galvin, the leader is the person who takes the organization elsewhere, and who leaves a mark on the company. "Leaders must spread hope. Leaders leave legacies."

- *Education and Training.* Galvin affirmed Motorola's historic commitment to heavy expenditures intended to develop and maintain an educated workforce. He argued that training is an investment rather than a cost: "If people are trained in proper sequence to their needs, the cost borne early in a period is earned back in a short number of months thereafter." As much of Motorola's future growth will largely occur outside the United States, education and training programs of comparable scope and quality have to be conducted worldwide.

Forging Change: Individual Dignity Entitlement (IDE)

Motorola escaped the fate of many other companies in the 1980s and early 1990s by avoiding the major downsizing and restructuring associated with corporate reengineering (Hammer and Champy, 1993). By 1995, however, it was clear that global markets and the American workplace were changing in ways that Motorola could not ignore.

As Motorola designed its strategic approach for global growth in the 1990s, four critical success factors stood out. First, the company needed to achieve rapid and significant quality improvement; many of its competitors were achieving comparable, or superior, product quality. Second, the company needed to radically improve customer service; it had developed an unwanted (and unwelcome) reputation as an "arrogant" supplier. Third, the company needed to achieve breakthrough operations improvements, especially cycle time reduction. The fourth requirement was development of a changed relationship with employees that would enable the company to rapidly respond to the other challenges through a company-wide process of change and renewal. The first three initiatives were necessary to meet competitive challenges and insure the company's continued growth and profitability. But the fourth initiative—creating wholehearted employee support for change—was crucial, and perhaps the most difficult to achieve. The critical challenge was to mobilize the efforts of the company many stakeholders—and particularly employees at all levels—for mutual benefit.

Individual dignity entitlement (IDE) was both a critical ingredient of the new strategic direction and an expression of Motorola's historic commitment to respect for the individual. The IDE initiative was designed as an attempt to develop stronger links between the needs, goals, and behaviors of individual employees and the long-term objectives of the corporation as a whole. David Pulatie, Director of Management Change Services during this period, was explicit about the IDE goal: "We want people to say 'Motorola is the best corporation in the world.'" The central leadership challenge was to fit desired outcomes for the company with desired outcomes for employees in the midst of the powerful forces shaping Motorola's business, including competition, technology, global economics, changing demographics, legislation, the balance of work and personal life, and the preparedness of individuals. Pulatie believed that the critical drivers for the company were its values, behaviors (how values are put into action), and survival needs (growth and innovation). Employees were driven by their own wants, needs, and reward expectations. Critical outcomes for the company were growth, profitability, and reputation; and for employees, economic security and personal dignity and satisfaction (Pulatie interview, 1995, pp. 23–24).

The goal of the IDE program was to change attitudes about human resource management from an emphasis on entitlement to an emphasis on commitment. Motorola articulated its "social contract" with its employee stakeholders through a continuous conversation regarding the company's future. Global competition did threaten job security, it was true, but the company could continue to grow. Employees needed to understand that they were not just doing a job, but were doing work that was vital to Motorola's success. Job security could not be guaranteed, but skill training could guarantee that each individual would be employable. Motorola could not guarantee a long career path within the company; individuals needed to develop a personal career plan. Loyalty to the company was no longer the highest compliment; now, professional knowledge mattered more.

The IDE initiative was also intended to supplement Motorola's traditional emphasis on "team" relationships, activities, and goals. "Teams are a marvelous way to run an institution," said Pulatie, "but teams are made up of individuals." Motorola tried to respond to the needs of individuals, but also encourage them to develop and utilize their fullest potential. When the IDE program was started in the mid-1990s, some employees were cynical. That reaction underscored Motorola's need to renew an emphasis on individual involvement and achievement and promote an ongoing dialogue to strengthen the alignment between each employee's needs and the goals of the company. The goal was to encourage entrepreneurial risk taking, productivity enhancement, openness, and sharing of information and concerns within the workplace. Pulatie and others believed that too great a focus on short-term goals discouraged those behaviors. One-to-one dialogues between each employee and his/her supervisor were designed to promote communication and build the trust needed to engage employees in more ambitious goals, both for themselves and for the company.

Respect for Families

Respect for the individual employee necessarily extends to the families and dependents of employees as well. Motorola has recognized that the modern work environment creates many pressures on personal and family life, and has instituted extensive work-family programs and initiatives throughout the organization. It offers fitness and wellness programs at many locations, and provides incentives for preventive healthcare. It also operates child day care centers in Schaumburg, Scotland, and Taiwan. Still, the reality of trying to be a high-performance organization wherever it operates forces employees to make hard choices. At the beginning of the new century, Motorola became a "24-7" corporation: Business is conducted twenty-four hours a day, seven days a week. According to Glenn Gienko, senior vice president of human resources, "When your largest market is 12 time zones away, there's no such thing as a workday anymore. It doesn't begin at eight and end at five. . . . We expect people to call whenever there's a problem. That's just the new world. If you can't accept this, you can't be part of it." Gienko acknowledges that even the most family-friendly policies cannot eliminate the demands of a dynamic and highly competitive environment: "Not everyone will be successful here. . . . Work/family balance is a priority, but this is not an easy place to work. We can help people, but ultimately, it's their responsibility" (Gienko interview, 1999).

New realities can force companies to alter longstanding practices. Major changes often require significant stakeholder cooperation and a willingness to interact with the corporation on new terms. The late 1990s were years of difficult change at Motorola, and a new understanding with employee stakeholders was crucial to re-establishing the company's competitive position. The company might have adopted the popular reengineering ideas of the day—reduce workforce, redesign processes, restructure operations. Instead, it pursued a more complicated process of dialogue and engagement with employees that facilitated a company-wide process of change while maintaining the company's tradition of shared values. Through a process it calls "renewal," Motorola developed new competency in working with its employees and other stakeholders. This process is further discussed in Chapter 8.

CUMMINS IN THE COMMUNITY[2]

Cummins Engine Company offers a model of commitment and innovation in corporation-community relations comparable to Motorola's leadership in human resource management. Respect for the community involves recognition of needs, acceptance of interdependencies, and willingness to take action. From the time of its first contributions of architectural services in Columbus, Indiana, during the 1950s to its support of community organizations and development initiatives in all of its operating locations in the 1990s, Cummins has pursued an expansive concept of community involvement and responsibility.

Cummins' role as a corporate citizen has evolved through several distinct stages and the dimensions of citizenship have changed markedly in recent decades. Its active community involvement began with its willingness to invest in physical improvements for its headquarters community. Architecture was a passion of J. Irwin Miller, Cummins' chairman, and for its first two decades (1950–70) the Cummins Engine Foundation (CEF, funded with shares of company stock) focused on bringing modern architectural design to Columbus— first for new school buildings and later for other structures and areas (Cruickshank and Sicilia, 1998, pp. 236–7). The company's support for the architectural and physical landscape of its rural hometown has earned international recognition, and recently brought the downtown Columbus mall area the rare designation of a "National Historic Landmark" (Meredith, 2000, p. 14).

In the late 1960s, CEF's mission was broadened to include issues of race, poverty, and the physical environment. The company hired black field officers to represent the black community in major metropolitan areas (Los Angeles, New York, Atlanta, Detroit, Chicago, Washington) and began funding local community organizations in those cities as well. This involvement proved controversial, and its direct benefits remained unclear; but the company's mostly

---

[2]This section is based on Cruikshank and Sicilia (1997), with additional interviews, documents, and data provided by Sicilia and the authors.

white managers gradually recognized and responded to the legitimate grievances of black employees, customers, and neighbors. During this same period, J. Irwin Miller rose, somewhat unwillingly, to national prominence as the first lay president of the National Council of Churches and a leading spokesman for business responsibility in society. In 1968 his picture appeared on the cover of Esquire with the headline: "This man should be the next president of the United States" (Cruickshank and Sicilia, pp. 10–11).

By the mid-1970s, Cummins reorganized and combined a number of separate functions into a "Corporate Action Division (CAD)" under the leadership of a vice president who reported directly to the CEO. Corporate philanthropy, government relations and public affairs, community relations, human resources development, and affirmative action programs were integrated into the division, which was intended to provide a coherent focus for the company with respect to social and community responsibilities. The CAD's stated mission was to "serve as an in-house resource for understanding the social and political context in which the company does business." The CAD began as a headquarters unit, but quickly decentralized to serve the various functional areas of the company (such as finance, purchasing, and operations) where specific initiatives could be launched. This process enabled Cummins to develop a highly successful affirmative action program, establish a significant minority purchasing program, and link social and community considerations to its strategic planning. During the 1970s Cummins, through CEF, was one of only two Fortune 500 companies to allocate 5 percent of its pretax net income to charitable contributions; the Fortune 500 average was 1.3 percent.

From Local to Global

Cummins' focus on local community responsibilities eventually led to broader concerns with its global business conduct, including the application of ethical norms in various parts of the world. By the end of the 1970s, Cummins was producing a series of "country reports" that tried to look 10 years into the future and answer key questions about a country's economic, social, and political prospects. (10 years was selected because experience had shown it took that long for an investment in a diesel plant to make a return.)

The critical questions, in which the term "stakeholders" was explicitly used, were:

- Within that 10-year period, would Cummins be able to "treat the stakeholders for whom it is responsible (particularly its employees) in accordance with minimal Cummins standards"?
- Would Cummins "have the opportunity to conduct a profitable business without engaging in activities which violated Cummins' ethical practices policy"?
- Would Cummins "make a contribution to the host country's development process"?

This analytical process eventually influenced key business decisions, including the decision to invest in South Korea rather than the Philippines, and to forego a potentially lucrative manufacturing opportunity in apartheid-divided South Africa in the late 1970s (Cruikshank and Sicilia, 1997, pp. 328–9). Cummins' understanding of its responsibility to potential stakeholders thus affected both its choice of operating locations and its practices within the locations in which it chose, or had previously chosen, to operate.

As Cummins expanded its international operations from the 1960s onward, it placed primary emphasis on collaborative arrangements, limiting its own investment and risk, and maintaining flexibility, even at the cost of weakened management control. As a medium-sized company, Cummins lacked the resources to establish widespread foreign operations on its own. Moreover, Cummins learned that it needed to approach each foreign operation as an individual case, remaining sensitive to local conditions and learning to adapt its operations to market opportunities as they evolved. According to a 1974 internal memo by CEO Henry Schacht, the basic strategy was to establish "preemptive positions" in new markets slightly ahead of demand, but to limit capital commitments by using local partners and "networking" its plants for maximum efficiency (Cruikshank and Sicilia, 1997, p. 367).

The pattern for Cummins' entry into international operations was established by its experience in India, where it began discussions, based on prior personal contacts, among a Cummins executive, a major private investor, and government officials in 1960. Development of local investment opportunities was a major government concern, and one-fourth of the shares in the company were eventually sold to the public with great success. The Indian investor retained another fourth, and Cummins held a half interest. The use of unskilled labor at the construction site was a second government goal, and resulted in some delays, but production facilities were eventually completed and the project proved highly successful over the long run.

Cummins' involvement in Mexico began in 1963 and, like its later entry into China, took the form of a licensing arrangement in which engines were assembled from kits manufactured in the United Kingdom. This evolved into a manufacturing joint venture with 60% ownership by DINA, a state-owned enterprise. In 1987 Cummins acquired 100% control of the company and set out to transform it into a modern, efficient, and socially responsible operation. Steven Knaebel, who became president of "Cummsa" at the time of the takeover, described the situation this way: "It was clear to me that my first task . . . was to let everyone know that many changes would take place . . . [and] would never cease: We would see Mexico as a country, an economy, and a marketplace undergo dramatic transformation. And we would have to change at an equal or faster pace in order to survive and prosper" (Knaebel, 1994, p. 49). Extensive reorganization, basic changes in management culture and processes, and external transformations were involved. Landscaping of the barren plant environment and major improvements in working conditions were followed by a new emphasis on training, based on principles developed by the Cummins Production System (CPS) unit in Columbus. The "Mexicanized" version of the CPS training course was eventually required for every Cummsa employee. The culture of the operation was changed to the point that not only Knaebel but even Cummins CEO Henderson wandered the shop floor and conversed with the production workers. According to the workers themselves, this experience was unprecedented (p. 50). Cummins' commitment to Mexico has also included significant philanthropic activity not directly related to its business operations. Beginning with financial aid provided after the 1985 earthquake, Cummsa has become involved in aid to the blind, rescue and support of street children, education, and protection of natural resources. Cummsa has established its own foundation, and largely finances its philanthropic activities without parent company involvement. All of these external involvements are audited with a scorecard prepared by the Cummins Engine Foundation; the results for all foreign operations are compiled and reviewed at company headquarters.

Cummins was among the first group of U.S. companies opening up contacts with China after President Nixon's historic visit in 1973. After participating in the sale of heavy construction equipment for open-pit mining, Cummins executives visited China in 1975 to establish service arrangements for the equipment in use and to establish commercial relations with the Machinery Import and Export Corporation. Two Chinese-born Cummins executives helped to develop contacts, and the acceptance of Cummins' products soon spread beyond the mining industry into other uses. Negotiations for the production of engines under a license agreement began in 1978 and were eventually concluded in 1981. Throughout the negotiations, Cummins was wary of over-commitment, whereas the Chinese had difficulty deciding which ministry would be assigned responsibility for local operations. The initial plan was for local assembly of engines from kits produced elsewhere, with manufacture and assembly by the Chinese licensee to follow. Establishment of a new technical support and distribution center was subsequently added to the project. This initial venture, though small and narrowly specialized, was viewed as successful. By 1985 Cummins began looking for a new licensee to manufacture other types of engines, and eventually made an agreement with China's largest manufacturer of on-highway trucks, which also proved successful. Cummins' use of licensing arrangements rather than JV partnerships, although giving it less control over local operations, not only limited capital requirements and risks but also permitted immediate repatriation of earnings. Throughout its negotiations and operations, Cummins tried to recognize and respond to the goals and concerns of its Chinese stakeholders. One executive explained the success of the Chinese ventures as follows: "I think we were respected for how we went about doing it" (Cruikshank and Sicilia, 1997, p. 376).

Cummins' experience in Brazil during the 1980s shows how a flexible shift in its stakeholder focus enabled it to achieve long-term success. Although the company had been interested in this large Latin American nation since the late 1950s, Brazil's poor roads, underdeveloped trucking industry, and established competitors deterred any move. In the early 1960s, Cummins—not wishing to take the plunge into Brazil on its own—tried to establish a joint venture with

International Harvester, but that effort failed. In 1971 Cummins bought an engine manufacturing plant near Sao Paulo from a German firm, while continuing to look for a local partner. With a total investment of some $10 million, Cummins planned to manufacture a modest 10 engines per day. Soon the Brazilian government persuaded Cummins to join a consortium with two other non-Brazilian firms to manufacture buses, for which Cummins would produce the engines, but this enterprise foundered. Cummins then formed a joint venture with a company controlled by Brazilian entrepreneur Augusto Antunes to make engines for Ford. That business also encountered problems, especially after Ford canceled its standing order for Brazilian-made engines. In the midst of their continuing search for the right formula to reach the Brazilian market, Cummins's managers discovered that Mercedes was supplying a large portion of the trucks it sold in the United States with engines made in Brazil. Cummins had not considered manufacturing in Brazil for export. In 1980, the company sent executives from Columbus to evaluate the situation, and they concluded that export production would increase output enough to make the operation profitable. Moreover, these executives felt that expanded production would make Cummins large enough to be taken seriously as a corporate citizen in Brazil (Cruikshank and Sicilia, 1997, p. 371).

At this point, Cummins' interests dovetailed with those of the Brazilian government, which was trying to expand manufactured exports in order to attract foreign currency. Through its "Befiex" (Brazilian Export and Financial Incentive) program, the state had begun to allow foreign manufacturers to import one dollar's worth of merchandise duty free for every three dollars of product that they exported. Cummins jumped at the opportunity to import an expensive component of its engines (the fuel systems) duty free. Meanwhile, Augusto Antunes urged Cummins to buy out his portion of the joint venture. "We've never been good at manufacturing" in Brazil, Antunes argued frankly. "Chemical processing, yes—but not manufacturing" (Cruickshank and Sicilia, 1997, p. 372). Cummins agreed in 1981, and restructured the firm as Cummins Brazil, S.A. The Brazilian government added further incentives— a 15% rebate on goods exported by foreign companies—and the Cummins plant moved into the black. Soon it was a highly profitable, low-cost operation. In the end, Cummins had forged a successful strategic alliance, not with a local joint venture partner but with the Brazilian government. Between 1981 and 1988 Brazil paid Cummins some $70 million to export engines and components, which the company reinvested—plus another $9 million—in two major expansion programs. It took a decade, but Cummins had found a major stakeholder with complementary interests.

The relationship between Cummins and the local and national communities in which it operates has evolved considerably over four decades, but the company has consistently emphasized respect for the people, organizations, and governments with which it comes into contact, and has favored public and social decision processes over unilateral actions. (Even in the case of Columbus school architecture, Miller has insisted that "we never pushed it; we waited to be asked" (Cruikshank and Sicilia, 1997, p. 236). On occasion company officials were frustrated by slow or seemingly wrongheaded decision making of external groups, but both its successes and failures contributed to a deeper understanding of how its business interests relate to varied cultural, social, and political situations. This knowledge became increasing valuable as the company expanded to new countries and cultures. The process of interaction that occurred between the company and its many local and national communities brought it a highly favorable international reputation and produced substantial "social capital," which in turn led to new business opportunities for Cummins. As discussed further in Chapter 5, it also generated new ways of thinking about the synergy between the competitive realities of the diesel engine industry and social realities of communities such as Columbus, Indiana.

Cummins' orientation to its stakeholders, and its philosophy of corporate responsibility, has had widespread recognition and impact. Its programs and policies have been cited as models of corporate citizenship, and executives who have spent part of their careers with the company have often transmitted its philosophy to other organizations. Henry Schacht, a member of Cummins' top management team for two decades, later became CEO and chairman of Lucent, a multibillion dollar telecommunications spin-off from AT&T. As at Motorola, Cummins' interactions with one group of stakeholders—in this case local communities—yielded new competencies and skills that proved to be useful in dealing with others.

CONCLUSION

Stakeholder management is an expression of the shared values and humanistic commitments of the corporation. These commitments—reflected in core values, ethics, policies, procedures, and practices of the organization—give meaning to our basic proposition that corporations are what they do. Every company must address issues of human interaction, within the firm and beyond. These issues exist at different levels—micro, meso, macro—in areas of fundamental business importance such as employment, customer relations, business alliances, and community relations. The impact of Motorola's shared values on employment, training and development, cultural maintenance, and strategic change is a defining aspect of the company's identity. The identity of the Cummins Engine Company is also defined through its behavior and interactions with stakeholders, including the communities in which it operates. Such relationships are an important resource for the modern corporation. The proposition that corporations are what they do is more than rhetoric. It guides the analyst toward a focus on observable actions that reflect humanistic commitments and stakeholder management.

5

STRATEGIC RESPONSE TO

COMPETITIVE CHALLENGES

According to the stakeholder view (SHV) of the corporation, the management of vital relationships can be a major source of competitive success or an important cause of failure; stakeholder linkages can enhance organizational wealth or, when they are dysfunctional, reduce it. This view has both conceptual and operational implications: it involves the way managers *think* about stakeholders, and the ways in which managers *interact* with stakeholders, both internal and external. It can focus on such direct and obvious linkages as those between a firm and its employees and customers, or can involve the creation of new relationships, including those with political groups, governments, and other companies and industries.

This chapter examines ways in which innovative stakeholder initiatives can protect and enhance a firm's position in its industry, and contribute to its success in the marketplace. During the past three decades, both Motorola and Cummins discovered that their long-run success required new kinds of external support—political leverage and renewed customer confidence for Motorola; financial and technical resources for Cummins—which, in turn, led each of them to develop relationships with new constituencies. While attempting to retain the humanistic commitments of their core cultures, both companies dramatically changed their strategies—and to some extent their structures—to accomplish their business objectives. Their efforts to reaffirm and adapt their core cultures in these new situations are further examined below and in Chapter 8.

MOTOROLA: MANAGING BY HIGH PRINCIPLES

During the period 1980–2000, Motorola transformed the way it thought about and managed stakeholder relationships. A number of major business milestones mark this strategic evolution, which involved a growing awareness of, and responsiveness to, an increasingly dynamic and volatile operating environment. Responding to this environment altered Motorola's relationships with traditional stakeholders (such as employees in its U.S. plants) and brought it into contact with new and nontraditional groups ranging from the government of the People's Republic of China to the exploding population of Internet users. During the 1980s, Motorola's relationships with traditional and new groups of stakeholders evolved in several different ways, but by the early 1990s a mature stakeholder orientation pervaded the entire company. The 1993 annual report recognized regular interactions with five "key publics"—customers, employees, suppliers, shareholders, and communities. (In 2000, Motorola chief executive officer, Christopher Galvin, took the further step of addressing "A Message to Motorola's Stakeholders" on the company web site [business code of conduct page].) Formal acknowledgment of these relationships confirmed the evolution of stakeholder thinking that had been taking place within Motorola for at least a decade.

The 1980s Transformation

Beginning in the decade that immediately preceded World War II, Motorola based its success on technological innovation by encouraging its researchers to attack the frontiers of electronics. The company's knowledge base grew during the 1940s and 1950s, and by the 1960s the company had become a formidable research enterprise. Management had also learned to redirect resources to the most productive uses. For example, after the war the company invested heavily in the development of television technologies, becoming one of America's leading manufacturers of television sets. However, after a considerable period of profitability, senior management concluded that price, not technology, would be the decisive factor in the television market of the future. The company stopped investing in the consumer electronics products that came to be dominated by Japanese competitors such as Matsushita, to which Motorola sold its Quasar™ television business in 1974. Motorola continuously focused on developing and exploiting a distinctive "strategic fit" between its technological capabilities and product markets, where its technological leadership would command a premium price.

At the beginning of the 1980s, Motorola had two primary sources of revenue—communications equipment and semiconductors—each of which accounted for about one-third of total revenue; the rest came from a diverse collection of products and activities. Motorola's international sales were significant, but still well below 25 percent of total revenues. But the company had already made commitments to new technologies and global markets. Motorola's operations over the next two decades involved the continuous interplay of new technologies, global markets, and worldwide production.

On the technological side, Motorola transformed its established position in the pager market into a leadership role in cellular phones. It began testing cellular phones in the Baltimore/Washington area in 1980, and introduced its popular DynaTac™ line in 1983.

The company had been exporting to, and licensing products in, Japan since the late 1960s, and in 1980 it delivered 150 advanced paging units for testing by Nippon Telephone and Telegraph (NTT). It was soon accepted as an NTT supplier, and subsequently became the only U.S. manufacturer qualified by Japanese officials to market cellular phones in that country. Although the strong dollar limited Motorola's international sales in many markets during the 1980s, the company's high-tech global business strategy was emerging in clear terms.

During this same period, Motorola's international—primarily Asian—production was also expanding. Other Asian markets were also opening for Motorola products. When, in 1980, Motorola entered into a major joint venture with Toko, Inc., to produce a semiconductor designed specifically for the Japanese market, a decision was made to reorganize Asian operations. All of the company's Japanese subsidiaries were combined to create Nippon Motorola in 1981, and a new headquarters position was created to manage both this business and the Toko joint venture. A new assembly plant was opened in Malaysia and the company signed an agreement with the government of Sri Lanka to build an assembly operation there. Motorola's first orders from the People's Republic of China were also received during the early 1980s; its expansion there—to the point where China came to be officially recognized as the company's "second home"—is examined in more detail in Chapter 7.

One stimulus for Motorola's strategic expansion was the growth of Asian economies. In addition, company executives recognized the increasing acceptance of foreign, primarily Japanese, products in its U.S. markets. Motorola, long a supplier of electronics to American automobile manufacturers, became convinced that some of Japan's success in the U.S. electronics market was due to unjustifiably low prices made possible by government subsidies. This conviction led to a dramatic addition to Motorola's strategic stakeholder network, and to notoriety for the company and its chief executive, Robert Galvin, on the national and international stage.

In 1982 Motorola filed an antidumping complaint with the U.S. International Trade Commission and the Commerce Department alleging that Japanese competitors were selling pagers at lower prices in the United States than in Japan. This signaled Motorola's determination to defend its domestic market against what it perceived to be unfair competition, and also to insist that Japanese markets become more open to U.S. competitors. Even many years later, Robert Galvin expressed anger at the attempt of Japanese firms to claim a "right of sanctuary" that protected them from competition in their home markets while they entered the U.S. market without serious barriers (Galvin interview, 1999). In January 1983, the Commerce Department ruled in Motorola's favor, setting explicit dumping margins on tone-only pagers. The company's victory, hailed in the American trade press and by other U.S. companies, produced anger in Japan, where the government responded by advocating more open international markets for Japanese products. Motorola's subsequent success in Japan, although validating the quality of its products, gave it only a small piece of a very large market. Galvin condemned Japan for the impediments placed before his company as it tried to establish and enlarge its market position there.

Creating Allies and Stakeholders: The Chip Wars

The seeds of Motorola's antidumping petition lay in trends that had been developing for a number of years. Motorola began losing semiconductor sales to Japanese competitors during the 1970s. By 1981 the damage was so serious that the company decided on a risky new course: launching a major media effort to dramatize the impact of Japanese competition. The multimillion-dollar campaign began with a two-page spread entitled "Is Japan's Challenge to American Industry Going Unanswered?" (*New York Times*, 1981). The campaign was aimed at business and opinion leaders and ran in the *Wall Street Journal*, *New York Times*, and *Washington Post*; spot television messages were also included.

The advertising campaign turned Motorola and Galvin into visible advocates of concerted action to beat back Japanese competition. A 1985 *Business Week* story entitled "Bob Galvin's Angry Campaign against Japan" focused on the Motorola leader's highly publicized call for a three-year, 20% surcharge on all Japanese manufactured goods imported into the United States. Galvin argued that U.S. businesses were forced to move their manufacturing operations abroad because of unfair competition from Asia. Worse, the U.S. government was not doing its part to keep manufacturing activities (and jobs) at home. "By failing to stand up for American industry," said Galvin, "the American government is inadvertently letting American industry walk out of this society" (Dryfack and Frons, 1985). By 1985, 30–35% of Motorola employees were located outside the United States; Galvin feared that less than half would remain in America by the mid-1990s. (In fact, U.S. employment held steady during the 1990s, but most of the 50,000 jobs the company created during the 1990s were located in Asia.) Reducing jobs at home while expanding them abroad conflicted strongly with Motorola's traditional "family culture," which emphasized respect and benefits for employees. However, Galvin insisted that Motorola and other multinationals really had no choice: "We will do what we have to in order to survive. But that survival includes a process of defection. We are defecting from this country."

Galvin was not counting on Washington to solve Motorola's competitive problems, but he believed government support was needed to create a more level playing field. Internally, he emphasized the need to draw on the company's "culture of renewal" in order to transform Motorola into a company that could survive and prosper in tough global competition. Meeting Asian competition became an obsession throughout the company; its 150 top officers took intensive seminars on Asian culture, economy, and politics. In late 1984 Galvin relieved six senior executives of their normal duties and closeted them away as a special task force to devise new strategies to meet the Asian challenge. Asia was the only topic on the agenda for the April 1985 meeting of the executive board. "We had to go back to the basics and make very sure that the leadership of our company genuinely understood what the Asia threat was," said Galvin.

Galvin's frustration was rooted in what he perceived as a double standard. An ideological advocate of free trade and open markets, he encouraged Japanese companies to enter and compete in the United States. But Galvin was angered by Japan's refusal to allow Motorola to expand there. During the 1970s, he had quietly lobbied both the Nixon and Carter administrations for policies that would offset or eliminate the home market protection enjoyed by his Japanese competitors, but without much success. Motorola's senior managers concluded that they needed to mobilize public support if any significant policy changes were to be made. The "Meeting Japan's Challenge" media campaign was designed to open a dialogue with a wide range of political, business, and opinion leaders in order to build understanding and awareness, and thereby create powerful allies for its position in the trade policy debate.

Galvin's campaign drew attention—and eventually support—from many quarters. Many industry leaders came to agree that government had an essential role to play in setting fair rules for international competition. The Reagan administration was reluctant to interfere with market forces, but the Office of the U.S. Trade Representative (USTR) gradually became more understanding of the pressures U.S. firms faced because of Japanese competition. Motorola and other manufacturers became more adept at filing formal trade complaints; in a number of highly publicized instances the validity of these complaints was acknowledged and remedies were imposed.

Political Strategy

Motorola's strategy in the chip wars was essentially to develop allies throughout the business community, government, and general public who would lend support to its policy proposals. Part of this strategy was to show how other organizations and individuals—and the federal government itself—also were adversely affected by foreign (particularly Japanese) competition. Motorola also increased its own understanding of the federal bureaucracy and the policy-making process so as to position itself as a leader in this arena. Motorola's Washington office was expanded and given senior leadership, in close contact with Galvin, and company personnel became actively involved with various congressional committees, staffs, and agencies.

A critical aspect of this campaign was moving Galvin into a conspicuous and influential spokesman on trade issues. As early as 1982, Galvin appeared before the Senate Foreign Relations Committee to explain the nature of the problem and the seriousness of the risks involved. Galvin contended that the Japanese government promoted the electronics industry "through protection-ist and other market-distorting" devices, and cited specific Motorola experi-ence as evidence. As mentioned, Motorola had broken into the supposedly closed Japanese pager market in 1981 with an order from Nippon Telegraph & Telephone (NTT). According to Galvin's testimony, shortly after that a new Japanese firm entered the U.S. pager market, "undercutting prevailing pager prices by over 50%," to a level about one-third of the price being charged in Japan. Within a few months, the newcomer had captured more than 10% of the U.S. market. The huge domestic market was of prime importance to Motorola, and Galvin testified that "[T]he revenues Motorola has lost as a result of meeting this new Japanese competitor will probably exceed the total revenues from the NTT business." Galvin believed that Motorola was facing Japanese government-sponsored exports in the open U.S. market, and was being prevented from competing aggressively in Japan's domestic market by government-erected barriers (see Murtha and Lenway, 1994; Yoffie, 1987).

More threatening to the United States than any specific incident, Galvin warned, was the Japanese model of government-sponsored trade support: "Not only has Japan become a serious competitive threat to U.S. high-technology industries, but it has also established a model that other nations are seeking to follow." To overcome what he termed "the tremendous inertia against imports in the Japanese system," Galvin recommended that the U.S. government adopt an "affirmative action program" in which targets for increased U.S. business participation in Japan would be actively pursued by both the U.S. and Japanese governments (*Industry Week*, 1982).

Galvin spoke to Japanese business and government officials as well as to U.S. leaders. In October 1982, six weeks after his Senate testimony and several months after Motorola filed its landmark dumping suit against Japanese mobile pager manufacturers, Galvin spoke at the Japan national press club in Tokyo. One of the causes of the U.S.-Japan trade friction, he argued, was the perception among U.S. executives that the Japanese market was closed to their companies' products. "We perceive the Japanese marketplace has been extensively protected over the period from the late 1950s until now and therefore it was not possible for most of our companies to compete during the formative state of your [that is, Japanese] industry." To remedy this, he said, the U.S. and Japanese governments should take "moderate measures" to improve bilateral trade relations. However, he called a "local content" bill before the U.S. Congress an "immoderate" action, thereby signaling a preference for actions that would facilitate fair competition rather than simply provide protection. Japanese trade officials had become quite concerned that local content legislation would pass, which would be a serious blow to their export industries. They therefore welcomed Galvin's characterization of local content legislation as being immoderate. His preference for more open competition, rather than protectionist measures, helped facilitate eventual government-to-government discussion of actions to open the Japanese market (Kyodo News Service, 1982).

Trust building between the United States and Japan was an important ingredient of Motorola's political strategy. The company recognized that trust is essential to any regime that would enable governments and companies to know the rules of the game (see Mahon and McGowan, 1996; also, the discussion of trust in Chapter 2). Throughout the first term of the Reagan administration (1981–84), U.S. government officials negotiated at length with Japanese officials to resolve trade disputes involving semiconductors and semiconductor products. The Reagan negotiating team included the U.S. Trade Representative, Ambassador to Japan, Secretary of Commerce, and many others. Japan's negotiations were conducted by officials of the Ministry of International Trade and Industry (MITI). The negotiators worked closely with trade associations for the semiconductor industries of both countries and the executives of leading companies involved in the disputes. Galvin, representing Motorola, was an active participant throughout the year-long negotiations. When the agreement was announced in July 1986, Galvin said, "The Japanese have been steadfastly earnest in finding a solution based on trust. The stage is set for a more beneficial trade and investment relationship" (PR Newswire, 1982).

Motorola saw itself as one of the U.S. firms most affected by this agreement, and when it appeared that violations occurred almost immediately, the firm took fast action. In 1987, believing that the credibility of the agreement was at stake, Motorola persuaded the U.S. government to impose formal sanctions on Japan, including 100% tariffs on about $300 million of Japanese imports. Two years later, President Bush announced that more sanctions would be imposed because of Japan's failure to open its markets to U.S. telecommunications products such as cellular telephones and mobile radios. This high level of involvement in national policy required personnel with highly specialized knowledge and experience. A *Los Angeles Times* profile in May 1989 pointed out the "revolving door" through which a significant number of experienced U.S. trade officials passed on the way to positions of various kinds at Motorola. During this time, two Motorola executives became assistant secretaries of commerce with trade-related responsibilities; one was Michael Galvin, a son of the chairman (Pine, 1989).

The complexity and sophistication of Motorola's "chip wars" strategy was not fully appreciated by either adversaries or observers until several years after the semiconductor agreement was negotiated and implemented. As a political strategy, it had at least six key elements:

- Clear message—"Meeting Japan's Challenge"
- Credible spokesperson—Robert Galvin
- Public leadership—prominent political and business figures
- Effective communication—both print and oral, at home and abroad
- Expertise and learning—technical knowledge; administrative and political skill
- Execution/follow-through—Legal complaints; political initiatives; internal practices, such as renewed emphasis on quality and customer satisfaction.

Motorola learned important lessons about the role of political decision making on international trade issues. Galvin's example of tireless, personal leadership of the campaign became a symbol of business leadership and commitment to the global economy and free trade. The Motorola management team understood the complexity of the global marketplace and the proliferation of new stakeholders with which a company would have to interact if it were to succeed. The decade-long chip wars forced Motorola to learn new lessons about politics and markets. To deal effectively with each stakeholder required knowledge, expertise, and deep understanding; to deal with all of the stakeholders at once required a strategic mindset. At many points the company could have slowed its efforts, allowed others to lead, or deferred to government officials to shape the new rules. But it never did so. In a recent interview, Galvin (1999) commented that "our company's first job was rewriting the rules" and creating the principles by which commerce could be conducted.

Customer Stakeholders: The Quality Crusade

A frequent and sometimes legitimate criticism of American business in the 1980s was that there had been a significant decline in manufacturing quality. Foreign automobiles, for example, soared to nearly a quarter of all U.S. sales as American consumers determined that the quality of Toyota, Honda, Volkswagen, and other imports was superior to Ford, General Motors, and Chrysler vehicles. Lordstown, Ohio, home of a troubled GM assembly plant, became the symbolic link between poor product quality and poor labor relations. A popular cartoon read: *Price . . . Quality . . . Service . . . Pick any two.*

There were many excuses for America's manufacturing weaknesses in the 1980s: labor problems and motivation; weak supply chain relationships; safety and environmental regulations; subsidy and promotional policies of foreign governments; lagging technology; and so on. Motorola, which supplied electronic components for the space program as well as for domestic consumer goods, understood the importance of quality. Its executives knew that high quality standards were not commonplace throughout the economy, and the company became a champion of a national effort to raise quality standards (Dertouzas and others, 1989).

Throughout the 1980s, industries such as automobile manufacturing struggled to repair the damage from decades of neglect. Capital spending increased; old and inefficient facilities were closed; production processes were reengineered. The government became involved by trying to deal with a series of international trade issues, as one of the defenses offered by foreign manufacturers to charges of dumping was that U.S. companies were inefficient and had inflated cost structures. American consumers suffered when they paid inflated prices for domestic products that could be more cheaply manufactured abroad. When the federal government highlighted the efforts of U.S. companies to "show the way" on quality improvements by establishing a national competition and prize for quality (The Baldrige Award), customer satisfaction suddenly became an obsession for American manufacturers.

As far back as 1958, Motorola had established a Corporate Quality Council to strengthen the commitment to quality across its divisions. The council nurtured a quality-management process and tried to cultivate a corporate culture that placed a premium on excellence. Although Motorola's business focus primarily emphasized technology and innovation, quality has been one of its top ten corporate goals since the early 1970s. The company had been gathering, analyzing, and reducing the cost of poor quality for over a decade before the Baldrige Award was conceived. Systematic reviews were conducted in each plant by the Corporate Quality Council, and the quality theme became part of the company's landmark "Meeting Japan's Challenge" campaign. In 1981, Galvin, noting pockets of customer dissatisfaction with Motorola products, set the goal of a tenfold improvement in quality in five years, along with a sharpened focus on the customer.

The Baldrige Award's annual national competition became the keystone of quality efforts in the United States. The award was created by national legislation in 1987 and named after the late former Secretary of Commerce Malcolm Baldrige. Sixty-six companies competed for the award in the inaugural competition in 1988. Two companies won awards in the manufacturing category: Motorola and Westinghouse. Motorola's approach became a model for manufacturers in many industries.

The Baldrige Award is based on seven criteria, each of which is allocated a number of points to generate an overall score. Customer Satisfaction is the most heavily weighted (300 out of 1,000 total points), with Quality Results (measurement) and Human Resource Utilization following. Motorola's emphasis on human resource development and training (see Chapter 4) supported systems that focused on customer satisfaction and the achievement of "virtual perfection" in product and service quality. To reach this goal, the company launched the "Six Sigma Quality" initiative, which set a standard of no more than 3.4 defects per million instances of any activity.

Motorola's customers are heterogeneous and the company faces a wide range of stakeholder expectations. The company's business lines involve products and services for government, commercial customers, and the general public. In some uses, such as emergency communications, reliability problems could have life-threatening consequences; in others, Motorola products become incorporated in the products and services offered by customer-users, for whom reliability problems could be commercially disastrous. The "Six Sigma" quality standard placed primary emphasis on the interests of customers of all types. It was intended to demonstrate a major source of competitive advantage for Motorola, and to enhance quality as a core value for employees as well. The company's traditional focus on individual motivation and employee training fit perfectly within this framework, encouraging innovation, change, and "renewal" at every level of the firm.

Motorola publicized the goal of total customer satisfaction both inside and outside the organization. To meet this goal, it was important to know the customers and understand their true needs, desires, and expectations. It was also essential to measure satisfaction against expectations. The process of achieving total customer satisfaction really began to gather momentum at Motorola when executives, including Galvin, began a series of visits to key customers to find out from the ranks of actual users of Motorola products what they liked and disliked about Motorola. This was so successful that the company institutionalized the process of senior executive visits to key customers. In each Motorola sector and group, a senior manager was appointed "customer champion" with a mission to become the customer's advocate in Motorola's decision making. These actions helped focus the entire organization's energies on serving the customer.

Formal analytical tools were adapted to improve customer satisfaction as well. In addition to traditional market research techniques, Motorola worked to translate the voice of the customer into meaningful engineering specifications. Tools such as "value research," "multi-attribute evaluations," "quality function deployment," and "conjoint analysis" were introduced long before most other companies did so. Quality Assurance (QA) staff were considered "customer advocates" and the QA function was transformed from "doing, checking, controlling" into facilitating and guiding the internal organization in interpreting customer needs and wants. Another innovation of note involved training the customer's technical staff in techniques to help diagnose and solve problems. "Coaching customer employees in solving chronic quality problems is a bold move for a supplier to make," according to one trade journal (Bhote, 1989).

One notable innovation was Motorola's adoption of a new definition of "customer" to include the concept of Next Operation as Customer (NOAC). The external customer is, in many respects, the ultimate customer who transfers some of its wealth to the seller. But in a chain of operations to produce a product, information, or paper flow, there are many internal customer-supplier links. At each process step, there is a "process owner," or internal customer, for that process and an internal supplier of that process. The ultimate external customer is better served if each internal customer is also served to the fullest—in terms of accuracy, timeliness, completeness, and lowest cost (Bhote, 1989).

Motorola's quality crusade is a striking example of the way stakeholder relations can influence the structure and core values of an organization. There is no doubt that the company profoundly changed its thinking about customers, their role, and their expectations during this period. The result was not simply corporate rhetoric about customer satisfaction, but a deep change in the way Motorola thought about, and acted toward, these critical stakeholders.

Mobile Phone Users

Motorola's late-1980s experience with mobile phone users taught a valuable lesson: That satisfied customers could become valuable allies in the policy arena as well as in the marketplace. Motorola manufactured and sold radio technology for public safety uses (such as police and fire services) through its

Land Mobile Products Sector. Public safety agencies pioneered the use of two-way mobile communications to ensure the maintenance of secure connections, but by the late 1980s these communications links were threatened by the limitations of the radio spectrum (a 1982 study estimated that there would be 285,000 public safety radio stations on the air by the end of 1992; in reality, there were more than 483,000 by then. See "Dial 9-1-1 for Spectrum," *Communications*, August 1993). Public safety agencies, acting through the Associated Public-Safety Communications Officers, demanded that the Federal Communications Commission establish frequency standards that would minimize interference and meet public safety requirements.

Motorola had a large stake in the FCC's decision on this matter because it had invested heavily in several technical approaches to frequency standards. Police departments throughout the country were among the most important customers for mobile phones at this time, and Motorola had established user groups of police chiefs and other public safety officials that convened periodically to share information on a range of emergency planning and communication topics. Motorola's initial purpose in organizing these groups was to improve its understanding of customer needs and concerns, as a guide to product development and marketing. Members of these groups naturally had a strong interest in the frequency standards issue, and strongly supported the standards Motorola had adopted. The views of these groups proved to be highly influential on the ultimate FCC decision, which confirmed Motorola's approach and enabled the company to harmonize mobile communications standards with those of the emerging wireless systems. The full payoff would not become clear until the late 1990s, when wireless telecommunications experienced extraordinary growth.

The 1990s: Growth, Crisis, and Reorganization

Motorola addressed the major challenges of the 1980s with strategic initiatives involving both external and internal stakeholders. By the early 1990s, it was a global company with a strong public image, including an international reputation for quality and customer satisfaction. A number of executive changes took place at the end of the 1980s, including the election of Christopher Galvin as president and chief operating officer. Revenues grew at a vigorous pace, tripling between 1990 ($10 billion) and 1999 ($30 billion). During the 1990s, the number of employees increased to more than 140,000, 70% outside the United States.

Unfortunately, Motorola's record of growth and success during this period was tarnished by a number of severe problems that seriously affected key stakeholder relationships. The most dramatic issue involved the company's global growth strategy. Motorola's rapid growth and concentration in Asian markets made the company vulnerable to the financial crisis that swept that part of the world during 1998. Asian customers reduced their orders or closed their doors entirely, eliminating millions of dollars in potential sales. To make matters worse, Motorola had made a major strategic error by betting on analog products just as the demand for digital products was about to explode. With more than two-thirds of total revenue coming from wireless telephones, pagers, and microchips, the shift of demand to digital devices had serious financial implications. Nokia of Finland and Ericsson of Sweden both had proven digital technology for the wireless market, and were ready to seize market share from analog device manufacturers such as Motorola. In 1994 Motorola dominated the cellular telephone market, with more than a 60 percent share in the United States. Nokia, which had only 11 percent of the U.S. market in 1994, had 34 percent in 1998 while Motorola dropped to 31 percent. In July 1998 Motorola took a $1.8 billion charge against earnings and its share price plummeted from a high in the $80s to $38, and stock analysts issued bleak forecasts for the future. The Iridium debacle of 1998–99 (see Chapter 3) added to this tale of woe. In retrospect, Motorola should have responded to three distinct problems that cropped up in the late 1990s.

First, it should have closed technology gaps, especially regarding the shift from wireless analog to digital modes. Insiders say that the culture of "warring tribes" that Motorola had encouraged as a basis for internal technological competition became too powerful, and therefore destructive. Engineering groups competed fiercely for funds and opportunities, leaving customer needs secondary to Motorola's internal politics. Instead, teams were needed that could work across traditional boundaries within the company, and technological partnerships would have to be formed with other firms as well. The competitive landscape was rapidly being transformed from separate worlds of telephone, broadcast, and Internet into what would be called "broadband" communications.

Second, the company should have become more open to external information and developments. Merle Gilmore, an executive vice president, said: "Motorola had an insular attitude. We need to change that view. Things are happening too fast. Customer demands are too exacting. Now you need to be part of an overall echo system"[1] (*New York Times*, 1999). Motorola had slipped badly in its treatment of customers, with product delays, marketing miscues, and repeated charges of bullying tactics. "They used to be very arrogant," said one market observer. "They used to push phones on people and say, 'If you want our phones, you have to buy so many.'" But by then partnerships with customers were essential, and Motorola should have invested in repairing damaged relationships.

Third, the company's cost structure should have been revamped. Its severe financial losses forced a major restructuring by late 1998. The low-end chip manufacturing business had been losing money for years, but Motorola did not sell off that business until 1999. Always reluctant to lay off personnel, Motorola was eventually forced to lay off more than 17,000 employees, challenging the company's vaunted human resources reputation. The workforce reduction was done with as much care as possible for individuals, according to Glenn Gienko, Executive VP of Human Resources, who likened the downsizing process to "brain surgery" (Gienko interview, 1999). The relocation of talented people from one part of the company to another was accompanied by a shift of emphasis from hardware to software. As Dennis A. Roberson, chief technology officer at Motorola at the time said, "It's a very significant break for us. There are more software capabilities in the devices we produce, and we're expanding into the Internet space" (*New York Times*, 1999). During the reorganization, for example, more than 3,000 engineers were shifted to the development of new digital handsets.

Motorola's reorganization during 1998–99 was costly and time consuming, and it took a toll on many stakeholders. Employees, customers, suppliers,

---

[1]"Echo" refers to a feedback system in which customer needs and concerns echo back to the supplier, as in echocardiogram or ultrasound medical procedures.

community organizations, business partners, and investors all shared the company's reorganization pains. By the end of the decade, however, Motorola had accomplished the turnaround, and had done so through actions and processes that matched its stakeholder thinking. No single class of stakeholders bore a disproportionate share of the pain, and by 2000 the company's economic fortunes had improved, generating benefits for all. At the end of December 1999, the stock price had climbed to an all-time high of $150 per share; in January 2000, the company announced that its 1999 revenues and profits had broken previous records ($1.3 billion of earnings on $30.9 billion of revenues).

The reorganization of Motorola in the late 1990s demonstrates the continuous, sometimes turbulent, nature of stakeholder relations in the modern corporation. Externally, companies must reconfigure themselves to meet the changing needs of customers and to take advantage of new opportunities through partnerships, alliances, and other business relationships. This trend will become more pronounced as the Internet facilitates business-to-business commerce. By the end of the 1990s, Motorola had become a broadband communications provider, with its major businesses providing wireless communications products and microchips (embedded processors) for a growing range of products (broadband refers to the convergence of telephone, cable, and Internet communications via one wire or wireless connection).

The company trademarked the name Digital DNA™ to describe its vision of the way chips could penetrate all aspects of human activity. Motorola entered dozens of partnerships, alliances, and joint ventures to press the use of its embedded processors in a large variety of applications. In 1999, the company took another dramatic step by spending $11 billion to acquire General Instrument Corporation, a provider of cable boxes and broadband communications equipment. This merger presented new technical, administrative, and cultural challenges to a company that had weathered crisis by renewing its sense of purpose and committing itself to making all of its stakeholder relationships productive. Motorola's experiences in identifying, understanding, and responding to its stakeholders took time, and often involved costly lessons. But by the end of the 1990s, the cumulative learning coalesced into a management philosophy the company called "Managing by High Principles" (see Figure 5.1).

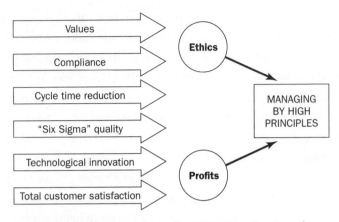

Figure 5.1   Motorola: Managing by High Principles. (Based on a presentation by R S Moorthy at the 1998 Business Ethics Conference, The Conference Board, 1998.)

CUMMINS ENGINE COMPANY: REINVENTING THE COMPANY

Throughout its history, Cummins has had to deal with extreme cyclical fluctuations in the demand for diesel engines and constant pressures to innovate, while keeping prices competitive with alternatives—all within a context of high capital requirements and heavy sunk costs. These macro-environmental features led Cummins to undertake a major redefinition of itself as part of a network of stakeholders during the 1980s.

Diesel engines were extremely popular during the 1970s when truckers sought fuel-efficient and cost-effective alternatives to conventional gasoline engines during a decade of rising oil prices. By 1979 U.S. customers purchased 215,000 heavy-duty diesel engines, roughly double the annual levels of the early 1970s. Cummins dominated its niche, with more than 40 percent of the market and record levels of output; but executives worried that the company was overly dependent on this highly cyclical market. Cummins executives recognized threats in the social and political environment. While working to resolve conflicts and threats arising from external sources, Cummins' senior management also worked during the 1980s to reinvent the company as the central unit within a new network of supportive stakeholder organizations.

Although the oil crises of the 1970s resulted in spectacular gains for Cummins, its managers—like most U.S. executives—realized that these turbulent years marked an important economic transition. The "glory days of robust postwar economic expansion were over, supplanted by instability, uncertainty, and stagflation. For Cummins, as for many other U.S.-based manufacturers, the happy combination of stability and rapid growth had given way to uncertain markets and new constraints" (Cruikshank and Sicilia, 1997, p. 331).

By the end of the 1970s, U.S. domestic demand for diesel engines was virtually saturated, accounting for nearly 95% of all heavy-duty trucks. New producers had entered the market in response to rapidly growing demand; but now growth had stopped, and any increase in sales would depend on Cummins' ability to take customers away from other firms. National policies aimed at slowing inflation would place additional brakes on growth in engine demand. Henry Schacht, Cummins' CEO, later recalled the situation: "In the equation, nothing worked as we looked forward. Slower growth, increased competition, more costs, more international competition, overcapacity pricing for the first time, and huge new EPA demand that was going to generate much larger capital requirements—we had no growth available to us" (Cruikshank and Sicilia, 1997, p. 335).

To survive and prosper under these dramatically changed circumstances, Cummins embarked on a risky, and very expensive, strategy to develop new products, markets, and technology in the early 1980s. The idea was to develop several new classes of diesel engines that would broaden Cummins' sales in European markets (which used lighter diesel engines); appeal to U.S. auto manufacturers that were selling more diesel-fueled autos as gasoline prices continued to rise; and attract new nonautomotive customers seeking efficiency advantages. The three prongs of the strategy, each directed at a new market segment, required massive amounts of capital—more than $1 billion, according to some inside sources. In retrospect, Cummins officials admitted the approach amounted to "betting the company."

Cummins saw the need to draw new partners into this venture, both as sources of capital and as potential customers or channels of market access. Many of its key customers—Ford, GMC, International Harvester, and other original equipment manufacturers (OEMs), as well as European firms such as Daimler Benz and Fiat—were approached as potential allies, but none agreed to participate. Finally, Cummins found a willing partner: J. I. Case, a world leader in manufacture of agricultural and light construction equipment.

Domestic joint ventures were unusual in the early 1980s, and Cummins and Case had to learn how to make the new arrangement work. Both were proud of their history and technical expertise, and each was reluctant to defer to the other. In time, however, Cummins got nearly half its financing from Case, plus a commitment to purchase 50 percent of the engines manufactured, which was critical for achieving manufacturing-scale economy. The company built new manufacturing facilities in North Carolina and began training people in team concepts that became the core of a new approach to state-of-the-art manufacturing. According to one manager: "Many, or most, aspects of the Case/Cummins project are different from the way Cummins normally operates." These differences included the venture's research and design processes, manufacturing methods, and financial arrangements, as well as the marketing and distribution innovations required by the new products (Cruikshank and Sicilia, 1997, p. 347).

Cummins executives learned a great deal from working with their new stakeholder-partner. There was technical learning about the mechanics of structuring a multidimensional relationship that covered all aspects of a "bet-the-company" new venture. Cummins executives also learned much about the administrative barriers and obstacles that had to be overcome when two strong cultures were being melded together. Finally, the company's leaders took away valuable lessons about the institutional challenges of negotiating, executing, and sustaining vital stakeholder relationships. This knowledge of stakeholder management skills would become a crucial asset during the next decade, when the company organized many new partnerships and alliances, defended itself against two hostile takeover bids, and tried to maintain its identity in an industry that was becoming increasingly amalgamated and concentrated. The reinvention of Cummins as a global manufacturer of a full range of diesel engines could not have been accomplished without the development and application of an active process of stakeholder management.

Stakeholder Threats

The 1980s also produced a number of serious threats to Cummins survival, and challenged it to establish a new network of stakeholders that could collaborate for mutual benefit. As with Motorola, an established business relationship with a Japanese partner turned sour amid pressures on both firms to defend themselves against turbulent global competition. In addition, Cummins was subjected to the threat of hostile takeover from an international raider.

The first challenge to Cummins arose from its relationship with the Japanese equipment manufacturer Komatsu. In 1961, Cummins and Komatsu signed a fifteen-year license agreement in which Komatsu agreed to produce engines for tractors and construction equipment. The companies subsequently created a joint venture—Komatsu-Cummins Sales Co., Ltd. (51 percent Cummins-owned)—to sell and service Cummins engines and parts in Japan. These agreements enabled Cummins to import its engines and parts into Japan at a time when the country was still strongly protectionist. Komatsu had sought alliances with technology leaders such as Cummins to combat an alliance between Mitsubishi, the Japanese industrial and automotive giant, and Caterpillar, the world's leading producer of construction equipment. But the Komatsu-Cummins arrangement was filled with tensions, and the parties renegotiated the agreement several times in the 1970s. The companies had a mutual need to compete against Caterpillar but were separated by differences over technology, pricing, and new opportunities such as entry into China. However, as Cruikshank and Sicilia note, "In spite of their differences over two decades, Cummins and Komatsu had sustained a nexus of relations that were mutually beneficial. As a licensee, distributor, parts producer and—especially—as a customer, Komatsu was one of Cummins' most valuable partners worldwide" (1997, p. 384).

But before long Komatsu transformed itself into a serious Cummins competitor. Komatsu revolutionized its manufacturing capabilities during the 1980s in order to directly challenge Caterpillar in the construction equipment business. The tensions with Cummins were multifaceted, but rested on Komatsu's belief that success depended on more than technological superiority: reliability and competitive pricing also were essential, and Cummins did not meet Komatsu's test. Cummins did not realize, or acknowledge, the problem until Komatsu and other Japanese firms made inroads into Cummins's American customer base in the mid-1980s. A turning point came when Komatsu won an especially important contract for generators: "Cummins is out, Komatsu is in," wrote a senior Cummins executive.

The Komatsu experience taught Cummins executives an important stakeholder lesson: all such relationships are temporary and need continual reevaluation. The Japanese entry into Cummins' home market shook the company out of its lethargy. It cut prices, cut costs, and invested in quality improvement. A major turnaround would take years to complete. Importantly, the reinvention of Cummins as a premier manufacturer drew heavily on the knowledge and wisdom of its Japanese competitors, including Komatsu.

Despite the tension caused by their new rivalry, the two firms managed to preserve some aspects of their collaborative relationship. Komatsu still collaborated with Cummins in manufacturing, in marketing engines in Japan, and in service of customers. Most importantly, Komatsu was willing to help Cummins improve the quality and efficiency of its operations, including process-control systems that lay at the heart of Japanese manufacturing success. In the mid-1980s, Cummins sent 100 of its technicians to study Komatsu operations.

Why did Komatsu and Cummins engage in this strange dance of competition and cooperation? The explanation, according to company historians Jeffrey Cruikshank and David B. Sicilia (p. 408), is tied to the underlying stakeholder relationship between the companies. Komatsu placed a special value on its relationship with Cummins, based on a history of trust, cooperation, and success. The joint venture arrangement had been negotiated by revered leaders of both firms, and their successors were uneasy about ending a relationship that had been so hard won. Despite a host of issues and conflicts, the complex relationship between Komatsu and Cummins was useful to both firms as they competed with their biggest rivals, Mitsubishi and Caterpillar. Komatsu evidently considered itself one of Cummins' important stakeholders, and worked to restore it to economic health; Cummins executives agree that the company would not have been able to reinvent itself without Komatsu's assistance. The Cummins-Komatsu story makes clear that the way a company manages agreements and disagreements with its stakeholders, and nurtures processes that enable it to communicate effectively, ultimately influences how those stakeholders value the relationship.

Unwanted Stakeholders

But just when this competitive conflict was resolved, Cummins became the focus of an international corporate raider. Hanson PLC, a British-based holding company, acquired a significant block of Cummins stock in December 1988. Cummins stock was put in play, and Wall Street anticipated a lively battle for the company. Cummins stock clearly was undervalued, and a Hanson acquisition or a bidding war for Cummins would yield gains for shareholders. In early 1989, Cummins officials dealt with the prospect of a full-fledged Hanson takeover attempt. The key to fending off the unwanted suitor was to find other investors willing to pay the premium price Hanson sought, yet patient enough to let Cummins management complete the turnaround without interference. In the parlance of the day, Cummins was being cornered into paying "greenmail." For months, Cummins executives traveled the globe visiting customers, suppliers, and other potential investors. Many of these parties were interested in working with Cummins, but a suitable deal could not be structured.

Finally, over a few months, Cummins succeeded in forging innovative agreements to stabilize its ownership base with two very different sets of longstanding stakeholders. The Miller family, descendents of the founders, still owned 5 percent of the company's shares in 1989. The Millers concluded that if Hanson prevailed, Columbus would suffer job losses and economic hardship that would prompt them to step forward with expanded philanthropy. They reasoned that the purchase premium on the Hanson stock would be less than the charitable expenditures they would likely feel obliged to make in the event of a Hanson takeover. Hence, purchasing the Hanson stock was a form of "preventive philanthropy." A complicated agreement was negotiated between the company, the Miller family, and Hanson PLC in July 1989. Eventually, all three would achieve their intended goals and the arrangement would be declared a "win-win-win" (Cruikshank and Sicilia, 1997, p. 423).

Meanwhile, Cummins' top executives finally were beginning to make headway in talks with three long-time stakeholders, each with a distinct relationship and set of interests with the engine company. One was Kubota, Ltd., a farm-equipment maker based in Osaka, Japan, with annual sales of more than $5 billion. Kubota was looking for a way to gain a foothold in the European market and to break into the market for farm and construction equipment engines in North America, where it had been selling about $10 million worth of smaller (10–90 hp) "loose" diesel engines per year. But the Japanese company was extremely conservative about investing in heavy manufacturing beyond Japan's borders. Through a series of meetings and discussions on both sides of the Pacific, including a critical visit from Cummins CEO Henry Schacht—who had been so adept in negotiations with Komatsu—and key shareholder Will Miller, the two companies moved toward a definition of mutual interests. Their connections through other stakeholders helped as well; Kubota was a close business partner with J. I. Case, and had been selling engines to Onan, a leading generator set manufacturer bought by Cummins in 1986. In the Spring of 1990, the Kubota board agreed to invest up to $48 million in Cummins stock, an amount roughly equal to the capitalization of the diversified company's own engine business. Schacht sagely acknowledged the step as a strategic departure for the new partner, calling it "a very significant 'first time' for this sort of investment by Kubota" (Cruikshank and Sicilia, 1997, p. 437).

The Kubota agreement, which covered about 7.5 percent of Cummins' capitalization, was an important beginning, but only that, and Schacht was nearly out of options. "We had been to almost all the U.S. guys, with the exception of Ford," Schacht later recounted. He had hesitated to contact Ford because various proposals for collaboration between the two companies over the previous two decades had failed to work out. Still, Ford was a major customer; in 1989, it bought two-thirds of the 12,000 diesel engines for its heavy-duty trucks from Cummins. As it turned out, four days before Schacht visited the Detroit giant, Ford executives had decided, after reviewing their commercial options, to approach Cummins about forging some sort of alliance. As with Kubota, this major new investor was looking to improve its emissions control technology, and to expand into horsepower ranges in which Cummins was stronger (in this case, down the horsepower scale into the middle ranges). Along with its commitment to buy up to 20 percent of Cummins' stock, Ford agreed to purchase as many as 27,000 (midsized) C-class Cummins engines.

That purchase agreement, in turn, helped Cummins land a third major investor: Tenneco Inc. of Houston. Tenneco had been losing money on the J. I. Case portion of its Consolidated Diesel joint venture with Cummins. The new Ford deal, by dramatically boosting production volume at Consolidated Diesel's Rocky Mount plant, made an investment in Cummins much more attractive. Tenneco signed on for a 10% ownership stake.

Each of these three deals made sense individually, but the key challenge was to effectively balance one set of stakeholder interests with another. This tension became immediately clear in the Ford-Tenneco-Kubota relationship. As larger shareholders, Ford and Tenneco demanded and were given seats on the Cummins board, whereas Kubota was not. Cummins sought to assuage Kubota's fears that the American companies might disadvantage its own interests by pointing out that the three companies sold almost exclusively into separate markets and assuring the Japanese managers that "both Ford and Tenneco understand" the importance of Cummins' ability to function as "an independent engine supplier that does not favor any customer to the disadvantage of another."

Cummins' experiences with Komatsu; with Ford, Tenneco, and Kubota; and with the Miller family illustrate several points about the practical implications of the stakeholder view. Had Cummins not repeatedly invested in its relations with Komatsu, it is unlikely the Japanese company would have shown any restraint in entering the U.S. market. But the residue of goodwill earned over two decades—a reservoir of social capital—enabled the firms to find new common ground even as they competed. It was an unconventional arrangement at the time, but one that enabled Cummins to reinvent itself as a global leader in diesel engine manufacturing.

The complex and delicate task of putting together the three-way agreement with a large customer (Ford), a disgruntled joint-venture partner (Tenneco), and a recalcitrant foreign diesel engine maker and potential competitor (Kubota) demonstrates the great value of transforming one kind of stakeholder relationship into another. In forging a new sort of tie (major investor), Cummins both exploited and reinforced prior stakeholder linkages. Together, the three agreements secured more than a third of the company's capitalization in the hands of three partners whose interests extended beyond the purely financial, for each held additional vested interests in Cummins' ongoing success. Little wonder that some business analysts lauded the Ford-Tenneco-Kubota deal as a model for how corporations under siege by raiders might safeguard their independence.

As for the unprecedented "preventative philanthropy" of the Miller family stock buy-back of the Hanson stock, no episode better exemplifies the business-society dynamic that defines Cummins as a stakeholder-oriented corporation. Had the Hanson takeover bid not been thwarted, the company's economic success could have been snatched away from its long-term stakeholders.

Interestingly, it was Cummins' relationships with long-term investors and the headquarters community (see Chapter 4)—a philosophy in action dating back to the company's first decades in business—that eventually brought forth this unconventional solution.

CONCLUSION

Motorola and Cummins faced complex, difficult competitive challenges in the last quarter century. Both firms encountered business slumps, with consequent reductions in profits and employment; and both developed ways to renew or reinvent themselves for success in the new business environment. Each firm engaged in stakeholder management processes that helped it redefine problems, develop creative approaches to those problems, and succeed in the marketplace. The leaders of each company embraced stakeholder thinking, in part because of their historic commitment to humanistic principles and values, and in part because they believed that mutually beneficial collaboration with stakeholders was the key to future success. Their responses to competitive challenges involved imagination, creativity, and flexibility. Both companies maintained their basic humanistic commitments to respect for individual employees, customers, and business partners, while modifying their strategies and, to some extent, structures, to remain successful under new operating conditions.

6

STRATEGIC RESPONSE TO

SOCIETAL CHALLENGES

Changing societal concerns and expectations, in the context of instantaneous worldwide communication, have greatly increased the exposure of corporations to external criticism and societal challenge. These effects are intensified for large multinational firms, where complex interactions among distant and diverse constituencies have become commonplace. The pattern for these challenges emerged in the 1970s, as worldwide concern about the racial separation (apartheid) policies of the government of South Africa turned into a full-fledged global campaign for change.

Corporations were caught in the controversy. "Campaign GM," for example, was a shareholder effort to force General Motors to withdraw from, or significantly change its behavior in, South Africa (Sethi and Williams, 2000). At the same time, pressures were being put on other multinational companies to change their business practices in the name of corporate responsibility. Nestlé's aggressive infant formula marketing practices in developing nations generated criticism in Europe and the United States, leading to an international consumer boycott that lasted from 1977 to 1984. The chemical industry became the target of pressure from environmentalists and governments to improve plant safety after an explosion at Union Carbide's Bhopal (India) plant killed more than 2,000 people in 1983. Firms in the electric utility, steel, forest products, pharmaceutical, and financial services industries also became targets of activist campaigns in this era. Public concerns about business practices involve government policies as well, as in conflicts surrounding the pricing of essential pharmaceutical products, the safety of nuclear power plants, and the sale of genetically modified food products.

Broad social concerns such as these challenge the core strategies and behaviors of corporations and require thoughtful responses that sometimes fundamentally alter the company's strategy and operating practices. And this important challenge-response process cannot be analyzed within the conventional resource-based (RBV) and industry-structure (ISV) views of the firm. The stakeholder view (SHV), however, provides a framework for the analysis of past experience and the development of future policies and practices with respect to such strategic challenges. The two preceding chapters show how the humanistic commitments of Motorola and Cummins influenced their behavior with respect to both internal and external stakeholders, and affected their competitive strategies. This chapter shows how external challenges stimulated Shell to reexamine its stakeholder relationships and establish comprehensive new policies and practices that ultimately brought about a transformation of the entire organization that is still in progress.

SHELL: HISTORICAL BACKGROUND

The profile presented in Chapter 3 shows that the entire Royal Dutch/Shell Group has from its beginnings been affected by, and intimately involved in, social issues and processes wherever it has done business. Development of the international petroleum industry over the past century resulted in global technological, social, and environmental transformations that continue today. Shell's wide geographic scope brought it into contact with diverse political regimes. In the Shell tradition, these social and political contacts were managed at the local-regional level. Early on, Shell adopted a colonial organizational structure, with powerful "barons" taking primary responsibility for policies and practices within their spheres of activity, and with little direct control from the management centers in London and The Hague.

World War II

The first serious challenge to this arose during World War II. From the company's origins, the London headquarters had been headed by a member of the founding Samuel family, which was Jewish. As reports of Nazi persecution of Jews became widespread, the relationship between Shell London and Shell Germany became tense, and this situation worsened after the German occupation of the Netherlands. In a formal statement at that time, Walter Samuel wrote: "I cannot refrain from referring to all those members of our Group who now find themselves in enemy-occupied territory, particularly our Netherlands friends. The happy relationship which has always existed between the Royal Dutch and your company makes the present unhappy position of the Netherlands and of our Netherlands colleagues particularly sad and a great anxiety to us. Many of our friends of many years standing are thus affected, and our sympathy goes out to them" (Howarth, 1997, p. 207). Most of The Hague headquarters operations were transferred to the Dutch colony of Curaçao, and the laboratory was evacuated to the United Kingdom. Shell Germany's facilities were eventually bombed out by the Allies; Shell London itself provided the locational coordinates.

The Shell Group's involvement in World War II was totally on the side of the Allies. Under Shell's leadership, the British Petroleum Board known as "The Pool" was established. Howarth describes this arrangement as follows: "The oil men of Great Britain have fashioned an effective 'monopoly' of oil for the purposes of prosecuting the war, but they also, they feel sure, have arranged to ensure the return of a truly free and competitive oil industry when the war is concluded. Perhaps the most striking feature of this 'monopolistic' arrangement and the plans for return to a free industry is the most informal way in which the legal side has been handled, not only as between the oil men but with their government" (Howarth, 1997, pp. 193–4).

Shell Germany's involvement with the Nazis, although inevitable under the circumstances, was seen as a disaster for the Group. The World War II experience led Shell to adopt a global policy of minimizing involvement in domestic political affairs within the more than 100 countries in which it was operating. Concentration on business operations and arm's-length dealing with all national governments was seen as the most satisfactory policy for such a complex multinational firm. However, within Shell's highly decentralized and diverse structure, many different patterns of business-government contact inevitably emerged in individual locations and time periods.

Rhodesia

The hazards of Shell's noninvolvement policy, in a setting of increasing world-wide communication and awareness, were clearly revealed in connection with its operations in southern Africa. In 1965, the independence of the former British colony of Rhodesia was proclaimed by a white minority government headed by Prime Minister Ian Smith. The British government declared this act to be illegal and asked for trade sanctions, especially with respect to oil and oil products. Thus, it became illegal for a U.K.-registered company such as Shell to supply oil to Rhodesia.

During the following decade there were worldwide reports that Mobil, Shell, and BP were conspiring to violate the sanctions and supply Rhodesia with oil. A report prepared by Thomas Bingham, Lord Chief Justice of England and Wales, in 1977 revealed that Shell Mozambique Ltd., jointly owned by Shell and BP, had participated in swap arrangements with the French company Total to supply Rhodesia and were currently providing half of Rhodesia's oil. Many of these transactions were made via South Africa. The report even mentioned that some of the senior managers in Shell London had been familiar with this arrangement, as were some members of the British government. Public concern with this issue in Britain became so great that it was discussed in Parliament. A Shell shareholder resolution was initiated on the matter, but was rejected by the shareowners (Howarth, 1997, pp. 327–31).

The Rhodesia issue became moot when the independent Republic of Zimbabwe was established, with black majority leadership, in 1980. However, this experience highlighted the difficulties and dangers involved in operating within diverse national laws and policies when directives from various sources were clearly in conflict. These potentials for conflict retained prominence in management thinking because of Shell's involvement in an Italian government bribery scandal during 1969–73 (Howarth, 1997, p. 323). And they became even more prominent as worldwide attention focused on foreign business operations within the apartheid environment of South Africa. Shell was one of the few major international firms maintaining its normal South African operations in spite of extensive criticism and pleas for withdrawal. Both the Royal Dutch/Shell headquarters and the local operating unit, Shell South Africa, publicly condemned the apartheid regime; but Shell argued that its continued business presence and influence would eventually prove to be more effective than withdrawal. The South Africa issue became crucially important for Shell Oil Company (Houston), which was made the target of a boycott in the United States. The Houston firm responded that it was not able to control the policies of the RoyalDutch/Shell Group on this matter.

Shell's Position, Circa 1990

At the end of World War II Shell missed the opportunity to simplify its structure with a single world headquarters and clearer lines of authority. The Dutch government, however, strongly supported the return of the dual headquarters to The Hague and even tried to alter the historic 40:60 British/Dutch ownership ratio. The major step toward greater integration was creation of the Committee of Managing Directors (CMD), which ultimately became the dominant global management group. However, extreme decentralization continued to prevail, as the Rhodesia and South Africa experiences clearly illustrate. Stronger central policy direction began to emerge with the development of the "Statement of General Business Principles" (SGBP) in 1976, first published externally in 1984. This document committed Shell to a broad and explicit company-wide stakeholder orientation, but no serious efforts to implement that commitment were made at the time. SGBP also affirmed the postwar policy of noninvolvement in local policy issues, stating that "Shell companies endeavor always to act commercially, operating within existing national laws in a socially responsible manner, *abstaining* from participation in party politics" (emphasis added). The 1994 version adds "and interference in political matters."

Thus, until the early 1990s the "Planet Shell" metaphor (see Chapter 3) remained valid, with a decentralized organizational structure and with strategy and culture focused primarily on technical issues. New developments were occurring, however, which made fragmented, locally focused direction and limited external involvement increasingly inappropriate operating modes for one of the world's largest corporations.

TRANSFORMING EVENTS: BRENT SPAR AND NIGERIA

As noted in Chapter 3, Shell began a company-wide reorganization in 1994. This was initially focused on structural changes intended to improve the rate of return on investment and to shift toward a global, rather than international (or, as sometimes said, "colonial"), management model. Just as the reorganization process began, however, it was dramatically influenced by two unexpected external challenges, both of which occurred in 1995. First, Shell encountered strong opposition from environmental protection groups in continental Europe when it announced plans to dispose of the oil storage buoy Brent Spar in the North Atlantic. Second, Shell's operations in Nigeria were charged with environmental irresponsibility, disrupting the lives of the indigenous Ogoni people, and indirectly supporting a military government that executed nine Ogonis, including their charismatic leader, Ken Saro-Wiwa. These incidents provided telling evidence of the strategic impact of unfavorable stakeholder relations, and led to the evolution and implementation of new stakeholder management policies throughout the corporation. The two incidents and their aftermath therefore merit careful scrutiny.

Brent Spar

After the discovery of oil in the North Sea, many offshore drilling and production facilities (oil rigs) were placed in operation before pipelines to carry oil to the mainland were ready for use. In the Brent field, jointly operated by Shell UK and Esso, a floating oil storage terminal was used to store oil produced by the undersea wells and to enable tankers to anchor and take on oil for transport. This structure, known as "Brent Spar," was 463 feet high and weighed 14,500 metric tons. It extended about 100 feet above the sea surface; the storage compartment itself was constantly filled with either oil or water, so that the entire structure would maintain a vertical position in the sea.

After three years of operation, a pipeline to the Brent field became available, and Brent Spar was no longer needed for its initial purpose. It continued to be used, however, as a tanker loading terminal and backup facility. In 1991, Shell and Esso determined that the 15-year old structure was not worth refurbishing and decided to discontinue its use. Because the Brent Spar was not suitable for redeployment and not worth dismantling for scrap, it had to be disposed of in some way. Reuse of the structure outside the oil industry was apparently not considered a significant alternative.

During consideration of this matter, a number of studies by technical and environmental experts were commissioned, and local fishermen's associations and conservation groups were consulted, all in accordance with relevant U.K. regulations. The principal external stakeholders involved in the decision process were the U.K. regulators, who ultimately accepted a proposal for deep-sea disposal. They selected a site 160 miles west of Scotland, where the structure could be sunk to a depth of some 2,000 meters. It was understood by all parties that some residual oil would remain in the structure at that depth, but the environmental effects were considered minimal. This decision was announced in late 1994, and EU governments and authorities, as well as other interested parties, were given an opportunity to comment during a required 60-day waiting period.

In February 1995, after the 60-day waiting period was over, Greenpeace, an international environmental activist organization headquartered in Amsterdam, charged that undesirable ecological effects might result from the planned disposal. They also believed that this action might have a precedent-setting impact on the disposal of the more than 400 oil rigs then floating in the North Atlantic. Although four years had passed from the time Shell and Esso decided to discontinue use of the facility, and the disposal method and site had been formally approved by U.K. authorities, Greenpeace leaders felt that the decision had been made too quickly, with insufficient consideration of alternatives, and also with inadequate publicity and public discussion. Between February and April Greenpeace started a media campaign to draw attention to the Brent Spar issue on the European Continent. In late April 1995, Greenpeace activists occupied Brent Spar in an attempt to prevent the planned disposal. This provided considerable television coverage and dramatic photographs, which were widely reproduced. The approved disposal plan proceeded, however, and a brief second Greenpeace occupation took place while the structure was being towed toward its scheduled destination.

Other than attempting to protect its property against trespassers, Shell UK's response to the Greenpeace attack was restrained. Its managers did not realize at first that the Brent Spar disposal had become more than a technical problem, to be resolved between themselves and U.K. regulators. They clearly believed, as all of their studies had indicated, that deep water sinking would be the best solution from both economic and ecological viewpoints. However, although the backup studies were made available to outside parties on request, no active effort was made to clarify the situation or to explain the basis of the final decision to the public. The matter was perceived as a U.K. issue, although the principal critics were operating from the Continent, outside the purview of U.K.-based managers and regulators.

As a result of this lack of attention to the primary source, as well as the intensity of criticism, Shell was surprised when its attempt to proceed with the offshore disposal plan led to massive public outrage in Europe. Greenpeace became increasingly accepted as an information source, and Shell's reactions and clarifications were often inadequate and tardy. Although some of Greenpeace's challenges and allegations were based on inadequate information and misunderstanding, and apologies were later issued for misinforming the public about various matters, the damage had already been done. Consumer boycotts were initiated in several countries; some were supported by prominent politicians, including Germany's Chancellor Helmut Kohl. Dramatic, but brief, declines in Shell's European retail sales occurred. In Germany, several Shell gas stations were firebombed and more than thirty threats against Shell facilities were reported. In the course of this controversy, Greenpeace gained considerable public support and media attention, while Shell was perceived as insular, irresponsible, and reactive.

The entire Brent Spar experience turned into a tragic drama for Shell, whereas Esso—its Brent field partner—remained untouched. Shell found itself trapped between the U.K. authorities, who expected Shell to carry out the original plan, and Continental public opinion, which was openly supported by German leaders. Eventually Shell agreed to reconsider the dumping. In a press announcement, Shell declared: "We will change. . . . We have learned that for some decisions, [public] approval is as important as the opinion of experts or the official consent of authorities" (Duncan, 1995).

To honor this public commitment, Shell initiated a new program called "Way Forward" consisting of three elements:

1. Independent outside analysis of the entire problem

2. Open search for alternative solutions

3. Public dialogue to assure acceptance of the outcome

The Norwegian foundation Det Norske Veritas (DNV) was brought in as a source of outside expertise. Although DNV's work confirmed the accuracy of the earlier studies and the appropriateness of the prior disposal plan, Shell solicited alternative proposals and received a large number of them. Eventually it was decided that Brent Spar should become part of a quay extension at the port of Mekjarvik, Norway. (Initially intended to be used as a facility for loading/unloading cars onto ferries, Brent Spar ultimately became a docking facility for oil service vessels.) This solution appeared to satisfy the concerns of all interested parties.

Although the Brent Spar storage terminal was unique, and its disposal not directly relevant to the fate of the numerous oil rigs operating in the North Sea, this episode became an important learning experience for Shell. It exposed the potential consequences of resolving externally relevant issues on purely technical grounds, without adequate public explanation and justification; and it revealed the ultimate cost of reactive, rather than proactive, approaches to matters of public concern. "Way Forward" was seen as a potentially useful model for dealing with other controversial issues. Most important, the Brent Spar controversy made the entire Shell organization acutely aware that it is operating in the "global village" created by instantaneous worldwide communication, in which decisions and actions in one area may have unanticipated but far-reaching effects elsewhere. These lessons would be reinforced by contemporary events occurring in Nigeria.

Nigeria[1]

The controversy surrounding Shell's operations in Nigeria presented in dramatic form the kind of problems that can arise for large, complex multinational firms that are inevitably involved in situations in which their knowledge is inadequate and their capacity to influence outcomes severely limited. The situation that arose in Nigeria is quite different from the Brent Spar problem. However, both issues demonstrated the wide impacts that may arise from seemingly localized management decisions, and both showed the importance and difficulty of identifying relevant stakeholders and comprehending their

---

[1]This section is based on many primary and secondary sources. The main compendium of company data is available at the Shell website, www.shellnigeria.com. See also L. Paine, "Royal Dutch/Shell in Nigeria (A)," Harvard Business School case, N9-399-126, 1999.

interests. Shell eventually recognized and responded to its problems in Nigeria as international issues, not simply as matters of local concern.

Oil was discovered in the Niger Delta in the 1950s and Shell became an active producer in partnership with British Petroleum (BP) in 1958. The Nigerian government took a 35% stake in the venture in 1973, and appropriated BP's share in 1979. Shell—operating as Shell Petroleum Development Company of Nigeria (SPDC)—reached an agreement with the democratically elected Nigerian government then in office to carry out nationwide onshore exploration and drilling operations as part of a government-dominated consortium. Ownership shares in the consortium in 1995 were: Nigerian National Petroleum Corporation (NNPC, 55%), Shell (SPDC, 30%), Elf (10%), and Agip (5%). This consortium accounted for about half of Nigeria's total oil production; Mobil, Chevron, and Texaco are also active in the country. SPDC is a major employer in Nigeria, with a staff of more than 5,000, only 300 of whom are expatriates. It has long operated a substantial social development program, including support for schools and hospitals, and the development of agricultural and water resources.

Nigeria produces only about 3% of world oil output, but the industry is extremely important for the country, generating 90% of its exports and 80% of government revenue. Oil revenues have played an important role in Nigeria's economic and social development, but have diverted attention from the development of indigenous agricultural industries and other resources. For the past couple of decades Nigeria has been viewed as one of the most corrupt countries in the world.

The population of Nigeria is roughly 100 million; about 7 million people, comprising 20 different ethnic groups, live in the Niger Delta. The half million Ogoni, the group that became the focus of publicity about Shell's activities in Nigeria, occupy an area of about 400 square miles containing some 100 oil wells and interlaced with ground-level pipelines and other oil production facilities. Like the great majority of people in Nigeria, the Ogoni are very poor. By the late 1980s some of their leaders became politically active in pursuit of their interests. In 1990 they formed MOSOP (Movement for the Survival of Ogoni People) in an attempt to gain greater political autonomy, as well as a greater share of oil income. The Ogoni felt that they had suffered severe environmental damages due to oil production in their area, and that oil revenues had been diverted to other areas of the country and largely misused or dissipated.

Although the Ogoni received some attention from a government commission reviewing conditions in the Delta, the matter was still unresolved at the time of the 1992 Nigerian elections. Ogoni leaders disagreed about how to use the elections to further their interests, and as a result split into two parties, one more moderate and the other more radical. Ken Saro-Wiwa, a well-educated and sophisticated Ogoni, became a leader among the radical faction. Initiating a change in strategy, he addressed a public demand to both the oil companies and the Nigerian government for $10 billion in compensation for environmental damages and lost oil revenues. This attracted some media attention in Europe and North America, although it was rejected by the parties to whom it was addressed.

The conflict between the two Ogoni groups led to physical attacks, including vandalism at Shell facilities and harm to its employees. The company therefore stopped its operations in Ogoniland (while continuing to operate elsewhere in the Delta) and issued the following statement: "SPDC does not support violence and has frequently and publicly expressed its concern about the actions of both sides in the dispute. We reject such violence as a means of settling disputes and we will not return to Ogoniland unless we can work in harmony alongside the communities" (Shell Nigeria Brief, 1995). In an effort to pacify the Ogoni and other tribes engaged in conflicts in the Delta, the Nigerian government—by this time a military dictatorship—inflicted organized terror throughout the area, killing around 1,800 people and making 30,000 homeless. During this turbulent period there was a clash between the two Ogoni groups during which four senior moderate leaders were killed. As a result, Ken Saro-Wiwa and eight members of the more radical party were arrested and accused of criminal offenses under the Nigerian legal system. In spite of widespread international protests, all nine were executed. Shell expressed formal objection to all of these actions, but nevertheless was accused of complicity in the brutal practices of the national government and was criticized for not actively supporting the Ogoni cause, particularly the effort to obtain a reprieve for the executed leaders.

Concern about these human and civil rights issues drew considerable attention to problems of environmental degradation in the Delta. Oil exploration and production inevitably alter the physical environment, and much of the activity in Nigeria took place before technical practices and environmental standards reached their current levels of development. Many facilities were outdated, and land and water pollution due to pipeline leakage was commonplace. The need for renewal of facilities and remediation of environmental legacy problems was generally recognized, but substantial expenditures were required and the Nigerian government was no more eager than the oil companies to pay its share of such costs in an era of falling oil prices. A major problem throughout the period was the inability of the oil companies to work out satisfactory collaborative arrangements with the Nigerian government. The companies had also made little effort to develop satisfactory relationships with other stakeholders, such as the various ethnic groups.

The combination of human rights and environmental concerns about oil company operations in Nigeria led to widespread international commentary and criticism. Greenpeace called for a boycott of Nigeria and demanded that Shell end all of its activities there. Shell rejected most of the accusations, and confirmed its policy of noninvolvement in the domestic affairs of countries in which it operates. It argued that withdrawal would have no effect, as almost all of its employees were local citizens and the consortium could continue operations under the direction of NNPC and/or other foreign oil companies. The company insisted that most of these matters were strictly between the Nigerian government and the Ogoni people, and not subject to control by foreign companies.

Nevertheless, Shell attempted to maintain open communications during the course of the dispute; and Brian Anderson, head of SPDC during the period, willingly met with Shell's critics and reporters. Shell acknowledged that the Nigerian oil industry as a whole was responsible for some of the environmental degradation, but pointed out that some damage was due to sabotage and some to the agricultural practices of the indigenous people. Shell acknowledged that oil industry profits were, indeed, the lifeblood of the Nigerian government, a relationship that gave the oil industry unusual responsibility, but not control. With respect to the compensation of the Ogoni people, Shell committed itself to an ongoing effort to create wealth in Ogoniland. The company also promised that older facilities in poor condition would be replaced piece by piece. "The company recognizes the gap between its intention and its current performance. It is working hard to renew aging facilities, reduce the number of oil spills in the course of operations, the amount of gas that is flared, and to reduce waste products" (Shell Nigeria Brief, 1995). SPDC began publication of an annual report on "People and the Environment" in 1996, at which time Shell CEO Moody Stuart expressed regret that the company had not started this project some years earlier, in the hope of reducing domestic tensions. He assured the public that Shell would conduct business in Nigeria with integrity, pointing out that its record of immediate damage compensation was already excellent (*New York Times*, 1996).

IMPACT OF THE EVENTS

The incidents involving Brent Spar and Nigeria eventually led to a reexamination of Shell's relationship with society at large and resulted in changes in its strategy, structure, and culture that are continuing up to the present. Some of these developments are discussed more fully in Chapter 8, in the context of organizational learning and renewal. Here we present a general analysis of these two experiences and show their impact on a subsequent Shell venture, the Camisea Project.

In the cases of both Brent Spar and Nigeria, Shell's response to external challenges was in every sense reactive and clearly lacked a coherent international focus. Shell's decentralized structure, together with its strong technological and rationalistic internal culture, left it unable to perceive and respond to challenges arising from outside its normal decision processes. To put it another way, Shell's strategic posture was grounded in its resource and technological base, and in its industry position; the possibility that broader external stakeholder concerns could have significant strategic impact simply did not fit within its analytical framework, and left it vulnerable to damage from surprising sources.

In the Brent Spar case, Greenpeace—which both Shell and the British government initially underestimated—adopted a "moving-targets" tactic that proved highly effective. Because Shell failed to offer a comprehensive analysis of the situation, Greenpeace was able to shift from one accusation to another, leaving Shell to play "catch up" with narrowly focused facts and explanations. Greenpeace did not necessarily deal with these responses, but shifted focus to another isolated aspect of the situation with a new accusation. As a result, Shell was always one or two steps behind. Shell also focused on U.K. media, whereas Greenpeace's primary contacts were with Continental publications and a network of relationships with customers, politicians, and other activist groups. Management separation between Shell U.K., where operating responsibility was lodged, and Shell Germany, where the principal public reaction was occurring, resulted in a disjunction that Shell's decentralized structure could not cope with.

The situation in Nigeria was, of course, vastly different in detail, yet there were many similarities. Shell did not reject MOSOP entirely, as it initially did Greenpeace, but its commitment to working with the established government—even though it was not by then the democratically elected one it had initially contracted with—prevented it from responding directly to Ogoni concerns. As with many firms operating in South Africa during the apartheid period, SPDC attempted to follow appropriate practices within its own operations, but tried to avoid involvement with the larger social and political setting. *The Economist* (December 2, 1995, p. 18) subsequently analyzed the situation as follows:

Against such complexities, it is tempting to argue for a simple division of labor. Let governments perform the complex moral calculus; let multinationals observe international law, comply with international sanctions, observe international environmental standards, avoid outright oppression of local people—but behave otherwise as political neutrals, free to make business decisions on business criteria alone. . . . And yet, in the end, asking for this simple division of labor may be too simple. This is because for many multinationals, and especially for oil and mining companies, politics is part of their daily business. The activities of such firms will sometimes alter a country's geography and ecology, or change the balance of riches between its regions. In Nigeria it was probably inevitable that Shell would be drawn into the murky politics of the local Ogoni people and their grievances against the central government. It is part of a multinational's job . . . to cope with such conflicts.

The two situations could also be described as failures in stakeholder identification and communication. In the Brent Spar case, Shell UK failed to recognize the potentially critical role of stakeholders on the Continent. As late as May 1995, *after* a Greenpeace occupation of Brent Spar had already occurred, the head of Corporate Communications for Shell Germany admitted to a local television station that he had no information about the matter. Subsequently Shell Germany announced that disposal of Brent Spar had been "deferred." Shell UK responded that there was "no change of plan," while Kurt Doehmel, the head of Shell Austria, publicly called the disposal plan "unacceptable."

In Nigeria, although there was no similar confusion among members of the Shell Group, SPDC saw the established government, whatever its origins, as its principal stakeholder, ignoring the obvious evidence of domestic divisions and conflicts.

Widespread media attention and public criticism of Shell also attracted attention from some shareowners. In 1995 and 1996, Shell executives met with people from the Pension and Investment Research Council (PIRC), representing a small group of shareowners, to discuss their concerns about a number of corporate responsibility issues, particularly those involving Nigeria. The PIRC urged Shell to revise its Statement of General Business Principles to emphasize currently critical issues, and also to move actively to repair its relationships with the Ogoni. Shell responded that these matters were under study, but the PIRC staff were dissatisfied and joined with the Ecumenical Council for Corporate Responsibility (ECCR) in preparing a resolution for consideration at the 1997 Annual General Meeting. This document, which became identified as "Resolution 10," asked Shell management to establish internal procedures for implementing and monitoring environmental and social policies, to establish independent external review and audit procedures for such policies, and to report to shareholders on these matters. All of these developments were actually underway at Shell at the time, but Shell management opposed Resolution 10 and succeeded in defeating it. This was perceived by some observers as wholesale rejection of the concerns raised by PIRC and ECCR.

In spite of the blunders involved in these two cases, there is some evidence of organizational learning; the communications mistakes of Brent Spar were not repeated for Nigeria. As soon as the Nigerian situation emerged, Shell headquarters in London recognized that it was dealing with an international situation that would attract a great deal of attention, and media services and external reporting were expanded correspondingly. This did not achieve the broad organizational transformation needed, but it enabled the company to make reasonable and informative responses to its questioners and critics.

The Brent Spar and Nigerian events, occurring almost simultaneously, challenged Shell's fundamental structure, strategy, and culture. They showed that decentralized and largely independent units—although legally sound and operationally effective in purely technical terms—could inadvertently create serious problems for each other and for the company as a whole. They also showed—as the Rhodesian experience had foreshadowed—that Shell's historic commitment to noninvolvement was not always a feasible option, no matter how much managers at all levels might wish otherwise. Shell's foundations of technical expertise and detached rationality were shaken by the deeply held beliefs of apparently powerless individuals who chose to "put their bodies on the line."

The broad transformation of Shell that resulted from this experience, which can be viewed as the long-overdue implementation of the stakeholder commitments made in the original 1976 General Statement of Business Principles, are examined in Chapter 8.

Here we conclude with an analysis of a specific instance in which the lessons of Brent Spar and Nigeria were put into practice: The Camisea Project.

THE CAMISEA PROJECT

The Camisea project became Shell's "laboratory" for demonstrating what it had learned from the Brent Spar and Nigeria experiences. A broad stakeholder-oriented approach to Camisea was already planned at the time the transforming events occurred, but experience with Brent Spar and, particularly, Nigeria strongly influenced its evolution and implementation. The results were so successful that Shell won an award from the Issues Management Council, a U.S. organization, for its "leadership in integrating constituent concerns into corporate decision-making" (Interchange, 1999, p. 15).

Camisea is an environmentally sensitive area in the upper Amazon region of Peru. It borders on the Manu national park, is rich in biodiversity, and is home to a number of indigenous peoples, primarily Machiguenga. In 1994, Shell and Perupetro, the Peruvian government agency responsible for hydro-carbons, agreed to a new evaluation of the commercial potential of the Camisea gas fields. Gas has great economic potential for Peru, which is heavily dependent on energy imports; increased use of domestic gas promises both fi-nancial and environmental benefits. There is enough gas in the Camisea fields to meet Peru's energy needs for more than a hundred years.

Shell discovered exceptional, world-class gas fields located on either side of the Camisea River during the 1980s. Peru had no legislation or policies at that time with respect to hydrocarbon exploitation, environmental protection, or the protection of indigenous peoples. But the Peruvian government then had some general hostility toward foreign multinationals. As in other parts of the Amazon basin—and elsewhere in the world—commercial and exploratory ac-tivity disrupted local physical and social environments, resulting in defor-estation, pollution of rivers, disturbance of communal lands, introduction of disease, and social dislocation. Insufficient marketing prospects for the gas—perhaps along with mounting criticism and local operating problems—caused Shell to abandon the project in some haste. Against this background, and with the recent experience in Nigeria clearly in mind, it was clear that renewed activity in Peru would require careful attention to local conditions and concerns—economic, social, and environmental.

During the 1994–96 period of preliminary appraisal, Shell developed a comprehensive program of stakeholder analysis and impact assessment that provided a framework for negotiation with the Peruvian government and other interested parties, both local and international. On May 17, 1996, Shell Prospecting and Development (Peru) B.V. (SPDP) and its minority partner, Mobil Exploration and Producing Peru Inc., signed a 40-year license agree-ment with Perupetro, the state-owned petroleum company, to undertake a "full well appraisal," including drilling and full project development. A com-prehensive stakeholder analysis and consultation program was implemented during 1996–98, during the course of this operation.

Shell's holistic approach to Camisea, as contrasted to its partial and narrowly focused reactions to Brent Spar and Nigeria, is clearly reflected in its focus on four interrelated "key issue" areas—Business, Society, Politics, and Environment. Within each area, and where areas overlap, specific issues of stakeholder concern were noted and critical stakeholder groups identified (see Figures 6.1 and 6.2). These charts, which have been modified from the original Shell documents for clarity, became the "maps" for development of detailed policies and action plans for Camisea.

The Camisea project was committed from the outset to conform with the highest international standards. Exploration and development would be isolated from the indigenous communities; no roads would allow for access into

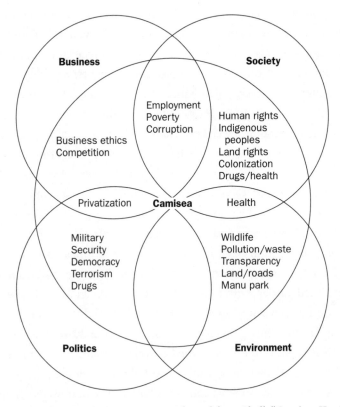

Figure 6.1 Camisea Key Issues. SOURCE: Adapted from Shell, "Camisea Key Issues: The International Dimension." Used with permission of Shell International Limited.

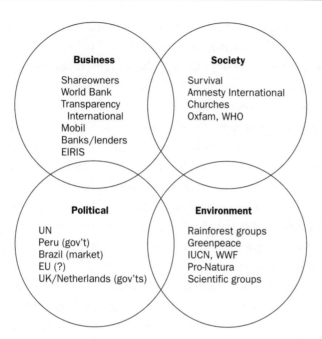

Business
Shareowners
World Bank
Transparency
    International
Mobil
Banks/lenders
EIRIS

Society
Survival
Amnesty International
Churches
Oxfam, WHO

Political
UN
Peru (gov't)
Brazil (market)
EU (?)
UK/Netherlands (gov'ts)

Environment
Rainforest groups
Greenpeace
IUCN, WWF
Pro-Natura
Scientific groups

Figure 6.2 Camisea Key Stakeholders. SOURCE: Adapted from Shell, "Camisea Key Issues: The International Dimension." Used with permission of Shell International Limited.

the region; socioenvironmental impacts would be minimized or avoided wherever possible. SPDP adopted an Environmental Impact Assessment (EIA) process that, in many respects, went beyond legal and regulatory requirements. The process involved a self-regulatory approach and was intended to be adaptive, continuing throughout the life of the project, gathering new information and responding to changes taking place over time. A series of detailed EIA's were required for different parts of the project, and long-term biodiversity studies and social diagnostics related to regional community planning were also undertaken.

A central aspect of the EIA process was consultation with a wide range of interested parties. A total of 350 different stakeholder groups were identified at local, national, regional, and international levels. SPDP's Health, Safety and Environment (HSE) policy included an intensive and transparent stakeholder consultation process involving the indigenous people and emphasizing conscientious response to their concerns. In accordance with guidelines from sources such as Shell International's own EIA and Social Impact Assessment procedures, the World Bank's EIA consultation guidelines, the Exploration and Production Forum's guidelines, and other sources, SPDP developed an interactive consultation process that was transparent and widely understood. This process not only ensured the identification of the relevant stakeholders but also established a framework for a two-way flow of communication. Stakeholders were encouraged to make their own analyses and contribute original information and ideas. Local communities were to be involved throughout, not simply in the final public hearings required by law. The EIA process also provided for training SPDP staff to be sensitive toward external messages and to give regular feedback to stakeholders about the ways in which their concerns were being addressed.

In June 1996, the key steps for initiating the consultation were specified: Identifying the relevant stakeholder groups, prioritizing them, establishing modes of interaction, defining procedures for responding to their specific concerns, and securing feedback to both the stakeholders and SPDP (see Exhibit 6.1).

Exhibit 6.1
Objectives of SPDP's Stakeholder Participation Program

- To ensure proper identification of stakeholders.
- To ensure availability of timely information.
- To make all environmental and social studies publicly available.
- To ensure two-way communication of information.
- To ensure that SPCP staff listen to external messages.
- To identify changes in the project that will help to alleviate or minimize concerns.
- To provide feedback to stakeholders showing how their concerns have been addressed.

SOURCE: Jones, 1997.

SPDP identified its stakeholders as "any individual or group who is affected by the project or can themselves affect the project." Primary stakeholders were those "directly affected" (local communities, for example), whereas secondary stakeholders were other individuals or groups who, although not directly involved or affected, may have influence or interest. After assessing the identified stakeholders as well as the key issues on the national and international level, SPDP contacted about 200 organizations representing different areas the project would affect (May and others, p. 11). The groups contacted had varying levels of interest in the project, and Shell used a variety of techniques in dealing with them. Some groups wanted to be significantly involved; some only wanted to be informed regularly; others distanced themselves from the project.

Shell's consultation process focused largely on primary stakeholders, including local communities and their associations, indigenous federations, and advisory organizations. Starting from an original list of 10 groups, these gradually expanded to include about 40 entities of various kinds. A number of nongovernmental organizations (NGOs) were invited to work actively with the indigenous communities and to monitor the project. These included the Red Ambiental Peruana (RAP), a network of nearly 40 Peruvian NGOs that conducted an independent assessment of the project and monitored socioenvironmental procedures and impacts. Special studies were undertaken concerning the region's biodiversity and health and socioeconomic conditions. Several consultation rounds and two sets of international stakeholder consultation workshops were held to discuss the results of this work, and the information generated was constantly fed into the process and was made publicly available. These procedures often generated new ideas that modified Shell's original plans. For example, a large electricity generation facility was initially intended to be sited within the rainforest. Opposition to this location, coupled with technical and environmental considerations, led to abandonment of this plan. Community concern with river transport by hovercraft caused plans for use of this mode to be modified, and anticipatory complaint procedures to be established.

Successful implementation of the broad, participative approach adopted for Camisea required skilled personnel and specific organizational arrangements and responsibilities. Individuals at different organizational levels and locations had to be selected and trained to deal with the project's challenges. These people were chosen for their ability to promote an open-minded way of conducting the project through all of its phases. A Camisea "issues team" was organized at Shell International Exploration and Production in The Hague, with responsibility for insuring cooperation between SPDP and the international headquarters. One of its members with a strong EIA background became the health, safety, and environment (HSE) manager for Camisea in Peru. At the local level, SPDP organized a community liaison team that acted as the interface between the company and the community, with the specific purpose of ensuring compliance with HSE policies. A specific innovation for Camisea was that community liaison officers (CLOs) were based within the HSE department and charged with seeking meaningful stakeholder feedback, not simply clearing the way for the company's operations. Although this arrangement demonstrated SPDP's strong commitment to stakeholder involvement, it departed from the usual assignment of CLOs to the operations department and sometimes led to misunderstandings and technical difficulties.

Another crucial feature of the project was the use of technical assistance from independent external organizations operating in partnership with SPDP. Pro-Natura, an international NGO founded in Brazil, advised SPDP on internalizing socioenvironmental concerns within its operations and developing corresponding capacity within communities.

One of the greatest challenges of the Camisea project was to ensure that Shell's commitment towards sustainability and social responsibility was transferred to the Bechtel-Cosapi-Odebrecht (BCO) alliance, which had the task of designing and constructing the field facilities and pipeline through the rainforest and highlands to the coast. This pipeline would involve other groups of stakeholders, and other processes, than those involved in the Camisea basin itself. To insure that these consultations were adequate, BCO had to develop its own HSE structure; Shell personnel were placed in critical HSE posts within BCO and a separate CLO team for the pipeline was established.

Throughout the Camisea project, consultations with concerned third parties—NGOs and international organizations—were extensively utilized, although only a small number of these remained active over time. Some withdrew because they believed that the project was being well handled; others because it demanded too much time and effort; others because their positions could not be accommodated. After several consultation workshops in Lima, Washington, and London, it appeared that Shell had established trust with a number of potentially critical groups. Some third-party responses also included criticism of the project, including fears that, in spite of good intentions, creation of a large-scale industrial operation within this fragile ecosystem could not fail to be harmful. In addition, some parties doubted that Shell's new social and ecological commitments would ultimately prevail over its historic technical and commercial orientation.

In 1998 Shell announced its decision *not* to proceed with full field development of Camisea. Gas marketing and distribution issues were cited as the explanation for this decision, rather than the human rights and environmental issues that were the focus of its stakeholder analysis and consultation program. A major effort was made to explain the decision to local stakeholders, and to ease any negative impact it might have upon them. Although Shell continues to market petroleum products in Peru, the 40-year license for appraisal and development of the area was returned to the government, which ultimately sold it to other parties.

In spite of the decision not to proceed, the Camisea Project represents a major change in strategy, structure, and culture for Shell, with continuing impact throughout the global organization. Shell's new posture clearly involves greater social and environmental awareness, including recognition that the technical and commercial success of any new project depends critically on the acceptance and support of local, national, and international stakeholders. Social impact assessment was made an additional element of Shell's already mandatory environmental assessment processes.

Structurally, the Camisea Project broke away from the traditional decentralization and independence of Shell units, and emphasized the management of organizational interfaces at many levels, with strong leadership from Shell Centre in London. Culturally, the project implemented the commitment to a proactive stakeholder management orientation that Shell had formally declared over the previous two decades.

It also developed and applied leading-edge standards for ecological and human values within a setting of open communication and consultation. The entire experience was then communicated throughout the Shell Group through presentations and publications by Murray Jones, a leading participant in the project (Jones, 1997). Summary results of the lessons learned from Camisea were incorporated in revisions of Shell's manual for External Affairs.

CONCLUSION

Shell's responses to societal challenges over the past half century illustrate the importance of particular sequences of events, so-called "path dependencies," in determining corporate attitudes and behaviors. Experience during World War II and in connection with the Rhodesian sanctions reinforced Shell's policy of minimizing local political involvement. Experience in Nigeria revealed the danger of this posture. Although former CEO Herkstroeter insisted that Shell should not be blamed for the situation in Nigeria, he admitted that "when we say we do not have the power, they [Shell's critics] simply do not believe us" (1996, p. 8). Shell's actions in Nigeria can be better understood against the background of its prior experience, even though the critics were probably justified in believing that Shell had greater ability to influence this corrupt political regime than it chose to utilize at the time. Shell's experiences during the 1990s clearly illustrate both the dangers arising from neglect of stakeholder interests, and the substantial effort involved in conducting and implementing comprehensive programs of stakeholder analysis and management. The value of the approach adopted for Camisea cannot be demonstrated directly, as the project itself did not go forward, but it seems clear that—if it had done so—there would have been much less basis for the type of criticism and confrontation that arose with respect to Brent Spar and Nigeria. Shell's challenge at the end of the 1990s was to diffuse and institutionalize the learning gained from these experiences throughout the Group.

The cultural transformation underway at Shell, further discussed in Chapter 8, is clearly motivated by these experiences. The new "Shell Business Framework" statement of 1996 emphasizes the need for change: "Today's business environment is characterized by fierce competition on a greater scale than ever. In addition, society's expectations for business are changing. Companies that fail to respond effectively to these challenges will simply decline. . . . In the longer term, we seek to continue to create value for society and for our shareholders, recognizing that there will be further significant changes in our business because fossil fuels are a finite resource, and because society and its needs will continue to change" (Shell, 1996, pp. 6–8). By 1997, Shell's leadership recognized the need to articulate a new "core purpose" that would express a societal vision and go beyond conventional commercial and technical objectives. The result was a commitment to "helping people build a better world" (Shell World, Dec. 1997, p. 8). The 1998 "Management Primer" on "Business and Human Rights" affirms the new perspective: "The distinction between 'business' and 'society' is artificial. Businesses and corporations are social entities, created in the context of larger interdependent cultural, political and sociological systems" (Shell 1998a, p. 15).

The varied cultural and economic settings in which multinational corporations operate raise fundamental issues—such as human rights—in unfamiliar forms and challenge the ability of organizations to maintain and implement core values in diverse situations. As Shell CEO Moody-Stuart has remarked, "In this boundaryless and multicultural world, others wander—so to speak— into every corner of our businesses. Equally, Shell people interact with every part of society in a multitude of political and social systems—often having to react rapidly in difficult situations without consultation" (Moody-Stuart, 1998, p. 4). As Shell accepts the need to create value for society, as well as for the firm, it has to reconsider its role. Again, according to Moody-Stuart, "In earlier days we used to concentrate purely on the commercial role of firms. Of late there has been a great acceptance of the need to consider the environmental, social and even cultural impact of companies. We now acknowledge that we have to take the broader aspects into account" (Moody-Stuart, 1997, p. 3). The challenge of implementing a corporation's core stakeholder commitments within dissimilar economic systems and cultures—that is, the challenge of stakeholder management in a world of diversity—is explored in the following chapter.

7

GLOBALIZATION: MULTINATIONALS

IN CHINA[1]

Chapter 3 noted that one of the critical challenges to stakeholder management is globalization. Firms that operate in more than one country cannot simply utilize the stakeholder-oriented policies and processes that work at home. They must adapt to the cultures and norms of their operating environments. Yet they must not betray their fundamental principles.

Consider the difference between Shell's experience in Nigeria and its subsequent development of the Camisea project, explained in the last chapter. The shift in stakeholder management technique was dramatic, just as it was for Motorola and Cummins in unfamiliar circumstances over the years. This chapter examines how Shell and Motorola are operating within the culture that is perhaps most different from those of the West: China.

Most large multinational firms are already doing business in China; Cummins, for example, has had a substantial franchise there for many years. More and more smaller companies are trying to do the same. When it comes to adapting company policies to the distinctive features of doing business in China, Motorola and Shell are excellent examples, and this chapter details their experiences. Both of these companies have been extremely active in China for more than a decade, and Motorola has declared China to be its "second home."

---

[1] The analysis of the role of foreign multinationals in China utilizes field reports and other material prepared by Daniel H. Rosen during 1997–99. Important additional background sources include Rosen, 1999; Steidlmeier, 1997; Overholt, 1993; Chen, 2001; and Luo, 2000. Frans Ryckebosch, who served as Xerox country manager in China, also provided valuable assistance.

THE CHINESE SETTING

China is different from advanced Western countries in many ways, and some of the fundamental features of Chinese culture are often believed to be inhospitable to Western management practices. Traditional Chinese society, like that of many other emerging economies, is strongly hierarchical, with status often determined by age, title, or social position. Chinese society is also highly relational, placing great value on familial and interpersonal contacts (*guanxi*) and cultural cohesion. At the same time, and in sharp contrast to the age and strength of traditional Chinese culture, social and economic relationships in contemporary China have been disrupted by instability and dramatic change. During the 20th century, Chinese socioeconomic structure has been violently torn apart, first by war and then by politics, and then forcibly (and repeatedly) rearranged under the Communist regime. Political and economic instability is characteristic of many emerging economies, including the former Soviet Union and the developing regions of Africa.

The complexity of governance and management in foreign operations in China is suggested by the schematic diagram in Figure 7.1. This diagram specifically applies to international joint ventures, but would be the same for a wholly foreign-owned enterprise if the Chinese partners were omitted. Major influences include:

- Chinese Communist Party (CCP) and local Party units
- Trade unions, both at the national (All-China Federation of Trade Unions-ACTFU) and local enterprise levels
- Ministry of Foreign Economics and Trade (MOFERT)
- Other national government ministries and agencies
- Regional and local governments and agencies

Since 1978, Chinese social and economic structures have become more flexible and more diverse, and government decisions now tend to give greater weight to economic considerations—employment opportunities, potentials for growth and productivity increase, and international competitiveness, for example—than in the past. However, central, regional, and local governments

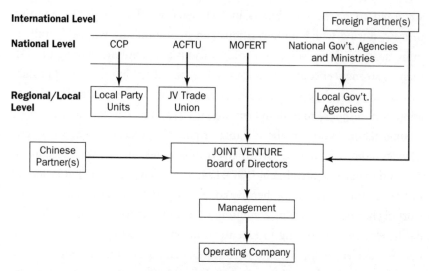

Figure 7.1 International Joint Venture in China: Governance Structure.
SOURCE: Adapted from Nyaw, M. K., "Managing International Joint Ventures in China," in Kelley, L., and Shenkar, O., *International Business in China*, London: Routledge, 1993, pp. 172–190, Fig. 9.1.

are deeply embedded in both state and nonstate enterprises, and government power and political considerations continue to play dominant, and often unpredictable, roles. Formal law governing business activity in China tends to be fairly brief and seemingly transparent, but implementing regulations tends to be voluminous, opaque, and subject to widely varying interpretations and levels of enforcement in different regions and industries.

China's official guidelines stipulate three principal ownership-control possibilities for a foreign investment enterprise (see Rosen, 1999, Case Study A):

- Wholly foreign owned enterprise (WFOE), controlled and managed by foreign interests
- Joint venture with majority ownership by the foreign investor, and with foreign control
- Joint venture with majority Chinese ownership and Chinese control

In some sectors the acceptable structure is specifically prescribed by law; in others the matter is left to the parties involved. In many cases the structure is supposed to be elective, but is in fact determined through the approval process, during which authorizations can be unofficially withheld until requirements, such as ceding control in various areas, are met. Foreign investment is strongly encouraged in some areas, permitted in others, and prohibited in some; and specific industries are shifted from one classification to another in response to both internal and international developments.

International concern about human rights in China over the past several decades has proved to be a particularly troublesome issue for Western companies and managers (Steidlmeir, 1997). Levi Strauss entered China in 1986, and in 1991 established a comprehensive code of conduct to ensure that the wages, working hours, and working conditions of its contractors met acceptable standards. However, according to executives interviewed as part of this project, Levi Strauss leadership became so concerned about the human rights climate in China that the firm withdrew entirely in 1993. In 1998 the company returned, joining with Mattel and Reebok in endorsing a new statement of "Business Principles for Human Rights of Workers in China" that was developed by a group of nongovernmental organizations focused on international worker rights (International Labor Rights Fund, 1999).

As in the case of South Africa, many firms have encountered considerable international pressure because of their operations in China and some other Asian countries. Some experienced analysts advise the foreign business community to "keep its head down," avoiding public debate on human rights issues while still trying to be "a model citizen" within its own sphere of control (Scarborough, 1998, p. 525). Others, however, argue that foreign firms cannot avoid "exporting human rights" if they follow their own best practice guidelines, and particularly if they want to avoid criticism and backlash from their overseas customers, shareowners, and critics (Spar, 1998; Santoro, 1998). These issues are most prominent with respect to employment and personnel practices, including those of subcontractors and other value-chain partners.

The foreign firm operating in China must work within the local culture and must find ways to motivate and collaborate with local persons and interests. At the same time, the whole purpose of the foreign venture is to bring about change, both within business units and within their operating environment. The greater the magnitude and speed of change attempted, the greater the opportunities for conflict; but reducing conflict by conforming to traditional norms reduces the likelihood that the venture will accomplish its intended goals. Western firms have been struggling with this dilemma in China for at least two decades, and it has become increasingly clear that a comprehensive stakeholder approach, based on explicit recognition of the concerns and interests of local participants and emphasizing the potentials for mutual gain through collaboration, can contribute to long-term survival and success. The field interviews suggest that only a handful of foreign firms have been able to fully achieve this result—knowing and controlling their own operations sufficiently to implement effective policies, and making certain that the benefits obtained are clearly understood and greatly valued by their Chinese partners and collaborators. It is clear, however, that elements of Western stakeholder management thinking are slowly but surely penetrating the Chinese business environment.

Within this setting, the field research for this project has focused on two main questions:

1. Why and to what extent have Western multinationals introduced stakeholder-oriented management principles into the very different Chinese environment?

2. How have Western firms operating in China developed relationships with three important groups of stakeholders:

    Governments—national, provincial, and local

    Employees—blue collar and white collar

    Customers—business and consumer

In addition, with particular reference to Motorola and Shell, we also ask what their Chinese operations reveal about their fundamental and company-wide stakeholder commitments. The impact of global operations on organizational learning and responsiveness in those companies is further explored in Chapter 8.

MANAGEMENT CONTROL AND MOTIVATION

Foreign management control is essential if stakeholder-oriented policies (or any other Western management ideas) are to be introduced into new operating environments. Many foreign investors in China fail to secure management control, in spite of contractual arrangements in their favor, either because they must explicitly achieve consensus with local partners before taking any action or because they do not fully understand how decisions are implemented at lower levels and therefore cannot determine how the firm operates.

In China, the potential for foreign management control is greatest in a WFOE. However, the WFOE alternative did not become predominant until 1997; and even within a WFOE and its value chain linkages, there are usually matters that the foreign investor lacks the power (and understanding) to control. Well-managed Chinese firms are greatly sought after as foreign investment partners, and therefore have extraordinary negotiating leverage, no matter what the formal control arrangements. And local partners are critical not only because of government policies but also because they often have preexisting distribution systems and relationships with potential customers. Hence, even when firms adopt a WFOE structure (as in the case of Motorola in China), they often must employ a kind of stakeholder thinking to create the external support network that they could have obtained by going the joint-venture route.

Why, if at all, would Western enterprises attempt to introduce stakeholder management policies into China? In the field interviews, managers repeatedly mentioned their need to turn JV and governmental partners created during negotiations into supportive collaborators in a common enterprise, to develop employees assigned to them through bureaucratic procedures into productive workers, and to transform inefficient suppliers and distributors into active participants in the value chain. These concerns clearly suggest the potential contributions of stakeholder management techniques, whether explicit or implicit, to organizational effectiveness and success. Other important stakeholder management motivations mentioned in the interviews included the following:

- *The need to look good to Chinese authorities.* The expectation that foreign firms will engage in social and philanthropic activities is commonplace at all levels, and firms make serious effort to show a philanthropic face to government authorities and the general public. Reformist authorities must constantly weather charges of pandering to foreigners; and foreign firms of conspicuous size constantly need to demonstrate their virtues. Motorola, for example, regularly updates its fact sheet showing dollar value of purchases from Chinese companies, taxes paid, number of state enterprises invited to its Quality and Productivity Institute, training provided to government officials, and so on.

- *The need to look good to customers and "social auditors" back home.* Avoiding situations that might lead to public scrutiny and unfavorable publicity provides strong motivation for proactive stakeholder policies in foreign multinationals. The great majority of larger American firms operating in China employ a statement of practices and behaviors similar to the "Universal Business Principles" issued by the American Chamber of Commerce in Hong Kong (Exhibit 7.1), although adherence to these standards is highly variable.

- *Avoiding future economic costs.* Many of the early foreign activities in China were "screwdriver" operations, in which foreign firms used China's cheap, unskilled workers to transform imported materials into re-export products. Under those conditions, the foreign firm had little control of the situation and little involvement in local affairs. But as foreign firms have become more permanently and profoundly involved in Chinese operations, this situation has changed dramatically. For example, Chinese subcontractors used to pick up toxic by-products at the factory door; their ultimate disposal was beyond the knowledge and concern of the foreign producer. Now the specter of the U.S. superfund experience—in which originating firms were held jointly and severally liable for environmental damages, regardless of the promises of intermediaries—hangs over Western managers. Similarly, firms have discovered that they can prevent damage to their brand names and quality reputations only by active involvement in the activities of distributors and retailers. Training and teamwork programs are frequently used to enhance stakeholder relationships where more active direct involvement is infeasible.

- *Achieving economic benefits.* Expatriate managers in China almost uniformly observe that there are limitless opportunities to improve

Exhibit 7.1
American Chamber of Commerce in Hong Kong: Universal Business Principles

It is fundamental to the philosophy of the American Chamber of Commerce in Hong Kong that good ethics and good business are synonymous. AmCham believes that American business plays an important role as a catalyst for positive social change by promoting human welfare and the principles of free enterprise. AmCham recognizes that American companies already set the highest standards for ethical business practices. We encourage members to communicate information about their existing programs and practices relative to good corporate citizenship in the markets in which they operate.

AmCham endorses the following business principles and encourages member companies to embrace them in all their operations, in the context of existing statements of corporate values of individual companies. We adopt these principles as a foundation for dialogue and action by business leaders.

1. We shall abide by the laws of the United States and the countries where we operate.

2. We shall aspire to be good corporate citizens, seeking opportunities to make positive contributions to the cultural, social, educational, scientific, and artistic life of the communities in which we operate.

3. We shall uphold the dignity of the worker and set positive examples for their remuneration, treatment, health and safety. To that end we shall not knowingly engage in business with firms which employ forced labor, or treat their workers in inhumane ways.

4. We shall endeavor to promote the highest possible standards of training and education for our employees. Training objectives derive from raising issues such as promoting self-confidence, independent and innovative thinking, self-improvement, and problem solving through teamwork.

5. We shall engage in environmentally responsible business practices in our operations and be proactive in promoting the value of such behavior in the communities in which we operate.

6. We shall be vocal in support of improved market access and intellectual property rights protection in the countries in which we operate.

7. We shall uphold high standards of professional and business ethics and incorporate these values into our employee training programs.

SOURCE: The American Chamber of Commerce in Hong Kong. Used with permission.

productivity and profitability through better management. The difficulty is often that economic agents inside the firm (Chinese partners, employees) or outside (value chain partners, regulators) are unwilling to make changes necessary to achieve the gains for fear that they will not be rewarded (or, indeed, may even be punished) for doing so. Many Western firms have tried to resolve such problems by trying to convert intransigent groups into collaborative stakeholders through proactive policies. This can involve simply "buying off" troublesome interests with the proceeds of greater operating success, but may also involve training, transfer of technology, guaranteed contracts, and other practices aimed at developing good long-term partners.

- *Implementing uniform global management policies and practices.* Restrictions on foreign business operations in China often make it difficult to integrate Chinese units into global management systems. However, many large foreign ventures enjoy some degree of administrative privilege and flexibility, particularly in the application of uniform company-wide policies. Access to these privileges is facilitated by a demonstration that the results will actually bring benefits to Chinese stakeholders. It may also be the case that the global practices being adopted are, in themselves, stakeholder oriented, as in the case of employee benefits.

- *Changing local operating cultures, particularly reducing corruption.* Many foreign firms express great concern over the corruption surrounding their Chinese operations. Uprooting these tendencies has proved difficult, especially outside the Special Economic Zones. In other areas, where foreign ventures account for only a small share of business activity, they are widely perceived as having "deep pockets" and are therefore prey to corrupt practices. Some firms have stated that their efforts to turn local authorities, partners, and employees into stakeholders is partly motivated by a desire to show them the benefits that can be gained by avoiding corruption, seeking an "ethical advantage." This can be a hard sell, but some larger firms have apparently managed to convince their immediate suppliers and value partners that saying "no" to corruption is essential if they are to become more deeply, and profitably, integrated into global networks.

In spite of these varied motivations, the introduction of stakeholder management practices into foreign ventures in China encounters significant obstacles. General problems arise from the number and complexity of government restrictions on foreign operations, and how these are interpreted and enforced from place to place and time to time. Because of the weakness of internal legal protections, foreign firms often avoid transferring critical technology and skills to value chain partners—actions that would strengthen their linkages and increase stakeholder benefits—for fear that the recipients will use these advantages to link up with other partners or become direct competitors. These concerns are commonplace throughout the world, but foreign firms operating in China generally feel that such behaviors are often encouraged, rather than discouraged, by government policies, and that the foreign interests involved have less protection from the legal system there than in many other countries.

STAKEHOLDERS AND *GUANXI*

The typical foreign investor in China confronts a large and diverse group of potentially important stakeholders—including Communist Party units as well as many other government authorities—and has a wide range of choice in developing relationships with them. All of these relationships evolve as the venture proceeds, but initial arrangements with particular stakeholders have significant impact on the flexibility of management over time. But the opaqueness of the Chinese business environment and the extraordinary rate of change and growth over the past two decades have made the development and maintenance of appropriate stakeholder linkages very challenging.

An additional factor complicating stakeholder management in China is the complexity of organizational structures. Managers in the Beijing office of a holding company may see the relevant *national* ministry as the primary government stakeholder, but operating managers necessarily give more attention to the concerns of *provincial* and *local* authorities. When different regulatory units give different instructions—requiring the use of a different set of suppliers or distributors, for example—even the most conscientious managers are stymied. Legitimate conflicts among the strategic linkages and regulatory requirements facing different joint venture partners are commonplace, and make the process of stakeholder identification highly problematic. (In addition, some executives interviewed have suggested that the home country headquarters of the multinational is often seen as a "stakeholder"—and not always a congenial one—by expatriate managers because of its remoteness and different perspective.)

Beyond these complexities, both formal and behavioral aspects of interpersonal and interorganizational relationships are more critical in China than in the West. For as long as foreigners have chronicled the Chinese scene they have fixated on the Chinese allegiance to the concept of *guanxi*. Family connections, common backgrounds, and longstanding friendships are often the basis of business arrangements all over the world, but these matters are much more important in China and respect for them is a distinct obligation. Whether in Hong Kong, Shanghai, or Taipei, Chinese executives spend considerably more time managing their contacts and connections than an analogous Western businessperson. Many expatriate managers working in China complain not about having to cultivate such relationships, which are both useful and universal, but about how much time and effort has to be expended on gifts, favors, and hospitality.

To Westerners, *guanxi* is often perceived as cronyism, but some understand that it is a reflection of trust, respect, mutuality, and commitment to common objectives among the parties involved (Lovett, Simmons, and Kala, 1999; Xin and Pearce, 1996). The latter view is more compatible with modern management concepts, and particularly with a stakeholder perspective. *Guanxi* relationships can be extremely enduring, lending stability and predictability to operations in spite of political and economic turbulence. Indeed, there is a tendency among Chinese to see the "stake" as the relationship itself, rather than as the objective benefits flowing from it (Fung, 1983).[2] At the same time, the web of connections just beneath the surface creates a sort of "shadow" system for the business enterprise in China that can prove problematic. For example, a manager might not take measures detrimental to a group of workers or dealers (such as firing some of them to reduce costs), even though this would be in the

---

[2]This material was brought to our attention by Paul Steidlmeier. Ming-Jer Chen helped to clarify our understanding of *guanxi*. See Chen, 2001, chapter 3.

best interest of the business, because some among them might use their *guanxi* to generate opposition among other workers, customers, or the community. The more market-oriented China becomes, the more conspicuous the impact of such restraints will appear. Nevertheless, these shadow relationships remain powerful. Incumbent firms have large sunk costs in the existing informal *guanxi* system and as long as it pays off they will continue to use it, even though it impedes the transition to more transparent management systems based on rational calculations and the rule of law.

Government Stakeholders

The structures and policies of governments influence the success or failure of business enterprises all over the world. However, the extent of government authority and involvement in the Chinese economy prior to 1978 went beyond anything ever experienced in any advanced industrial country, and even after more than two decades of reform, governments remain the most important participants in Chinese economic life. For four decades after 1948, governments at national, regional, and local levels were the principal owners of all urban businesses. In this role, they functioned as stakeholders on their own behalf, using their ownership status to achieve economic, social, and political objectives, and also purported to act on behalf of other stakeholders—employees, customers, and society at large. The reasons for this pervasive government role are not solely ideological. All land belongs to the state; many important economic activities and industries simply did not exist in China until after World War II and were first established by government initiative. Government control is therefore difficult to disestablish, because there are no prior arrangements or comparable set of market-based structures to serve as models for privatization. This is not uncommon among transitional economies all over the world.

A special feature of the Chinese economy is that governmental power and decision making is fragmented among multiple jurisdictions and levels, which are often in uneasy tension. The central government's primary interests include high and sustainable aggregate economic growth, with an emphasis on export earnings; acquisition of technology with minimal dependence on foreign firms; and global political status and national security. However, even at the national level ministerial portfolios often overlap, resulting in conflicting goals and priorities; and local and provincial governments tend to be focused on attracting new foreign investment and creating local job opportunities, without regard to export orientation or foreign dominance. The official Shanghai Investment Guide, for example, lists 185 industries in which foreign investment is encouraged, 111 "restricted" areas, and 30 areas in which investment is prohibited—in 25 pages of fine print (Shanghai Foreign Investment Commission, 1998). Local governments also try to increase their ability to manage their own affairs and to reduce their fiscal and regulatory dependence on Beijing. In addition, the pet projects of senior leaders at all levels inevitably receive special attention. These diverse motives lead to conflicts among government stakeholders, and account for some of the difficulties that Western managers inevitably have in dealing with them.

Units of government can also take direct stakes in foreign enterprises, either in pursuit of industrial policy objectives or as passive beneficiaries of the revenue flow. Special Economic Zone (SEZ) authorities may also take ownership positions, often using them to bring jobs, taxes, and revenues to their jurisdictions. The Tianjin Technological and Industrial Development Zone Authority is a good example, challenging the central government in Beijing on a number of occasions to assist its foremost corporate clients, such as Motorola. Singapore sponsored the formation of an entire industrial park at Suzhou outside Shanghai that was designed to make the local authorities explicit stakeholders and motivate them to support the enterprises based there. (The results of this experiment have been mixed; the benefits of in-park operation are said to leave firms ill-prepared for reality when they try to move outside.)

This suggests that governments are among the most important stakeholders in foreign ventures in China, but that the multiplicity and diversity of governmental units and arrangements gives the foreign investor a wide range of choice as to the identity and motives of its government partners. structural arrangements. In addition, whatever the initial choice tions, it is likely that the relationship between gove ners will mutate over time, for several reasons. Firs "obsolescing bargain" that evolves as the leverage of creases, and the investor's bargaining position declines.

a new $50 million plant cannot credibly threaten to take its operation elsewhere, although the host government can easily threaten to make the plant unprofitable, or to seize it and turn it over to other users. The Chinese legal system offers little recourse to parties impacted by changes in government policies at any level. Second, the entire structure of government in China is constantly in flux, in response to changing circumstances and political motivations. These changes in administrative structures—no matter how appropriate they may be—can easily damage or destroy preexisting stakeholder relationships between foreign ventures and their governmental hosts and partners. Finally, the performance of the venture itself will have an impact on its stakeholder relationships with government authorities, as with all others. Firms that consistently fail to achieve profit, employment, or export goals have seen their support from local and central authorities dry up. At the same time, there is some incentive not to appear too successful, since profitable firms are liable to have their tax rates arbitrarily raised and to be actively approached for assessments, fees, and philanthropic contributions.

Managing Government Relations in China

Whatever the structural relationships between foreign investors and units of government, government-business contacts in China, as everywhere else, require management. Richard Latham, head of United Technologies Corporation's China operations, has stated that his government relations staff visited more Chinese officials in a month than the U.S. Embassy political and economic division staffs saw in a year (Remarks at U.S.-China Business Council meeting, Jan. 13, 1997). Of course, such a high level of contact has its own hazards. Conspicuously close government relations can create the appearance of favoritism, generating antagonism from other firms and even from other units of government. Mixed signals from the business side are also problematic. Different subunits of a foreign firm, its Chinese partners, and even individual managers often appear to pull in different directions, each seeking to develop a separate relationship-oriented power base. Xiaolin Yang, head of GE's government relations in the Eastern China region in 1997, commented: "The trick [of go]od government relations is to deal with good and bad issues through one [pers]on. GE's problem is that its SBUs [strategic business units] all do their 'happy stuff' [philanthropy, contributions, etc.] through their own channels, then come to GE's overarching government relations department only to deal with the problems." Her point is that effective *guanxi* involves a balance of diverse elements. When different parts of the organization deal with different aspects—some with "happy stuff" and some with problems—there are few opportunities for compromises and trade-offs, and possibilities for the development of *guanxi* are correspondingly limited.

To access supporting authorities and stakeholders in government, expatriate managers are often said to "spread their dances around." This means breaking their overall operations into multiple smaller units, each tailored to pursue a narrow niche, with the relevant set of government authorities brought in as stakeholders. This has been a strategy of necessity for firms like GE that were anxious to get in quickly and establish market share, but it entails obvious loss of economies of scope and scale, not only in production and support functions but also in the management of government relations, with each unit handling its own affairs independently. Nortel officials suggested that a rival's 5% market share was entirely the result of distributing "rep fees" (quasi-bribes) to officials in various jurisdictions; without this dispersed local support, their product would have little chance of competing.

For other types of firms, the government relations function emphasizes specific benefits other than market access. ARCO China has relied on its central government partners to keep local bribe demands, unreasonable fees, and assessments under control. Senior financial managers at DuPont China Holdings stress that government partners are critical conduits for collecting information about customers' ability to pay, and for finding out where to focus pressure and publicity in order to get bills paid when they are delinquent. Government partners can also help firms to distinguish real business opportunities—big projects likely to receive funding and therefore worth cultivating—from proposals that are unlikely to emerge from the pipeline.

The Motorola legal staff emphasizes the importance of government relationships for getting the "right" interpretations of law. As noted earlier, there are significant ambiguities—and considerable gaps—in Chinese law, and numerous technicalities and exceptions need to be understood before serious planning can be undertaken. Government authorities take great risks if they allow a foreign venture to go forward and then discover that a Chinese venture has been negatively impacted. The presence of clear government stakeholder interests can provide offsetting justification. This kind of careful planning is particularly critical for major firms like Motorola, which inevitably have large and diverse impacts and consequently cannot expect to escape critical scrutiny.

To conclude, managing relations with government stakeholders is of foremost importance to foreign ventures in China. For small ventures far from Beijing, this may mean creating a "stake" for the person or agency with authority to grant a local operating license. For large and complex multinationals, it may involve complex issues of access and status, as well as financial arrangements. These critical relationships have to do with much more than money. They include the effect of the foreign venture on local markets and competitors, employment bases, technology transfer, and philanthropy. Particularly in the case of U.S. firms, relations with government stakeholders may include willingness to lobby on behalf of Chinese interests back in their home country as well. One peculiarity of these government-business relationships in China is that they have tended to be rather unstable, eroding, changing, or breaking up after a few years. These shifts have made the relationships all the more difficult to manage, but have done nothing to decrease their importance.

Employee Stakeholders

The nature of employment has changed radically since China's reform process began in 1979. Under the earlier regime, the concept of employees as stakeholders would have been meaningless, as the dominant ideology held that workers had complete power over their workplaces, with the Communist Party structure making decisions and interventions on their behalf. If a separate managerial hierarchy existed, it functioned alongside and in collaboration with the Party representatives. In reality, under this arrangement both responsibilities and benefits were so widely dispersed that there was little discernable connection among contributions, risks, and rewards—the essential elements of the stakeholder relationship. The benefits due employees were set in stone—the "iron rice bowl," which included housing, education, health and child care, old-age security, and even entertainment and leisure time activities. And it often appeared that the most likely way to lose one's personal entitlements was to take initiative or suggest some departure from standard procedures. These ideas are still pervasive in China, particularly in state-owned enterprises. However, the private sector—including indigenous firms and Taiwan/Hong Kong ventures, as well as foreign enterprises—now accounts for a large and increasing share of Chinese production, and these new and diverse enterprises are beginning to have widespread impact on employment practices and worker expectations (Benson, Debroux, and Yuasa, 1998). Human resource management (HRM) policies of foreign firms distinguish sharply among those involving non-Chinese expatriates, ethnic Chinese expatriates from Hong Kong, Taiwan, and other locations, and domestic employees. Our analysis focuses on domestic workers, but there is inevitably some interplay among the groups, particularly among the ethnic Chinese, domestic or foreign.

Human resource management in China has implications ranging from basic human rights issues to the most mundane details. The ability of foreign firms to manage their employees depends on their prior success in securing comprehensive control of their Chinese operations. After a foreign investor and its Chinese partners complete their own operating agreements and prepare their business plan, they develop a proposed labor contract setting forth their requirements, pay scales, benefits, and the like. This document requires approval by relevant authorities, who often introduce considerations other than the economic logic of the venture, particularly the local level of unemployment. Therefore, it has been very common for approval authorities to insist on higher levels of employment than the business partners deem necessary. Approval decisions are made outside of public view and cannot be appealed through normal channels. Under these circumstances, there is no way in which the balance of stakes and obligations, responsibilities and incentives can be explicitly introduced into the decision process. Hence, neither the number and character of the work force, nor the mix of base and performance-based elements in the pay scales, is likely to be what the foreign investor (and perhaps even the Chinese partners) intended. It is sometimes possible to trade off some employment restrictions for other things (technology transfer, export commitments, and the like) during the approval process; and staffing flexibility can be increased by establishing a WFOE rather than a JV, but that may involve foregoing other important stakeholder linkages that may be vital for success.

Whatever the staffing conditions may be, they are typically implemented in a labor market where skilled and semiskilled workers are increasingly scarce. The EIU (1997) survey confirmed a widespread impression that attracting and retaining competent workers is the single greatest management problem for foreign firms operating in China. This has two implications:

- Desirable workers will be able to demand high wages, status, and benefits
- Even with such commitments, there will be high rates of turnover among the most valuable employees

Foreign firms typically deal with this situation by providing generous support for competent employees, designed to increase their "stake" in the firm and therefore their productivity and loyalty. Abundant training and advancement opportunities are key elements in the package, along with housing (sometimes including home purchases and mortgage assistance), profit sharing, and other welfare enhancing benefits. Obviously, if investment in training programs is to prove worthwhile, the employees involved must be retained as loyal stakeholders and participants in the firm.

Some managers believe that an aggressive workforce training program is critical preparation for the "real" competition among market-oriented firms that will emerge in the future. Only a limited number of foreign firms are allowed to enter most sectors of Chinese industry, and the development of competitive indigenous firms is strongly encouraged. The challenge therefore is to develop a strong competitive posture, including a productive and loyal workforce, in order to survive in the future market environment. This strategy also leads to aggressive recruitment efforts, which contribute to high turnover in the upper levels of the domestic labor market. In high-growth cities, good people jump from venture to venture to achieve rapid increases in salary and benefits, as well as grander-sounding titles. In preparation for the launch of its Shanghai Buick production venture in 1998, General Motors ran recruitment ads in Shanghai papers offering hiring bonuses to financial managers, computer workers, accountants, and other specified professionals working at other local joint ventures. This tactic infuriated their foreign investor compatriots.

The problem of attracting and retaining talented workers is matched with the problem of avoiding overstaffing at lower levels. As foreign firms evolve from "screwdriver" plants into more sophisticated producers for both Chinese and export markets, the premium on skill and loyalty increases and the need for masses of unskilled labor correspondingly declines. This shift alone should increase the emphasis on stakeholder-oriented policies among foreign firms (and probably among Chinese firms as well). But reductions in the need for unskilled labor tend to exacerbate stakeholder relations with local authorities, for whom unemployment is a major and continuing concern.

Pressures to increase wages and nonwage labor costs have obvious implications for stakeholder management. In addition to raising wages directly in order to attract and retain desirable employees, foreign firms operating in China have tried to take greater control of their nonwage obligations and use them to build stronger bonds with critical employees. For example, in the past many foreign ventures did not provide housing, but paid housing fees to local governments comparable to the employee housing expenses incurred by state-owned firms. These fees often went into general municipal funds, with no direct impact on housing availability or quality. More recently, Motorola, DuPont, IBM, and some other large employers have taken control of these resources and used them to build housing and create employee home ownership plans (EHOPS). By 1997 Motorola had overseen construction of over 700 units, and more underway, with the stated objective of attracting and retaining qualified employees. Subsidized mortgages for employees increase the impact of these programs. Of course, programs of this type can be undertaken only by large employers.

Assuring and increasing quality in Chinese operations is an issue involving both skilled and unskilled employees. Chinese production workers are strongly disinclined to take initiative. They tend to be antagonistic toward incentive pay systems that result in inequalities; unwilling to use quantitative metrics to gauge task performance; and resistant to cost-saving, income-generating measures if they require changes in the way things are organized or require extra time or effort. Many of these behaviors can be understood in the context of the prior socialist system, and sometimes even in terms of current conditions, properly understood. One manager, irritated at lack of labor commitment to production goals, finally discovered that workers were reluctant to stay late because the last bus to the residential area would have departed, leaving them with a five-mile walk home. The workers involved had been hesitant to explain this for fear of losing face. It seems clear that an approach to such problems based on an understanding of employee interests and motivations would be more effective than insistent demands and heavy criticism. Company-wide training emphasizing open communication about organizational goals and the kind of collaborative behavior necessary to achieve them—in other words, HRM techniques designed to create and motivate stakeholders—is being introduced by some firms. Increased empowerment of employees—such as authority to interrupt an assembly line when necessary—is also consistent with a shift to greater emphasis on stakeholder-oriented policies.

Customer Stakeholders

Under the Communist regime, the interests of consumers or business customers were seldom considered on their own merits, but were determined in the state planning process and passed along to producers as directives. This has changed in recent years, with the appearance of better quality and selection and more direct attention to the needs and tastes of potential buyers. Many state-controlled firms have been told to focus on competing instead of expecting subsidies, and this may be one factor explaining changes in productivity measurements for state and collective enterprises in recent years (Rosen, 1999, pp. 122–5).

By contrast, foreign firms typically arrive in China with a focus on customers and do not require policy initiatives or changes in subsidy practices to adopt a marketing orientation. Although some foreign firms came to China thinking that the domestic market would welcome old products that were already mature or outdated in their home countries, competition among foreign producers—and rapid adaptation among Chinese enterprises—quickly increased competitive quality standards. Of course, some foreign product offerings were so clearly new or superior that customers would have purchased them without significant marketing effort.

Although recognition of customers as stakeholders is not yet the norm in China, it is clear that foreign ventures have led the way in introducing a customer orientation into the Chinese marketplace, particularly in their business-to-business dealings. Many foreign firms, especially those of small and medium size, have come to China because their important customers—larger multinationals with complex needs—were already established there. Examples include Hayworth Inc., Motorola's office furniture supplier, and McCormick, which produces the honey-mustard sauce used by McDonald's. These value-chain partnerships are particularly important in China, because the domestic marketplace is volatile and domestic suppliers often unreliable. Foreign partners then become strongly embedded in the stakeholder networks of their major customers, affected by their legal and political concerns as well as their product requirements, and often accepting less desirable locations, local sourcing requirements, and other derivative responsibilities. Successful operation for the whole chain of firms depends upon the fortunes of the lead multinational in the pack, such as General Motors in Shanghai, Motorola in Tianjin, Citroen in Wuhan, or Procter & Gamble in Guangdong. The analogy is often made that the lead firm is an aircraft carrier: the most important vessel but vulnerable without a flotilla of support ships.

Over time, indigenous companies have joined the "support ship" flotilla, and smaller foreign ventures have become thoroughly localized. Through this process, Chinese firms and managers have been led to adopt modern, customer-oriented practices with an emphasis on quality, reliability, and constant attention to changing customer needs. These attitudes are gradually spreading beyond the foreign venture networks and SEZs into the modernizing sectors of the Chinese economy. This gradual development of business-to-business links based on technical and economic considerations can be viewed either as a challenge to traditional *guanxi* relationships or as a natural evolution of *guanxi* to fit modern business conditions.

Relations between foreign ventures and household consumers are more tenuous. Chinese consumer markets are generally viewed as immature and atomized. Except for widely recognized names such as McDonald's, brand identification is weak, brand loyalty tenuous, and few branded products are available nationwide. Foreign ventures are still largely prohibited from distributing or servicing products other than those of their own manufacture, which means that most of them are dependent upon middlemen and have no direct contact with final consumers. Some firms are gradually circumventing these restrictions, first on the local level and then gradually more broadly, and their direct consumer contacts are increasing as a result. There is, however, very little evidence of a serious stakeholder orientation toward consumer goods marketing in China on the part of foreign firms, and even less among their Chinese counterparts.

OPERATIONS OF THE FOCAL COMPANIES

The situations and practices described in this chapter apply in a general way to most Western companies operating in China, and to foreign multinationals operating in many other developing country environments as well. In addition, each of our focal companies presents some special characteristics and experiences in their attempts to practice stakeholder management in such settings.

Motorola[3]

Motorola's operations in China present an extraordinary example of the activity of multinationals in emerging economies. During most of the 1990s, Motorola has been one of China's largest, most profitable, and most innovative foreign investors, with some 10,000 employees and $3 billion in annual sales from its China operations. The company has become deeply integrated into the Chinese national economy and into the communities in which it and its various partners and clients operate. Probably because of its success, Motorola has also been very open in documenting and discussing its China experience (Motorola, 1997). Its two-pronged strategy can be described as both committing itself to an important stakeholder role within China and creating a network of important and supportive stakeholders for itself within the Chinese economy and polity.

Strategy and Structure

Motorola was not inexperienced in international operations when it established a representative office in Beijing in 1987. Like most such offices, this

---

[3]This section is based on Motorola publications and interviews by Daniel Rosen, Lee E. Preston, and James E. Post. Special assistance from Dr. Eric Schuster, Motorola historian, is also acknowledged.

base served as a point of facilitation for import-export trade and as a learning center for making contacts and laying the groundwork for the development of a substantial presence. The foundation-building phase lasted four years; in 1992 Motorola (China) Electronics Ltd. (MCEL), a holding company, was incorporated as a WFOE. This was considered an innovative strategy at that time, because the JV structure was officially favored and because a WFOE might get little support from local business partners; however, the holding company form gave the venture considerable flexibility.

The conditions of Motorola's full-scale entry into China were particularly favorable. The Beijing government was attempting to offer a more accommodating face to foreign investors following the Tiananmen Square incident of 1989. Even before incorporating, Motorola developed a relationship with officials of the coastal city of Tianjin, which had been chosen as its initial operating location. Ground was broken a mere three months after incorporation; by March 1993 the firm was producing an array of pager and radio products for both export and the domestic market. Dismissing common wisdom that the highest value-added components of manufactures had to be imported, rather than made in China, Motorola's new facility started producing submicron integrated circuits in 1997. Today the firm has a national network of JVs operating alongside its flagship WFOE, plus several research and development labs, and is making an increasing effort to get into the service side of the business (which is so far prohibited). Motorola describes China as its "second home," and its China and Hong Kong operations account for more than 10% of its worldwide profits.

The fact that Motorola entered a sector with little domestic competition and brought substantial new technology to China helps to account for its favorable entry environment. From the beginning, Motorola's actions were closely coordinated with official government policy, and the company made every effort to create an atmosphere of mutual trust and favorable interdependence. In effect, Motorola attempted to "become part of the Plan," accepting the intentions of Chinese planning authorities as indicators of demand rather than making an independent analysis of market conditions and trends. This was appropriate and effective within a socialist planning environment, and created a strong stakeholder relationship with critical government bodies. As one Motorola executive put it, "You have to fit into *their* agenda, become one of *their* stakeholders."

Note that the initial WFOE structure did not mean Motorola was without partners in China. From the start it had a variety of commercial and regulatory collaborators; more equity JVs have also been developed over time. Motorola's customers include Chinese distributors and government-owned or -related network operators, all of which become "partners" to some extent, although all are subject to official regulation and other pressures. (Motorola takes no ownership interest in downstream enterprises.) Motorola attempts to maintain full management control over its JVs, and all of these entities become important stakeholders, serving and being served by Motorola's China operations. Local governments—particularly the Tianjin Economic Development Authority (TEDA)—are also critical elements in this mix. TEDA quickly became an active collaborator, working on behalf on Motorola in its dealings with other governmental levels and agencies. Curiously enough—and undoubtedly a sign of the changing situation in China—the Communist Party appears never to have become actively involved in Motorola's operations.

MCEL personnel use the term "stakeholder" freely in their discussions of JVs and value chain partners, such as suppliers and subcontractors. Its "China Center for Enterprise Excellence" tries to identify firms that meet both quality and ethical standards, and then to expand, upgrade, and strengthen their mutual relationships. In cooperation with the State Development and Planning Commission, this Center has offered programs to increase the efficiency of more than 1,000 state-owned firms, and to train some of them to become Motorola suppliers. The firm deals with almost 1,000 Chinese suppliers, and channels about 60% of its total procurement to local sources.

Motorola has also adopted a leadership position in China for community involvement and philanthropy. One executive commented: "If we didn't do things *for* China, we would not be able to do many things commercially. . . . We must project the message that we are stakeholders in China's future." A branch of Motorola University was established in Beijing in 1993, with subsequent expansion to other locations. Employees receive 10 or more days of training per year, and personnel from upstream and downstream organizations and government agencies receive training as well. Scholarships to both Chinese and foreign educational institutions have been provided. In addition, Motorola has placed great emphasis on the construction and occupancy of new facilities. The new Motorola North Asia headquarters building in Beijing, opened in June 1998, contains a branch of the Motorola Museum of Technology known as the "Beijing Gallery." Extensive support for schools, social programs, and other philanthropic activities is reported in Motorola publications and news releases. A particularly important example is the 1997 donation of three million yuan to Project Hope, a nongovernmental charity that supports schools and teacher training in poverty-stricken and underdeveloped areas. Motorola's Chinese employees were also encouraged to support this and other local charitable endeavors, an innovative practice in this setting.

Culture: Human Resource Management

From the very beginning, MCEL has made a determined effort to build constructive relationships with its local employees. Many of the original managers of its China operations were Asians who had been long-time Motorolans in Malaysia, Hong Kong, and elsewhere; some were native Chinese speakers. The strong mutually supportive relationship between these individuals and the company penetrated the China operation from the outset. In addition, three major programs—one entirely new to the company—were established to strengthen the link between Chinese employees and the company: Motorola University, the Employee Stock Ownership Plan (ESOP), and the innovative housing mortgage/financing program (Employee Home Ownership Plan, or EHOP). Motorola University currently presents more than 30,000 student days of course work, with hundreds of China-specific courses. These courses are made available to Motorola employees, joint venture partners, suppliers, distributors, customers, and Chinese government officials with whom the firm interacts. In 1996 MCEL employees spent an average of 70 hours in the classroom each year, and this number is expected to increase.

A key element of Motorola employee training has been a focus on ethics. Motorola believes that its long-term and worldwide ethical commitments, discussed in Chapter 3, gives it an "ethical advantage" over its competitors. But it has learned that it is necessary to adjust specific policies to local conditions.

For example, the corporation as a whole generally avoids the practice of gift giving. However, in Asia, where the presentation of gifts is a traditional part of business activity, the firm has created flexible but unambiguous guidelines for the giving and receiving of gifts, and has spent considerable time educating employees on their application. The emphasis on training—both in technical skills and in such cultural practices as gift giving—reflects the company's need for sophisticated personnel who are able to take initiative in responding to changing circumstances. In fact, "initiative taking" is an important emphasis in all of Motorola's training activities. The China Accelerated Management Program accepts about 100 young Motorola employees per year, exposing them to benchmark operations both within and outside the firm for six months, followed by six months of training in the United States and a final wrap-up period back in China. The goal is development of a substantial cadre of Chinese Motorolans who are deeply committed to the company and ready to take on positions of leadership and responsibility.

Motorola's employee stock ownership plan (ESOP) was not easy to deploy in China. A key obstacle is that China's closed international capital account prohibits Chinese citizens from holding financial instruments that can be exercised overseas. Senior Motorola executives are permitted to engage in off-shore transactions, but ordinary employees are not. Attorneys for Motorola have worked for several years with the China Securities and Exchange Regulatory Commission in an effort to get this policy changed, so that stock ownership could be used as an incentive for recruiting and retaining employees. In the meantime, Motorola has created a "stock equivalent," an accounting unit indexed to the stock price, which can be paid to employees to accomplish similar purposes. This program is primarily available to managers, but some lower-level staff are also included.

Motorola has offset the weakness of its normal ESOP policy with a special program to promote home ownership for its Chinese employees, the EHOP, which several other large foreign investment enterprises have subsequently adopted. Employers in China (largely state-owned firms) have long been responsible for providing housing for their employees, but the quality of such housing is often inadequate. Private housing alternatives are rarely available and there is no housing finance market. Private employers such as Motorola have been required to pay housing fees to local governments to finance the construction of housing for company employees. However, Motorola obtained permission to retain a portion of these fees to finance the construction of housing complexes that meet specifications determined by a housing committee of its own employees. Motorola then subsidizes and makes available a mortgage service to facilitate employee acquisition of units in these complexes. Motorola is not the owner of these housing complexes, but serves as the financial guarantor and project manager. The EHOP program gives MCEL employees a sense of control and responsibility, as well as a taste of democratic proceedings. It also creates strong incentives to stay with the firm, since the subsidies are not available to nonemployees. Chinese employees participating in these programs can, of course, still change jobs of they choose, and they often negotiate continued housing support from the new employer when they do so. The only notable downside of EHOP programs has been some damage to stakeholder relations with local governments, which lose some funds and some control over local housing conditions because of these changes.

Adaptation over Time

In the early years, Motorola had difficulty meeting both its export requirements and domestic demand for its products. However, since 1996 competition has increased as Nokia, Eriksson, and other manufacturers have entered the Chinese market with newer technology and aggressive marketing, challenging Motorola's leadership. In addition, some of Motorola's stakeholders—both governments and business partners—appear to have adopted new agendas or to be pursuing objectives that were previously secondary or suppressed, as their own positions have improved. The tendency of value chain partners to become independent, form links with other sponsors, or even become competitors is reflected in an often-heard comment: "We wish our JV [that is, the entire project] was getting stronger, not just our JV partner." In the "obsolescing bargain," as the competence of the JV or value chain partner increases, the control of the foreign investor weakens.

Motorola has responded to this by strengthening, rather than reducing, its commitments in China. In 1997 it moved its Semiconductor Products Sector Consumer Systems Group to Hong Kong, the first time such a unit was ever based outside the United States. At the same time, it named a leading Asian businessman, Ronnie C. Chan, to its board. In 1998 the firm announced plans to upgrade its Tianjin facilities with an additional $250 million investment, and in May 2000 Motorola requested permission to build a $1.9 billion semiconductor and telecommunications facility in Tianjin that would increase its total China investment to $3.5 billion. The company was an active participant in efforts to guarantee China's "most favorable nation" trade status with the United States, and also advocated China's designation under the Permanent Normal Trade Relations (PNTR) law. Motorola appears to be convinced that there is only one way to go with its involvement in China.

Shell[4]

Shell was an active distributor of petroleum products in China for many decades prior to World War II. In fact, the first joint venture of the two parent companies—Shell Transport and Royal Dutch—was the Asiatic Petroleum Company, formed in 1903, four years before the Royal Dutch/Shell Group itself was created. Shell reopened in China briefly after the war before turning all its facilities over to the PRC government in the early 1950s. During the 1970s it established a base of operations in Hong Kong.

Strategy and Structure

One of the first foreign firms to return to China after the major policy transformation of 1978, Shell opened an office in Beijing in 1980. An indication of the company's status at that time is the fact that the representative's office and residence were originally located in the "Clouds Gathering Pavilion" within the Imperial Summer Palace, which Shell restored to its former splendor and continued to use for special functions until 1999. Like other major international oil companies returning to China during this period, Shell believed that as the Chinese economy modernized it would become one of the world's largest markets for petroleum products, and possibly the site of the world's next great oil discoveries.

---

[4]This section is based on Economist Intelligence Unit, 1997; Howarth, 1997; *Looking at the Long Term: The Story of Shell in China* (1997); other Shell documents; and news stories and interviews.

Neither of these expectations has been fully realized, although Chinese companies have achieved some success in both; neither petroleum reservoirs nor product markets of world-class status have been developed yet. ARCO is the only foreign company with a major discovery to its credit; and until 1996, retail gasoline sales were entirely in the hands of Sinopec, a state-owned firm with retail outlets that were little more than pump stops. More recently, major firms, including Shell, have been allowed to open small numbers of more modern service stations, but Sinopec has responded by pressuring the central government to protect its monopoly status.

Shell's China operations expanded gradually until it became the largest foreign oil company investor and the largest international oil producer and trader in the PRC. Despite some downsizing and withdrawal from the liquid natural gas business during the 1990s, Shell China employs over 500 people and is engaged in multiple projects, both wholly owned and joint ventures. The head of Shell China is now an ethnic Chinese, as are nearly all the employees. In August 2000 Shell announced a new $4.3 billion joint venture with China National Offshore Oil Corporation (CNOOC), along with an intention to purchase an equity interest in that state-owned firm when it becomes available.

Shell's leadership position has not, however, given it free rein to pursue its own strategies. In the late 1980s Shell proposed to construct a large petrochemical complex and refinery at a coastal location in Guangdong province to produce output for the Chinese market from imported oil. This venture, known as the Nanhai Project, would have 50-50 ownership between Shell and CNOOC (with other local partners). The initial $4.5 billion petrochemical phase of the project would be the largest foreign investment ever made in China. Unfortunately, Nanhai became a perfect example of intrastakeholder conflict. Although it has powerful JV partners and strong support from the provincial government, central government approval of this project was held up for four years by a demand that most of Nanhai's output be exported to earn foreign exchange. (In the course of these negotiations, a Chinese employee of Shell was arrested and charged with stealing state secrets. Whatever the facts, this action and the publicity surrounding it was seen as a threat by many of China's most important foreign investors.)

China is a net oil importer, mostly in the form of refined products. Its leading area of market growth is in the south, far from the refinery centers in the north. Hence, Shell and its partners argued that domestic processing of imported oil, rather than importing petroleum products, would save foreign exchange over the long term even as it reduces the high level of petroleum products smuggling in South China. After four years of foot-dragging, the matter was finally resolved at the political level, and an agreement to proceed with the joint venture was signed in The Hague in the presence of then PRC Prime Minister Li Peng and Dutch Prime Minister Wim Kok on February 16, 1998. The petrochemical complex is currently scheduled for completion by the end of 2005, with the refinery to follow on the basis of domestic demand growth.

One way to avoid central government restrictions is to keep projects small (less than $30 million), and Shell has engaged in a series of these in the coastal provinces. It operates through seven main companies, including an important marketing unit in Hong Kong and others that have to do with all core areas of Shell activity from exploration through retailing, plus power generation and renewable energy sources. Shell China operates under the umbrella of Shell Companies in North East Asia (SCNEA), headquartered in Beijing; the chair and CEO of SCNEA is a member of Shell's Committee of Managing Directors (CMD) and is ultimately responsible for the implementation of Shell's global policies in China.

Culture

Shell's expanding operation in China has provided an important setting for testing and refining new stakeholder-oriented policies arising out of its experiences during the 1990s, described in Chapter 6. However, the transfer of some of Shell's most basic operating principles to the Chinese environment has proved problematic. Partially in response to its experience in Nigeria, Shell added a commitment "to express support for fundamental human rights" in the 1997 revision of its Statement of General Business Principles (SGBP). This phrase is not only hard to translate into Chinese but also can appear argumentative in that context. The same is true to a lesser extent of phrases such as "market mechanism," "free enterprise," "competition," and "sustainable development"—all of which appear prominently in Shell documents. After much work, a Chinese translation of the SGBP and related documents was developed to capture Shell's fundamental commitments without creating confusion or offending Chinese sensibilities.

Shell China has placed heavy emphasis on its external affairs function, which includes both community relations in locations where Shell has facilities and nationwide programs emphasizing environmental protection, road safety, education, and the development of sustainable energy sources. Shell views all these as both philanthropic and strategic. An example of the latter is its sponsorship and participation in technological conferences and research on paving materials and processes for roads and airports. It has also produced a broad statement on "sustainable development" in China, with an emphasis on energy needs and sources. In 1999 the Shell Foundation announced it would spend more than $1.5 million on new sustainable energy projects in China, including the use of rice straw to produce energy for remote villages ("Earning the License to Grow," address by Jeroen van der Veer, November 26, 1999).

The Shell Better Environment Scheme is a high school-focused educational program originating in Hong Kong and now functioning throughout China with hundreds of schools and thousands of student participants. All of these activities reflect Shell's new stakeholder-oriented management culture, as well as its increasing emphasis on renewable energy sources. They also are part of an effort to build a broad base of social acceptance for Shell in China as insurance against future changes in government policy and the emergence of competitors, both domestic and foreign.

CONCLUSION

Many foreign multinational corporations have made serious attempts to adapt their company-wide characteristics to the special characteristics of diverse local cultures and sociopolitical situations—to "globalize" their core commitments instead of making ad hoc responses or merely duplicating home country practices. Most Western firms operating in China have attempted to understand and adapt to its unique characteristics, and Motorola and Shell have clearly committed themselves to significant stakeholder positions. Both companies have attempted to identify themselves with China's successful economic and social development across the board, not simply with respect to their own activities and objectives. In particular, they have cultivated close and mutually beneficial relationships with local and regional authorities, and have established outreach activities—such as training programs—that provide clear benefits for domestic and state-owned enterprises, as well as for themselves and their employees. Extensive and innovative employee benefits programs and conspicuous commitments to national and local social and philanthropic projects help to make the stated "humanistic commitment" of these companies a reality within their China operations. Their activities in China clearly illustrate the challenging process of adapting company-wide commitments and policies to the special features of dissimilar operating environments, and thus give meaning to the idea of globalizing stakeholder management.

8

IMPLEMENTING STAKEHOLDER
MANAGEMENT: LEARNING
AND RESPONDING

Chapters 3, 4, 5, and 6 examined how Cummins, Motorola, and Shell identified critical issues and developed stakeholder-oriented responses in a variety of management areas—human resources, community relations, competitive developments, government relations, social and environmental concerns. A comprehensive commitment to stakeholder management involves continuously drawing lessons from such experiences, and implementing pervasive and permanent change throughout the organization wherever necessary. Stakeholder management is entirely different from ad hoc reaction to the concerns of a particular group or ex post resolution of some specific current problem.

This chapter examines two central issues: How and why did these companies develop a responsive approach to stakeholder issues? How have they sustained and institutionalized a stakeholder-oriented mode of management over time? The company-wide learning processes that have taken place at Cummins, Motorola, and Shell over the past quarter century have produced changes in strategy, structure, and culture. Our analysis confirms the results of the Business Enterprise Trust study (Bollier, 1996), referred to in Chapter 4, which shows the favorable impact of commitments to humanistic and social values on corporate performance. This study goes beyond that work, however, because we have examined these companies in depth, over an extended period of time, and with an emphasis on the challenges confronting their basic wealth-creating strategies. Hatten and Rosenthal (1999, 2001) have also analyzed the favorable impact of mutually beneficial corporate relationships with economic stakeholders in terms of competitive capabilities. Our research extends their perspective to include a full array of stakeholders, particularly those emerging from the social and political arena, along with those contributing to the firm's resource base and involved in its industry structure.

MODES OF LEARNING AND CHANGING

Learning is a process, not an event; the ability to extract information and insight from experience, and to accumulate and transfer knowledge among units and over time, is the distinctive characteristic of so-called "learning organizations" (Senge, 1990; 1999). Learning is a process that creates *path dependencies* within organizations. The learning process is a link between two states of knowledge, one that exists *before* a particular event or experience occurs, and another that prevails *afterward*. The second state is different from the first, but its specific characteristics depend significantly upon the conditions that prevailed earlier, as well as upon the character of the stimulating event or experience.

Corporations learn from both negative and positive experiences, as Shell's transformation following the Brent Spar and Nigeria incidents clearly illustrates. Effective organizations and their managers know how to integrate knowledge about internal and external change processes with prevailing assumptions about the organization's strategy, structure, and culture. As a result, basic features of the corporate core—strategy, structure, and culture—may change, as well as routine policies and practices. The ultimate result can be a fundamental change in the way that the firm pursues its goals of survival, value creation, and growth.

The experiences and events that generate learning can emerge from within or outside the firm. New leadership, changing resources (less or more), technological developments, acquisitions, and new administrative systems normally produce ripples of change throughout an organization, frequently leading to adjustments in its strategy, structure, and culture. External stimuli for organizational learning include new expectations, technology, political developments, changes in relevant regulatory policy, or critical incidents such as the

Firestone tire recall, Nestlé boycott, Exxon Valdez oil spill, or Microsoft antitrust trial. (Highly visible and conspicuous external developments often generate learning in organizations *other than* those directly involved; indeed, building knowledge from the experience of others is a valuable and sophisticated organizational skill.) New conditions also bring in new actors—competitors, customers, suppliers, or regulatory authorities—some of which may become important new stakeholders for a particular enterprise.

There is an extensive body of research on organizational learning, with numerous theories and data ranging from the anecdotal to the systematic. Of central importance is Argyris' (1977) fundamental distinction between single-loop and double-loop learning. Single-loop learning occurs when there is a mismatch between the organization's action and intended outcome. These mismatches are corrected by changing actions, but without the critical examination of variables that characterizes double-loop learning. Fiol and Lyles (1985) differentiate between lower-level and higher-level learning. The former involves developing cognitive associations that facilitate incremental organization adaptation, but without questioning of norms, assumptions, and frames of reference. Higher-level learning occurs when all these are challenged and altered, producing a more accurate understanding of causal relationships. Senge (1990) emphasizes the distinction between adaptive and generative learning, the former being incremental and involving coping within an existing frame of reference, whereas the latter is about being creative and requires new ways of perceiving the world.

Our research reveals that the learning processes involving stakeholders involve many elements of the generic types of learning. External change imposes different degrees of pressure on an organization to respond and, in so doing, promotes different kinds of learning. A corporation's interaction with its stakeholders typically involves a *responsiveness process* that includes generating internal awareness of the issue and the stakeholders involved; learning about the technical and administrative factors affecting the issue; commitment by senior management to policy and a course of action; and initiatives to institutionalize change. The classic discussion of this process is Ackerman (1973); see also, Post, Lawrence, Weber (1999), pp. 85–88, for current applications. The companies we have studied manifest three distinct forms of learning about, and responding to, their stakeholders. We refer to these as *adaptation, renewal,* and *transformation.*

- *Adaptive learning* involves adjusting routines and practices to avoid known mistakes and take advantage of recognized opportunities. Processes and behaviors are modified within an essentially unchanged configuration of corporate strategy, structure and culture. Adaptation is typically single-loop learning, although the Cummins Engine experience reveals an example of double-loop learning within an adaptive learning process.

- *Renewal learning* involves evolutionary and more proactive behavior, including the reexamination of assumptions and cognitive frameworks. Basic values and goals may be pursued in new ways, involving noticeable changes in strategies and structures. As seen in the experience of Motorola, learning that is focused on renewal can involve a mixture of both single-loop and double-loop dynamics.

- *Transformational learning* involves substantial change within the organization to increase its probablility of success within a changed environment. This type of learning may lead to substantial, even disruptive, change within an organization, including change in its core culture. Significant discontinuities, or new realities, can force such learning, producing major changes in an organization's strategy, structure, and culture (Drucker, 1989). This type of learning must involve double-loop processes, as the organization addresses the disrupted equilibrium that once prevailed.

As the analysis presented in this chapter makes clear, Cummins, Motorola, and Shell display these various forms of learning in dealing with stakeholders and stakeholder issues. Their learning experiences and responses to change are *path dependent,* involving interaction between prior conditions—history of the firm and preexisting strategy, structure, and culture configuration—and specific issues and events. All three firms were well aware of their stakeholder relationships before critical new developments occurred, but all of them learned from experience and changed in response to changing circumstances.

The path dependencies revealed by our analysis include both deliberate and (apparently) unconscious or habitual consideration of stakeholder interests in response to changing circumstances.

Organizations develop *patterns* of responsiveness, as well as specific responses to individual stimuli (Post, 1978). The cultures of Cummins, Motorola, and Shell evolved over many decades prior to the period analyzed in our research. The historic success of each company gave rise to a set of internally shared assumptions about how business should be conducted, what factors accounted for firm success, and what pitfalls were to be avoided in responding to change. Nevertheless, during the last two decades of the twentieth century the conventional premises and operating assumptions within each firm were challenged and modified in response to internal and external realities of operating within a global context. Cummins developed creative ways to respond to new global market opportunities within the framework of fundamental and long-recognized competitive characteristics of its industry. Motorola, by contrast, made strategic choices that resulted in substantial and widespread change; it became, in effect, a different company, involved in new technologies, operating locations, and markets. Shell, which had a global reach from the start, voluntarily transformed itself to better manage its increasingly interrelated worldwide activities, and then found itself forced to alter its basic strategy and culture in response to new kinds of external pressures. By 2000, each of these firms was addressing challenges and dealing with stakeholders in ways that would have been unimaginable only a few years earlier. The learning experiences and resulting organizational changes in the three companies under study, described in more detail in the rest of this chapter, are summarized in Table 8.1.

ADAPTIVE LEARNING: CUMMINS ENGINE COMPANY

Throughout its history, Cummins has operated within an industry composed of megafirms such as General Motors, Ford, Toyota, and Daimler-Chrysler, along with many specialized and innovative "niche" firms—including Cummins itself. Because motor vehicles, particularly commercial truck fleets, are capital goods, levels of demand are heavily influenced by the business cycle.

Table 8.1
Corporate Learning Processes and Results

	Cummins	Motorola	Shell
Initial stimulus for learning	Industry characteristics and global business trends	Strategic changes in products and markets; new stakeholders, internal and external	Internal reorganization (New Shell) and emergence of external crises and challenges
Learning mode	Adaptation—informal, unstructured, continuous	Evolutionary, with an emphasis on renewal; deliberate, but gradual	Transformational—formal and systematic; episodic (crisis driven) and substantive
Strategic impact	Maintain market niche focus; leverage core competencies with resources from alliance partners	Integrate critical stakeholders into strategic management system; strengthen external contacts and linkages	Proactive contact with stakeholders; develop collaboration for mutual benefit
Structural impact	Modifications include alliances; managing new issues; structure changes (internal: Corporate Affairs Division/CAD; external: joint ventures)	New processes (MERP, Global Task Force) leading to structured change (Office of Ethics Compliance, Code of Business Conduct)	Increase status and role of external affairs within "New Shell" framework; more global coordination
Cultural impact	Continuous learning strengthens traditional culture	Reaffirm and renew core values and apply to new situations; increase collaboration with organizational culture	Broaden culture to include social concerns; emphasis on "listening and responding" to stakeholders

Increased demand places a strain on production capacity; economic downturns leave facilities and employees idle. Maintaining facilities, retaining skilled personnel, carrying on research and development projects, and covering capital costs during slack periods place serious pressures on the financial structures of firms in such industries, and usually lead to intermittent periods of consolidation through closures, mergers, and acquisitions.

Strategic Adaptation

Cummins' success during the last decades of the twentieth century involved adaptation to the fundamental instability of its industry and development of an increasingly global system of production and marketing. Central to its strategy was the selection and development of stakeholder partners to share responsibilities and risks in various markets. This conserved capital for use in the company's own R&D and manufacturing operations, while taking advantage of specialized knowledge, productive capacity, and market access provided by others. From its first overseas venture in Scotland in 1959 to its more recent entries into India and China, Cummins has relied on functional partnerships to achieve its objectives. Cummins has also extended its strategy of "creating stakeholders" beyond market partners (discussed in Chapters 4 and 7) to include governments, labor unions, and local communities.

The company's effort to create favorable stakeholder relations with government regulators is well illustrated by its response to the emergence of new environmental concerns that began in the late 1960s. Diesel exhaust then had a mixed reputation in the eye of the public. On the one hand, it contained little harmful carbon monoxide or smog-creating unburned hydrocarbons; on the other hand, it was more visible and malodorous than automobile exhaust. The federal government had authority to control automotive emissions, including those from diesel engines. The Secretary of the Department of Health, Education, and Welfare was empowered to certify that all engine lines sold after January 1, 1970, met the new emissions standards.

Looking ahead to this deadline, Cummins' chairman J. Irwin Miller believed there would be little difficulty in meeting the deadline, and that the new regulations might offer "additional profitable business for the Company." But Cummins' stance toward the new requirements, and toward the government officials assigned to enforce them, extended far beyond simple market considerations. In 1969, the company announced it would not wait for "federal requirements or incentives . . . to fulfill our responsibility to improve the quality of our environment." Soon thereafter, Cummins made public its controversial position that engine manufacturers should *internalize* the cost of meeting pollution standards. Cummins' competitors sharply disagreed. The true test of

Cummins' commitment came in the 1970s, as air quality standards were ratcheted up. The Clean Air Amendments of 1970 demanded the removal of 90 percent of carbon monoxide, unburned hydrocarbons, and oxides of nitrogen (NOx) by model year 1975. The California Air Resources Board then imposed a hydrocarbon standard twice as stringent as that of the Environmental Protection Agency (EPA), a move that former CEO Henry Schacht declared "turned the industry upside down." Nevertheless, Cummins maintained its position on internalizing costs, to the growing dismay of its industry peers.

The stakes rose dramatically in 1975, as Congress focused on revising the Clean Air Act. Whereas diesel engines had previously been excluded from the heavier controls imposed on gasoline vehicles, new proposals would hold them to more stringent regulations. Legislative committees were defining their own standards. For Cummins, the process by which standards were set and enforced—in effect, the nature of relations between key public and private stakeholders—was as important as the standards themselves. As company historians Jeffrey Cruikshank and David B. Sicilia put it: "Was it fair and realistic, Cummins asked, to have and entire industry's fate hinge on the seemingly arbitrary processes of a single congressional subcommittee, or on the opinions of a single legislator?" The company's response was to try to redefine a more mutually beneficial relationship. To this end, it crafted a four-part set of recommendations for setting and maintaining standards, which soon became known as the "Cummins book." These were: (1) to restore the EPA as the sole standard-setting body (while leaving Congress authority to raise or lower those standards); (2) periodic review of standards to insure their scientific and technological currency; (3) redefinition of the certification process; and (4) imposition of financial penalties for noncompliance. After considerable debate, the Cummins standards were approved by both houses of Congress in 1977 and incorporated into Section 202 of that year's Clean Air Amendments.

This did not settle the matter, however. Soon it became clear that the question of who would conduct the research essential to setting standards was filled with complications. Diesel exhaust is more complex than gasoline engine exhaust, and researchers understood only a small number of its thousands of compounds. Industry interests—including Cummins—doubted that the EPA could conduct adequate research to set fair standards on its own, while the EPA reasonably did not wish to leave research strictly in the hands of industry. The issue came to a head when the EPA began to ask engine manufacturers to accept personal liability for every certified engine. Without conducting extensive animal and other toxicity tests, engine makers would be vulnerable to massive damages should their emissions be found to cause health problems. Seeking to work through the conundrum by building on mutual interests, Cummins' executive Henry Schacht approached EPA administrator Douglas Costle in 1978. The result was a unique business-government research consortium for research on mobile diesel engine emissions, the Health Effects Institute. Engine manufacturers paid for one-half of HEI's budget while the EPA paid the other half; and all research projects were to be conducted by independent experts. These matters took more than two years to work out, but when HEI was dedicated in late 1980 it drew applause from industry interests as well as from the EPA. "We have created, I believe, a new kind of institution," said the EPA's Costle at the dedication, "whose organization will give it both the competence and independence so essential for disciplined and credible scientific inquiry" (Cruikshank and Sicilia, 1997, pp. 302–3).

Structural Response

As Cummins grew from a family business into a giant, multinational corporation in the postwar decades, its internal structures of governance had to be reformulated. The personal, sometimes paternalistic, management style of J. Irwin Miller had to give way to a more formal form of organization. But neither Miller's successors nor the company's rank and file employees wished to see the core values of the company lost amid growth and change. If Cummins were to continue to sustain and nurture strong relations with key stakeholders, therefore, it had to fashion an appropriate internal structure.

In this domain, as in many others in which it departed from conventional methods, Cummins had to innovate. To begin with, the company's high-ranking executives continued to recruit and cultivate successors in a manner more befitting a small firm than a giant one. In more than eight decades, only a half dozen men have served as company president, each after a long period of mentoring. The company's geographical isolation from the east and west coasts also has helped preserve its distinctive corporate culture. Still, a genuine stakeholder orientation in governance must emanate from the inside out rather than from the top down. And that was becoming increasingly difficult by the 1970s, when Cummins employed more than 20,000 people, half of them outside its hometown.

Recognizing those realities, Cummins established a unique "Corporate Action Division" (CAD) in 1972. In its charter, the CAD was given this mandate:

- Serve as an in-house resource for understanding the social and political context in which the company does business.

- Interpret political and social issues, propose corporate policies, and coordinate public affairs programs.

- Work with management at all levels to ensure that all business analyses—new plant sites, new ventures, market penetration, product development, functional planning, etc.—include corporate responsibility considerations (Cruikshank and Sicilia, 1997, p. 315).

James A. Joseph, an ordained minister and former civil rights activist, was appointed first head of the CAD; he was soon joined by Charles W. Powers from Yale University, who had coauthored an influential book on ethical investing. The Corporate Action Division had the strong backing of senior management. Joseph was appointed at the vice-presidential level, reporting directly to Schacht, and at least two members of the group were assigned to each major functional area in the corporation. At times, the CAD struggled with how to codify its guidelines and policies. Management saw the need for uniformity, yet recognized that ethical situations often require subtle judgments. As a result, the CAD tried to promote what it called a "loose-tight" set of ethical norms.

The Cummins approach began to attract the attention of other large firms. "Cummins really plowed the first ground in this field," wrote CBS President Arthur Taylor, who asked to "borrow" James Joseph so that he could set up the same kind of program at his own company (Cruikshank and Sicilia, 1997, p. 328). The Corporate Action Division was an attempt to institutionalize Cummins' longstanding stakeholder-focused approach to business at a time when the company was feeling the effects of rapid expansion, particularly into unfamiliar and diverse operating environments abroad. Its policies, codes, and guidelines penetrated every layer and function of the corporation. Audit procedures were created to monitor and evaluate the external involvement of the firm's operating units. These structural and process responses produced both a better understanding of the world in which Cummins was, and would be operating in, but also generated a new set of capabilities and experiences for the company and its management.

EVOLUTIONARY LEARNING AND RENEWAL: MOTOROLA

As discussed in Chapter 5, Motorola has sought to be a learning organization throughout its history. Over seven decades, the company has emphasized the need to develop new products, technologies, and processes. Robert Galvin (1999) described the company's commitment as one of "creating new industries . . . to produce what has never been done before." Creating new knowledge, and learning how to do so, has been recognized within the company as essential to that process. The evolutionary development within Motorola over the past two decades highlights the distinctive role of renewal as a core value.

One impressive aspect of Motorola's success is that it has operated in industries that are noted for extraordinarily intense competition, constant entry and exit of significant competitors, and rapidly changing technology. "Indeed, remaining on the cutting edge of technology is often insufficient—firms have to anticipate and lead the changes in technology" (Peach, 1999, p. 3; see also Leonard-Barton, 1998). Motorola invests heavily in new technologies, and the timing of their introduction—or anticipation of new technology introduction by others—is critical. The cycle of change and innovation is a defining feature of Motorola's operating environment, much as the cycle of macroeconomic expansion and contraction is a defining feature for Cummins. And it may be an even less predictable environmental factor.

Culture

When Motorola's business was concentrated in the domestic market, the company's midwestern culture helped guarantee disciplined and ethical behavior among employees. The company was, metaphorically, a family of

"Motorolans" raised in the atmosphere of middle-American values and social norms. As discussed in Chapters 3 and 4, Motorola's culture is an extension of two fundamental propositions—respect for the individual and uncompromising integrity. Adherence to high ethical standards is a fundamental commitment that has been restated, and reinforced, by each generation of Galvin leadership.

Since 1973, Motorola has published and periodically updated a document entitled "*For Which We Stand: A Statement of Purpose, Objectives & Ethics.*" This document was originally created in response to what Galvin perceived as unfair criticism of American industry, condemning many firms for the sins of a few. The text has been revised several times, most recently in 1996; it became incorporated into the company's Code of Business Conduct in 1999. In a "Letter to Motorola's Stakeholders," for example, Christopher B. Galvin (chairman and CEO) stated that the "Code of Business Conduct highlights our important legal obligations, but we believe that obeying the law is a minimal standard. . . . [T]he Code also includes our Key Beliefs—Uncompromising Integrity and Constant Respect for People. We rely on all Motorola employees to be guided by these standards consistently and faithfully" (Motorola, 2000).

Motorola's growth from a midwestern American manufacturer to a global enterprise posed serious challenges to its humanistic values and ethical standards. With two-thirds of its employees living and working outside the United States, half in Asia and half elsewhere, the need to translate its culture into terms that would be understood and appropriate in foreign settings became critical. Motorola's basic commitments to humanistic values appeared to be universal; however, the meaning and behavioral implications of these commitments necessarily varied among diverse peoples and cultures. Retirement also claimed many of the long-term employees who had risen to leadership positions, increasing the pressure to review and update basic commitments and to translate them into terms that would be understood by a new generation of employees working all over the world.

An early response to these concerns was the issuance to all employees of a pocket-size card restating Motorola's Key Beliefs, Key Goals, and Key Initiatives (see Exhibit 8.1) The terminology used on this card is clear and straightforward, leaving no ambiguity about what behavior is expected of each

---

Exhibit 8.1
Content of Motorola Pocket Card

Our Fundamental Objective   Everyone's overriding responsibility

- Total customer satisfaction

Key Beliefs   How we will always act

- Constant respect for people
- Uncompromising integrity

Key Goals   What we must accomplish

- Best in class
  - People
  - Marketing
  - Technology
  - Product: software, hardware, and systems
  - Manufacturing
  - Service
- Increased global market share
- Superior financial results

Key Initiatives   How we will do it

- Six sigma quality
- Total cycle time reduction
- Product, manufacturing, and environmental leadership
- Profit improvement
- Empowerment for all, in a participative, cooperative, and creative workplace

[Motorola employees carried a pocket card with a statement of key ideas summarizing the company's objectives, beliefs, and strategic priorities circa 1997.]

Motorolan. The card has been translated into many languages and every member of the company's workforce is expected to carry the card.

MERP: A Learning/Teaching Process

Another significant step in the evolution of Motorola's stakeholder management capability was the development and implementation of the Motorola Ethics Renewal Process (MERP). As Motorola evolved into a full-fledged global business, ethical issues grew in number and complexity, especially as the variety of cultural practices and legal structures encountered expanded. Telecommunications operations often involve joint ventures and alliances, producing complex issues of ownership, control, and governance. By the mid-1990s, Motorola executives realized that it had become impractical—even impossible—to establish uniform rules of behavior covering all the circumstances that arose in its worldwide operations. Top management retained a strong commitment to Motorola's fundamental humanistic and ethical values, but realized that their application had to be adapted to diverse operating situations and circumstances.

In 1995 the board of directors asked a group of the company's senior retired officers to examine the status of ethics understanding and compliance around the world. The team spent one year interviewing people within and outside the company. They recommended to the board that an ethics renewal process be created and rolled out across the corporation. The intent was to surface issues that were keeping people awake at night, things they could not easily discuss even with coworkers.

The board of directors agreed to support the process, and put the weight of their personal reputations behind the initiative. At least three of the company's senior officers and directors, including the CEO, participated in MERP meetings. Management responsibility for MERP was placed with Human Resources rather than the company's legal department. "From the start, the objectives were to establish an honest dialogue on concerns about ethical compliance, ethical values, and the Code of Conduct," said Glenn Gienko, Executive VP for Human Resources (Peach, 1999, p. 33).

The study team recommended that Motorola create an ethics office specifically tasked with ensuring ethics compliance throughout the organization.

The goal was to be proactive, not reactive, in addressing Motorola's compliance with legal and organizational requirements. This recommendation was adopted, and the ethics office was established in 1998. The team also recommended that Motorola support the ethics renewal through a major educational effort, including development of customized study material tailored to its actual work situations. This resulted in the preparation of a book of company-oriented ethics materials and case studies that were subsequently published by Motorola University Press (Moorthy and others, 1998). The book applies the insights of a number of experts to the analysis of cases based on the experience of Motorola employees and stakeholders.

Maintaining an Ethics Advantage

The MERP process evolved into a sustained learning process—an "organizational conversation," in the words of one Motorola executive. The MERP workshops started in 1996 and continued through a series of regional gatherings across the world. The hands-on workshops were supplemented and supported by frequent executive visits. Overall, the process has captured a considerable amount of information about the challenges confronting Motorola employees in the field. As these ethical and business problems are discussed among Motorola employees, executives, and experts, responses are crafted that suit each region's facts and circumstances. According to company executives, MERP is not intended as a platform to teach ethics or provide specific training concerning Motorola's Code of Business Conduct, activities that take place in other ways. Rather, MERP is intended to help employees understand that it is "okay to talk ethics here" and to empower them to make ethically appropriate business decisions in their daily work. The goal is to enable Motorola employees to take ownership and accept accountability for infusing the company's key beliefs and ethical values into all aspects of the business. This could only take place on a foundation of understanding and commitment to a culture that values ethics and integrity. By 1999, senior management was sufficiently confident to authorize local Motorola Ethics Committees to make procedural interpretations of company-wide guidelines. These committees are also encouraged to suggest modifications of the guidelines for each region based on local culture (Bradshaw, 2000).

Motorola Ethics Committees have formal responsibilities and authority. Representatives from three of the company's staff groups—legal, human resources, and finance—have specific responsibilities for enforcing ethics standards. For example, complaints and allegations of misconduct are received by the legal department, which analyzes the allegations for action. The human resources office conducts investigations of internal breaches and allegations of wrongdoing. Motorola's financial officers, operating through the auditing function, monitor the company's financial activities for possible violations. These ethics committees operate at local, country, and regional levels, and attempt to address—and resolve—issues as close to the actual scene of events as possible.

The formal responsibilities of the local, country, and regional ethics committees are supported by the role of the MERP process. MERP is used to raise issues, discuss alternative responses, and reinforce creative efforts to harmonize the company's ethical beliefs and practices with actual operating conditions. As Christopher Galvin's "Letter to Motorola's Stakeholders" suggests, Motorola's ethics renewal process has been a focal point for disseminating, maintaining, and modifying Motorola's ethical posture, and for preserving its basic corporate culture in a world of diversity and change. This ethical posture, according to company executives, is a source of competitive strength in a world of constant challenge and change.

At the end of the 1990s, Motorola executives were grappling with a number of new ethical issues that had eluded the MERP discussion process. In 1997, for example, Motorola learned that a documentary aired on British television had identified the company as being involved in the manufacture of land mines used in the war between India and Pakistan. The disclosure occurred at a time when public concern about land mines was rising in the United States and internationally. Motorola discovered that its timing chips had been sold to a European buyer who, in turn, sold the parts to a company that assembled and sold land mines. Motorola claimed to be unaware of this commercial chain of relationships and vowed to halt such shipments. According to Motorola officials, the land mine episode bore some similarity to a number of other disturbing situations that appeared to have the same "information platform" (Moorthy interview, 1999). That is, policy decisions about sales, marketing, and distribution were being made with less corporate over-sight than seemed appropriate. Moreover, the company's strategy called for advanced wireless communications—with the potential for the unobtrusive monitoring of people—and the development of "biochips" that could hold vast quantities of human genetic information. These technologies were thought by some to contain the risk of more problems if review mechanisms were not improved.

To address these issues, a Global Corporate Responsibility Task Force was convened in 1998. Chaired by CEO Christopher Galvin, the task force in-cluded senior managers from legal, public relations, operating units, and fi-nance. The group's mission was to sort through these issues and recommend a process that would enable Motorola to maintain the "ethics advantage" it had achieved through previous actions. As one executive said, the point is that good ethics is good business—in other words, it is the right thing to do and the right way to do it. By 2000, the company had established a independent review committee to oversee developments in the area of biochip and "bioinfomatics" technology.

TRANSFORMATIONAL LEARNING: SHELL

The learning process that has transformed the Royal Dutch/Shell Group in the past decade contrasts sharply with the adaptive and evolutionary develop-ments at Cummins and Motorola (see Mirvis, 2000; Eccles and others, 2001, and Chapter 9). The initial pressures to create a "New Shell" arose from inad-equate rates of return on Shell's global operations, partially due to declining oil prices. (Petroleum prices had declined to less than $15 per barrel in the early 1990s, and would eventually hit $11 per barrel.) These oil price trends were reversed by the end of the century, but the movement toward greater global coordination within Shell responded to more fundamental stimuli and has continued up to the present. Indeed, whatever the specific level of Shell's prices and profits, the natural instability of the oil industry and the increas-ingly obvious global impact of all of Shell's actions favored development of a tighter global management structure more similar to that of other major in-ternational oil companies.

Awareness that "New Shell" needed to include an increased emphasis on global external affairs arose from the controversies surrounding disposition of Brent Spar and Shell's operations in Nigeria, both of which came to a head in 1995. These events had important consequences, such as Shareholder Resolution 10, presented and defeated in 1997 (see Chapter 6); the Camisea Project, which provided a laboratory for developing new approaches to both internal and external constituents; and the expanded Planning and External Affairs staff at Shell Centre London that was challenged to generalize this experience and ensure its impact throughout the entire Shell organization. The demonstrably serious impact that social concerns could have on economic performance— and even on the "license to operate" of the Shell Group as a whole—accounts for the strong stakeholder orientation reflected in the "New Shell." Although developments within the Shell Group during the 1990s inevitably flowed into one another in complex ways, the sequence of events can be much more sharply delineated as a transformation process than the other two companies, as indicated by the diagram of "Shell's Transformation Process" in Figure 8.1.

Structural Change

The shift toward a stronger central management structure and increased coordination among operating companies that took place within the Shell Group during the 1990s provided the context for the changes in stakeholder strategies and organizational culture that were to follow. As in the reorganization of the 1950s, McKinsey and Company was again retained to help develop the new design. Multinational corporations are typically "matrix" organizations, structured according to both product/function and geographic dimensions. The geographic dimension—with national/regional units managed by nearly autonomous "barons"—had been dominant throughout Shell's history. In "New Shell," emphasis shifted to five core business areas, each with its own CEO: Exploration and Production; Oil Products; Chemicals; Gas and Power; and the newly created unit, Shell International Renewables (SIR). Shell Oil Co., headquartered in Houston, Texas, which until the mid-1980s had been an essentially independent entity with majority Shell Group ownership, is being integrated into this new structure. The Committee of Managing Directors (CMD), a small number of top-level managers who are themselves members of one of the two

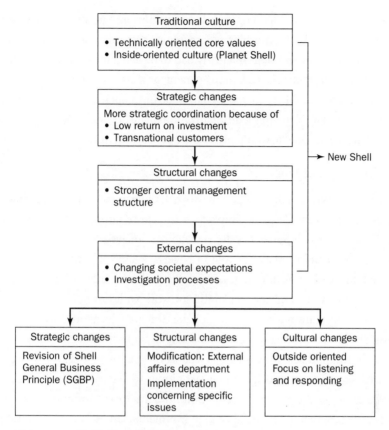

Figure 8.1 Shell's Transformation Process.

national (British, Dutch) national boards, is intended to function as a single unit with global responsibility and authority, not as a parliament of chieftains with independent powers. The five global core businesses and the more than 100 operating companies operate under the control of the CMD.

The Shell Group's external relations functions would undoubtedly have been reorganized as part of the transition to the new global structure. However, the Brent Spar and Nigeria incidents, occurring as they did while this structural transformation was in progress, increased the attention given to external affairs and affected the outcome. The fact that Shell executives in Germany and the UK were essentially unaware of each other's actions and concerns contributed to the scope and impact of Brent Spar, and criticism of

Shell's operations in Nigeria gave rise to business and political consequences all over the world. The complex repercussions that might arise from individual operating company actions clearly had to be taken into account within the "New Shell" framework, and management processes designed to anticipate and avoid unfavorable occurrences had to be put in place. In short, a new and explicitly stakeholder-oriented organizational culture was required, and new and transformational learning processes were used to develop it.

New Learning Processes

Increasing awareness that the actions of Shell units in individual countries and areas could have widespread impact on the entire Group's operations stimulated innovative approaches to stakeholder analysis within "New Shell." Worldwide criticism of Shell's role in Nigeria, against a background that included the earlier South Africa/Rhodesia problem, showed that changing social expectations and the availability of worldwide communications made corporate reputation a matter for global, not merely local, management concern. Shell has traditionally been a "learning organization" with a strong focus on technical and scientific areas, as well as on the broad trends captured by its well-known "scenario" planning techniques (de Geus, 1997). By the mid-1990s it became clear that these commitments to organizational learning needed to be extended to social and environmental issues, and on an anticipatory rather than reactive basis.

The proactive learning process began with a global study of changing social expectations concerning large, multinational corporations. A series of roundtables, held in different parts of the world, brought together approximately 150 Shell executives with a comparable number of external participants, including scientists, members of activist groups, researchers, journalists, and other opinion leaders. These discussions revealed considerable goodwill toward Shell, but a general lack of specific knowledge about the company. Corporate identity and reputation were not the assets they could be, nor the assets they needed to be, in "New Shell." It became clear that Shell had done very little to make itself known to external publics, including important stakeholders and sophisticated observers. This shortcoming reflected the historic "Planet Shell" mentality, implying social isolation and technical-scientific focus.

Shell Centre staff followed up by interviewing Shell executives and public policy experts in 10 target countries. They also reviewed existing research, including more than 60 relevant surveys that Shell had commissioned in 21 countries. To strengthen their understanding of the attitudes of young people, the team organized special Young Persons Focus Groups in London and Amsterdam. Finally, Shell surveyed 23 peer companies in Australia, Japan, the United States, Germany, Netherlands, and the United Kingdom to gather ideas and best practice models for reputation management.

Cultural Change and Stakeholder Strategy

This extensive research program led to the development of a new global statement of corporate purpose, articulated in 1997, as Shell's "core purpose": *Helping people build a better world* (italics in original). The implications of this broad commitment involved both substance and process, and were intended to produce fundamental changes in organizational culture. On the substantive side, issues of political responsibility and human rights were perceived as most important. As global oil exploration and development necessarily follows the path of geology, not politics, oil companies sometimes find themselves dealing with undemocratic governments in which basic human rights are not protected. The dangers to global operations and reputation that can arise from these situations were clearly illustrated by Shell's experience in Nigeria. Shell's analysts reached the conclusion that matters of this type should not be left to local management and ex post corrective actions. Instead, ongoing top-level attention to issues of political responsibility was required. More fundamentally, long-range development of mutual trust and understanding among relevant stakeholders was needed in order to provide a background for identifying and dealing with potential issues before they became critical. To emphasize the importance of these issues, a statement in support of basic human rights was included in the 1997 revision of Statement of General Business Principles, and a "management primer" on this subject was prepared and distributed in 1998.

The other major focus of Shell's new stakeholder strategy was health, safety, and the environment (HSE). The environmental impact of oil industry operations had been well recognized from its very beginnings, but Shell had traditionally left these matters to local management. Similarly, employee health and safety issues were primarily addressed at operating levels. By the 1990s, however, there was a new global awareness of the importance of all these areas, and increased concern with spillover effects and company-wide practices that might have widespread impact. Shell analysts believed that the company's traditional core competencies in science and engineering had become inertial barriers, resulting in a narrow technical approach to matters that might be of much broader concern. Results from the Young Persons Focus Groups pointed toward a shift in values, including overriding concerns about the sustainability of world resource use. According to these young people, the world seemed to be smaller, less secure, and less supportive than they had anticipated. These concerns, accompanied by a high level of global communications, led to new expectations—and possibly new suspicions—about the activities and motivations of multinational firms as they might affect health, safety, and the environment. The clear message from participants in the Young Persons' Focus Groups was "performance matters."

Attention to these important substantive issues required a change in management processes and culture. The new strategy emphasized the development of close working relationships with key strategic stakeholders at all levels, along with active monitoring of emerging issues throughout the entire organization. Continuous dialogue with stakeholders was viewed as critical for building long-term, sustainable relationships. In addition, in crises the company needed to speak with one voice, to avoid legalisms and defensive postures, and to develop an ability to respond to public concerns at an emotional and human level, as well as with technical competence. A culture of "listening and responding" needed to be developed, as opposed to a culture of technical superiority and engineering rationality. As one of Shell's consultants noted, it is not only important for companies to be "doing the right thing," but also to be "*seen* to do the right thing," if corporate reputation is to be preserved.

In order to achieve these results, greater global leadership and support in external affairs management was required. The findings from the peer companies study showed that Shell's highly decentralized mode of operation was unique, and was probably too weak to cope effectively with the challenges generated by new societal expectations. As a result, the Planning and External Affairs function in the London headquarters was reorganized and strengthened. Responsibilities were assigned to teams of headquarters and local personnel, relying on new electronic communications and information technology. Under the new "coordinated decentralization" arrangement, the external affairs organization in London has primary responsibility for global issues management, crisis management, and stakeholder dialogue at the international level (for example, United Nations environmental meetings). The operating businesses (and each country management team) focus on local stakeholder relationships, including government, regulatory bodies, and communities. Close contact between the two levels is intended to achieve continuous coordination and to avoid surprise, and the development of relationships with external stakeholders is reported throughout the internally complex Shell organization.

Shell's new stakeholder strategy includes a strong emphasis on open communication, both internal and external, based on the policy of "listening and responding." As CMD Chairman Mark Moody-Stuart has said:

> We recognize that the inwardly-focused Shell must become a thing of the past and are committed to become better at communicating, both listening and responding. As part of this commitment, we are changing the way we communicate as an organization and are making a long-term investment in a communications program, designed to keep all of our stakeholders informed, both about the issues themselves and the work we at Shell are doing to address those issues [Shell, 1999a, p. 1].

According to Shell, "stakeholders" are "any individual or group who is affected by the project or can themselves affect the project." The five categories of stakeholders named in the 1997 SGBP are: shareholders, customers, employees, those with whom Shell does business, and "society." Over the past five years Shell has vastly expanded its efforts to communicate with all these types of stakeholders, and has placed special emphasis on media relations, public statements, and active participation in business and other nongovernmental organizations in its various areas of interest and concern.

In 1999 Shell initiated a global corporate identity campaign intended "to establish or re-establish relationships with key special publics, enhance their knowledge of Shell, defend Shell's reputation and promote a more positive and real image of the company" (Shell, 1999c, p. 19). The annual Shell Report, summarizing the company's performance in a wide range of areas of stakeholder interest, is a part of this campaign. These publications are based on the annual reports of the operating executives submitted to the CMD and create the agenda for Shell's policy initiatives as well as for its public relations tasks. The quarterly external affairs review *Interchange* provides greater depth and detail on many of these issues and activities, and serves both as a source of public information and as useful information for managers and external affairs officers around the world. These activities are supplemented by a wide array of publications, speeches, press releases, and workshops, as well as internal documents, proprietary web sites, and consultations. A number of outside consultants, including Business Planning and Research International (BPRI), have been engaged to monitor the impact of these efforts at reputation management on an international sample of opinion leaders.

Implementing the Strategy

Implementation of the new stakeholder strategy, and ultimate transformation of Shell's organizational culture, required leadership from the highest management levels. Cor Herkstroter, Chairman of the CMD during the Brent Spar and Nigeria incidents, led the way by recognizing their potential impact on the operations and status of the entire Group. His successor, Mark Moody-Stuart and his CMD colleagues—particularly Phil Watts—became active internal and external spokespersons, acknowledging Shell's broader societal responsibilities and explaining the ways it was preparing to deal with them.

Responsibility for implementing the new stakeholder strategy reflected in the 1997 revision of the SGBP was vested in a new Social Responsibility Committee composed (like the CMD itself) of six members selected from the boards of the two parent companies. This group, later renamed the Sustainable Development Council, was charged with oversight and improvement of the Group's worldwide performance with respect to economic, ecological, and social issues, with a focus on *sustainability* in both physical and social-political terms. This council is responsible for the annual *Shell Report*, an assessment of the company's problems and progress in these areas. The *Shell Report* is a stakeholder-oriented document and makes a strong effort to stimulate stakeholder dialogue, including mail response cards and other direct contact information. The 1998 *Report* affirms Shell's stakeholder orientation in no uncertain terms: "Shell companies have responsibilities to a wide range of interested parties, such as shareholders, employees, customers, and others in society. And the responsibilities relate to our financial, environmental, and social impacts on each of these groups" (Shell, 1998a, p. 8). This issue of the *Report* also explicitly adopts the "triple bottom line" concept, involving economic, environmental, and social performance elements (Shell, 1998a; letter at pp. 46–47 by John Elkington, creator of the "triple bottom line" concept).

The commitment to *"Helping people to build a better world"* articulated in 1997 was supported by statements on identity, mission, and objectives (see Exhibit 8.2). Taken together, these statements constitute a strong acknowledgement that the fundamental purpose of the corporation is ultimately societal, rather than purely private, financial, and/or technological. The release of this material in December 1997 emphasized that Shell was making a *public* commitment, not simply restating internal policies. Subsequently, Shell attempted to communicate its commitment to the new stakeholder strategy, and its intention to take a global leadership role in this area through an extensive program of speeches, conference appearances, and executive interviews, as well as through publications and media relations. Phil Watts, a member of the

---

Exhibit 8.2
The Evolving Nature of Shell and Its Objectives

Core Purpose	*Helping people to build a better world.* (italics in original)
Corporate identity	The future is a better place. Shell believes in the future and will invest more than any other company.
Mission	Search for and develop sources of energy.
Objectives	Develop a proud staff of Shell employees. Create a better business portfolio. Achieve operational excellence. Develop the Shell Group's reputation.

source: Authors' assessment based on interviews and Shell World, December 1997, pp. 8–11.

CMD, confirmed the Group's view of the link between financial and social performance in a more recent address as follows: "Business can only contribute by being profitable and competitive. Otherwise it is unsustainable. But we will only remain profitable if we meet people's expectations and respond to their concerns" (Watts, 2000).

In a major departure from previous practice, adherence to the 1997 SGBP and HSE policies was made mandatory throughout the Group, and a regular system of monitoring, reporting, and external auditing was introduced. (Other practices made globally mandatory at the same time were uniform brand identification for all Shell products and a uniform system of financial accounts.) Shell's 140 company managers remain the front-line officers for all operations, but their annual reports are now expected to include a holistic view of the operating environment of their companies and their critical stakeholder relationships, both internal and external. These reports are integrated in order to produce a global overview for the members of the CMD. In addition, top regional managers analyze the individual reports of their subordinates and respond to them in writing, followed by face-to-face meetings, workshops and assistance from Shell Centre staff as needed. A regular cycle of reports, responses, and follow-ups has been created; the outputs of this process are utilized in investment proposal reviews and long-range planning. The ultimate goal, in addition to anticipating and avoiding unfavorable social and political developments, is more sophisticated overall risk management. A recent statement captures the essence of the change involved:

> Shell needs to talk consistently as a Group, although the individual Shell Operating Units in each local area will lead most stakeholder engagement. We intend to address stakeholder interest under three headings: The *commercial* perspective, the *public interest* perspective, and the *personal* perspective. These reflect the three legs of sustainable development: economic progress, environmental care and social responsibility (Shell 1999b; italics in original).

A special problem for most multinational enterprises involves the maintenance of global corporate performance goals and standards in joint ventures and supply chain relationships. (See further discussion of this issue with respect to multinationals operating in China in the preceding chapter.) This problem is particularly acute for the Shell Group because it is composed of operating companies that are coordinated—but not strictly controlled—by the worldwide headquarters, and these in turn are engaged in diverse alliances with other businesses. Shell acknowledged its responsibility within these varied and complex relationships by including a commitment to "seek mutually beneficial relationships with contractors, suppliers and in joint ventures and to promote the application of these principles in so doing" in the 1997 revision of the Statement of General Business Principles (SGBP). It also noted that the "ability to promote these principles effectively will be an important factor in the decision to *enter into* or *remain in* such relationships" (Shell, 1997a; emphasis added).

Shell recognizes a distinction between relationships in which a Shell operating company has effective control, so that implementation of its principles should be straightforward, and others in which conformance with Shell's standards depends on the ability of Shell personnel to induce cooperation from other partners, and necessarily involves compromise. In all situations, Shell makes an effort to explain its principles and concepts of corporate responsibility to the firms with which it deals. Companies involved in formal joint ventures with Shell units are offered assistance in developing appropriate policies and practices, and are required to provide relevant information to their Shell partners on an annual basis.

Two Sustainability Issues: Human Rights and Environment/Ecology

As noted earlier, two critical substantive issues identified during Shell's transformational learning processes were *human rights* and *environmental/ecological conditions*. These were seen to affect the *sustainability* of life, both in particular areas and on the planet as a whole, and also the *sustainability* of Shell as an organization and the kinds of economic and technological activities in which it is engaged. Neither of these issues was new to Shell managers, but both were now seen in a new global perspective, and with a new awareness of their interaction and broad societal implications. Thus, both were explicitly addressed in the 1997 SGBP revision, followed by extensive and on-going implementation efforts.

With respect to human rights, the 1997 revision of Shell's SGBP specifically acknowledges a responsibility "to express support for fundamental human rights in line with the legitimate role of business" This reflects a significant policy change within a short period of time. As late as 1995, the "Shell Management Brief About Human Rights" included the following text:

We are sometimes asked why we don't speak up against violence or other human rights abuses, with the suggestion that as a major multinational group of companies we must have a great deal of influence with governments. Clearly we always talk to governments about matters which relate to the legitimate pursuit of our business interests—such as oil and gas exploration licenses, the impact to legislation and so on—and we make no secret of this. However it would be quite different to interfere in political matters which are the preserve of the state as our business principles set out.

Many other Shell documents from this period contain similar wording.

The new commitment, although not heralding a new posture of social activism, explicitly affirms a significant level of responsibility that is confirmed, for example, in the *Shell Report* for 1999. This document presents a diagram of concentric circles as a "Human rights and business responsibilities map," which establishes the following hierarchy of human rights issues:

- Core: Employee rights, including reference to "ILO Declaration" (international standards)

- Intermediate: Community rights, including concern with indigenous people, social equity, and a "right to development"

- National rights: Macroeconomic and public policy issues, including "force for good by example"

- Advocacy: Rights to speak out, provide education and training, and engage other stakeholders on these issues

Robin Aram, Head of External Relations and Policy Development, Shell International, has stated: "Our job is to work out what realistically we can do to enhance human rights in the context of doing our business—and then do it" (Shell, 1999d, p. 30). Shell acknowledges that it can be influential in these matters, but cannot control the policies and behavior of others. Today, Shell accepts responsibility for human rights issues only with respect to persons with whom it is in direct contact. It has, however, issued a "management primer" on *Business and Human Rights* (Shell, 1998b) that addresses issues beyond the workplace and marketplace, including concern with the protection of indigenous peoples and child labor.

Shell's new external affairs strategy also recognizes *environmental and ecological issues*, grouped under the rubric "sustainable development," which also includes Shell's recent emphasis on the development of renewable sources of energy. These issues are analyzed along financial, environmental, and social dimensions. In a speech addressing sustainable development issues, Jeroen van der Veer, a member of the CMD, emphasized the importance of renewables to the maintenance of Shell's "license to grow":

> We don't invest in renewables because it's good PR (public relations). . . . We do it because over the next 20 years, customer demand in this area is going to grow significantly. We do it because it makes good commercial sense and it's good for the bottom line. We also do it because we believe it has a role in a sustainable future for us all ["Globalisation, Ecology and Economy," speech at the Bridging Worlds Conference, Tilburg, November 26, 1999, p. 2].

In implementing Health, Safety, Environment (HSE) standards, a sharp distinction is made between a "commitment" to certain levels of performance in this area, which is an expression of the company's aspirations and intentions, and a "policy," which is a formal operating requirement. Formal policies are backed by explicit implementation procedures, including coverage within the annual reports of each operating unit to the CMD. In general, Shell's goals are to do no harm to people, protect the environment, use energy and materials efficiently, and develop safe energy resources, products, and services. One of Shell's main emphases in this area has been the development of groupwide management systems for collecting and reporting performance data in ways that contribute to improved management within the organization and that are suitable for review and verification by outside auditors. Feedback from external stakeholders and observers is also an important part of the HSE management process, as the description of the plan for the Camisea Project presented in Chapter 6 makes clear.

The shift to greater global coordination and the greater emphasis on stakeholder relations gradually brought about a change in Shell's organizational culture. The traditional culture, based on technical expertise and engineering rationality, is giving way to an emphasis on "listening and responding" that would have been inconceivable within the old "Planet Shell." This transformation was only reluctantly accepted by Cor Herkstroetter and his contemporaries, but has been conspicuously embraced by CMD Chair Mark Moody-Stuart.

By the mid-1990s it had become clear that Shell's traditional culture had become a handicap—a source of problems and a barrier to solutions—in its contemporary global operating environment. The need for a more open and responsive relationship with stakeholders, both internal and external, was most apparent at the headquarters level. But the required changes in managerial behavior could only be achieved at regional and local levels. Therefore, greater and continuous interaction between central and peripheral elements of the Shell network was clearly required. These modes of interaction became, themselves, part of Shell's worldwide cultural transformation. A 1999 document captures the essence of the change involved:

> Shell needs to talk consistently as a Group, although the individual Shell Operating Units in each local area will lead most stakeholder engagement. We intend to address stakeholder interest under three headings: The *commercial* perspective, the *public interest* perspective, and the *personal* perspective. These reflect the three legs of sustainable development: economic progress, environmental care and social responsibility (Shell, 1999a).

CONCLUSION

This chapter addresses two central issues: How and why did these companies develop a responsive approach to stakeholder issues? How have they sustained and institutionalized a stakeholder-oriented mode of management over time?

Learning—and the creation of new knowledge—occurs in many different ways in the modern corporation. Some forms are deliberate and planned; others are unintended and even unconscious. Experiences that produce learning may be favorable or unfavorable, gradual or traumatic, and may involve the organization itself or its observation and interpretation of the experience of others. Our analysis of the stakeholder learning processes and their effects at Cummins, Motorola, and Shell highlights the different ways these companies gained new knowledge about their stakeholders, the substantive data they gathered, and the ways in which this learning had an impact on their strategies, structures, and cultures. In all of these respects, the companies could scarcely be more different. But together, they illustrate ways in which a stakeholder view emerges and is institutionalized in the modern corporation.

Some might argue that stakeholder learning is at the margins of the firm's knowledge base because many stakeholders are not at the core of the business and, hence, not at the center of top management thinking. That may be true in some companies. But the example of these companies suggests that a multitude of employees, customers, regulators, communities, investors, and business partners had profound effects on Cummins, Motorola, and Shell. Moreover, managers in these firms worked hard to learn how to understand and manage these relationships better. The stimulus for doing so may have been crisis, as occurred at Shell (Brent Spar and Nigeria), Cummins (Hanson PLC's takeover attempt), and Motorola (awakening to the reality of Japan, Inc.). It may also have come from the strategic understanding of managers like those at Cummins who recognized the high costs associated with hostile stakeholder relationships, and the potential values that could arise from labor peace and from collaboration with government regulators. Whether born in crisis or vision, some organizations will use their new knowledge to grasp the opportunity inherent in stakeholder networks. They will innovate and lead. Others will ignore the chance to learn, fail to see opportunity, and be left to cope with the results.

9

THE STAKEHOLDER
VIEW: CONCLUSIONS
AND IMPLICATIONS

The central proposition of this book is that the private business corporation needs to be redefined both conceptually and practically in order to clarify its status and purpose within contemporary society and the global economy. Following the empirical maxim that "Corporations ARE what they DO," we view the corporation as an organization with multiple constituents, for whom it creates wealth and other benefits. Most of these constituents are essential to the operations of the corporation because they contribute inputs, receive outputs, or—whether actively or passively—provide its "license to operate" as an institution within the economy and society.

We refer to these constituents as stakeholders because they have a stake—a benefit or a risk—attached to the successful operation of the firm. Every person or group with an interest in the affairs of a particular firm is not necessarily a stakeholder; and some claims to stakeholder status may be illegitimate. However, the number and diversity of legitimate stakeholders in the contemporary corporation's operating environment is large and growing. The scale, scope, and interdependence of modern economic activity generate new consequences, uncertainties, and risks—social, technological, ecological, and ethical—that challenge conventional concepts about the business corporation and stimulate dialogue about the responsibility and behavior of the corporation at both the societal (macro) and firm (micro) levels.

The contemporary large, professionally managed corporation—often with global scope and sales greater than the total output of some nation states—cannot be viewed as a microscopic enterprise at the mercy of market forces and government policies. Its accumulation of resources and its institutional presence and power inevitably give it the ability to influence its own operating environment in significant ways. Moreover, the wide array of constituents with which the corporation is engaged in a two-way flow of contributions and benefits, as pictured in Figure 1.1, gives it a role in society far beyond the narrow confines of individual product and service markets. Hence, it is essential to view the corporation as a more complex and multipurpose institution than conventional legal and economic concepts might suggest.

Our proposed stakeholder view is intended to provide a new basis for analyzing the role and operations of the large, modern corporation. We emphasize the position of the corporation as the center of a network of stakeholders, including those providing resource inputs and market contacts as well as those in the social and political arena. Looking at the firm from inside, we believe that successful management can build organizational wealth through the development and use of favorable relationships with the entire array of stakeholders. Looking at the firm from outside, we believe that its status within the economy and society depends upon its ability to respond to stakeholder interests and concerns.

This chapter brings together three central themes of our research. First, it reviews the learning processes and changing stakeholder relationships of each of our focal firms over the study period, which we describe as their "stakeholder journeys." We emphasize again that these companies are by no means faultless. Each of them has been, and will continue to be, criticized by unhappy investors, employees, customers, suppliers, communities, and others from time to time. But the experiences of these firms reveal efforts to become more effective in their interaction with their stakeholders and give specific meaning to the concept of stakeholder management.

Second, this chapter summarizes the key implications of the stakeholder view of the corporation, emphasizing their descriptive, instrumental, and normative aspects and their further implications for corporate governance. The stakeholder view (SHV) seems to be a distinct and significant addition to the strategic management literature, integrating and extending the resource-based view (RBV) and industry-structure view (ISV) of the firm. These established concepts do not address the central question about the position of the corporation within society: To whom and for what is the corporation responsible? Yet the answer to this question is critical to the governance and sustainability of the corporate system and to the operational success of the individual firm.

Third, the chapter examines the implications of the stakeholder view for management practice. Stakeholder management begins with the recognition that the participation of many different groups and interests, some of them involuntary, are vital to the success of the corporation. Therefore, the concerns and goals of all relevant stakeholders require knowledgeable and respectful consideration by corporate management. Effective stakeholder management involves organization-wide core commitments to humanistic values, continuous learning, and adaptive behavior. And these commitments have to be implemented through appropriate organizational structures, strategies, and practices over the long term. The stakeholder view also implies that varied interests will be appropriately represented, either directly or indirectly, within the corporate governance structure. The impact of stakeholder management is difficult to gauge because it involves different criteria for appraising success or failure, as compared to traditional short-term and shareowner-oriented management models, but evidence that it is relevant is summarized here.

The final section of the chapter comments briefly on the implications of the stakeholder view for the development of emerging sectors of the new economy of the 21st century.

STAKEHOLDER JOURNEYS: THREE FIRMS

Relationships with investors, employees, customers, suppliers, communities, governments, and other stakeholders are part of the history of every corporation. Cummins, Motorola, and Shell, from their different industries and situations, have developed management approaches that place stakeholder relationships at the center of their decision making. The decisions made about the acquisition of resources, development of competitive strategies, and actions in the sociopolitical arena during the study period reveal the impact of interaction between market and nonmarket forces, and the contributions of diverse stakeholders to the achievement of overall business success.

Chapter 3 introduced and compared the array of stakeholder issues that Cummins, Motorola, and Shell have faced over the past quarter century (summarized in Figures 3.2, 3.3, and 3.4). Subsequent chapters detailed the experience of these companies in addressing various of these issues, with a strong emphasis on the processes of organizational learning and responsiveness that these firms developed. The picture that emerges from this analysis is one of *reciprocal interaction* (Henderson and Mitchell, 1997). Each firm has had distinct impacts on the providers of its resources, on its industry structure, and in its sociopolitical arena. And stakeholders in all of these areas have had distinct impacts on the firms, leading to adaptation, renewal, and transformation within the strategy-structure-culture core of the corporation. The data confirms that each firm "has affected, and been affected by, its stakeholders" (Freeman, 1984; Clarkson Principles, 1999, p. 4). We refer to the results of these evolutionary and interactive processes as each firm's "stakeholder journey," described in terms of the expanding scope of its stakeholder relationships in interaction with increasing complexity and instability in its operating environment.

Cummins

We have presented Cummins Engine Company as an example of adaptive learning. The firm has maintained a high degree of continuity in its corporate culture, but its managers have learned from experience (both positive and negative) with various stakeholders and changed their policies and practices accordingly. Cummins has undertaken imaginative initiatives, but also recognized that its strategic choices were often constrained by larger forces, both within its industry and in the sociopolitical arena. After turbulent times during the 1970s, the company developed its workers into long-term strategic partners. It extended its collaborative approach to the creation of business alliances and to the establishment of new relationships with government regulatory authorities as well. It institutionalized a commitment to high ethical standards in the Corporate Action Division.

As shown in Figure 9.1, the scope of Cummins' stakeholder relationships in the 1970s was relatively narrow, with a focus on employees, investors,

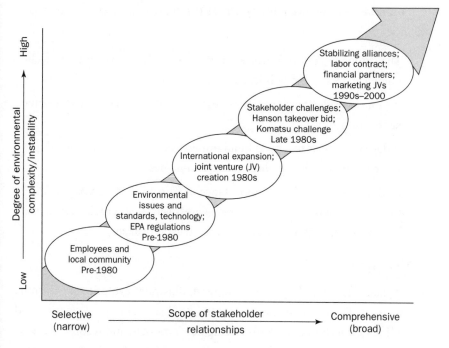

Figure 9.1 Cummins' Stakeholder Journey.

customers, and its local community. The company's approach to labor and community relationships was distinctive, reflecting the values of the founding families and the hard experience of a protracted and costly labor strike. From this critical experience base, Cummins built an iconoclastic, precedent-breaking organization with a management mentality that was prepared to challenge prevailing wisdom. To acquire market presence in international markets, it engaged in extensive joint venturing. To address long-term environmental issues and concerns, it committed to improved technology and collaborated with EPA regulators to establish fact-based processes for setting regulatory standards. To secure financing for its cyclical, capital-intensive business, it developed sources of patient capital and learned to fight takeover threats. Each experience moved the company a further step away from a narrow, selective way of thinking about individual stakeholders toward a wider, more comprehensive understanding of the contribution that a network of stabilizing stakeholder alliances involving its resource base, industry contacts, and social-political environment could make to its long-term success.

Cummins' stakeholder journey can be summarized in terms of four basic themes:

- The company's outlook evolved from local to global in economic, technological, social, and political terms.
- It came to understand that its success rests on both market and nonmarket relationships.
- It developed the capacity to build innovative stakeholder relationships as well as innovative products and technologies.
- It recognized the role and importance of trust to all stakeholder relationships, and the need to respond aggressively—either with corrective actions or through withdrawal—when trust is broken.

Motorola

Motorola, as the preceding chapter showed, illustrates evolutionary learning and renewal. The company has reinvented itself several times—creating and exploiting new technologies, introducing new products, and reconfiguring its structure and strategy to suit new conditions. Motorola differs from some other companies that have survived several periods of rapid change in that it has systematically affirmed its commitment to the core values of its founders—uncompromising integrity and respect for the individual—even while emphasizing a strategy of technological leadership and globalization. The company has tried to become the kind of "learning organization" described in the academic literature, and the central lesson seems to have been the importance of preserving and nurturing the culture that is the source of its corporate identity. To an extent rarely seen elsewhere, Motorola managers recognized the nature and importance of stakeholder relationships with political leaders, customers, suppliers, and partners, and evolved deliberate and successful strategies for interacting with them.

As Motorola has expanded the technological range and global scope of its operations, the complexity and uncertainty of its operating environment has increased, and the scope of its stakeholder relationships has expanded (see Figure 9.2). Beginning with the "chip wars" of the early 1980s, Motorola learned that the modern corporation can become the target of collective efforts to

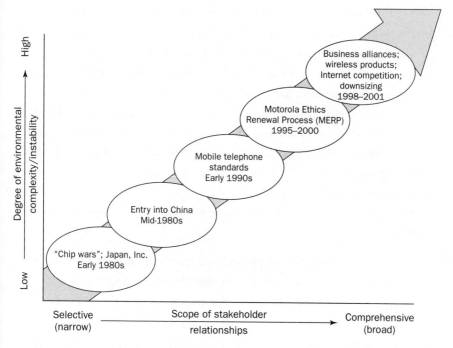

Figure 9.2 Motorola's Stakeholder Journey.

attack its market position. In such circumstances, leaders reached out to new stakeholders—government and the public—to demonstrate what was truly at stake. By the late 1980s, as the company negotiated its entry into China, the concept of society as a stakeholder (as well as the reciprocal dependence of the firm on its host society) was no longer foreign to Motorola. Its understanding of this reciprocal interdependence was a key element of its success in making China a "second home." By the 1990s, Motorola executives clearly understood that industry-wide technology standards were basic to product acceptance and market success. The company worked with key stakeholders to shape mobile telephone standards in the early 1990s, and engaged in elaborate efforts to establish GSM as the worldwide product standard for wireless phones. The company's ability to deal with diverse stakeholders was critical to the creation of Iridium, the satellite project that required permission from more than 100 national governments to establish the system's right to circle the earth. It has also become increasingly engaged in "coopetition" in its simultaneous involvement as both competitor and collaborator with other firms in the rapidly changing world of wireless communications and the Internet. As the 1990s ended, the company encountered business challenges—a corporate restructuring that necessitated layoffs, Iridium's bankruptcy, global operations, intense technological competition, and severe cyclical shifts in demand for its products. Each development challenged corporate values, testing the company's ability to adapt, improve, and extend its core commitments. In the face of such complexity and uncertainty, Motorola repeatedly drew on its renewal process to redefine itself in strategic and operational terms.

Motorola's stakeholder journey can be summarized as reflecting four basic themes:

- The company resolved to preserve and nurture its historic values and to find ways to implement its humanistic concerns and ethical standards in rapidly changing, and often unfamiliar, global business conditions.

- It learned to create new stakeholders (such as government) while continuing to respond to those that had already been recognized.

- It learned to create and utilize new stakeholder networks as a means of charting its own course and avoiding dependence on the inaction or leadership of others.

- It learned to use its stakeholder networks to define and develop new corporate strategies to address the competitive challenges of wireless communication and the Internet.

Shell

The experiences of Shell show how external challenges can lead to learning processes that transform even enormous and highly successful organizations. The impact of both a structural change to greater global coordination and a strategic change to greater emphasis on stakeholder relations is gradually transforming Shell's traditional corporate culture. A historic emphasis on technical expertise and economic rationality is being enhanced by a new commitment to "listening and responding" that would have been inconceivable within the earlier "Planet Shell" framework. Shell's top management has clearly accepted the idea that the firm has to demonstrate that it is creating value for society if it is going to be able to create value for its shareowners. This new orientation has been expressed by Jeroen van der Veer (1999), a member of Shell's Committee of Managing Directors, in the following way:

> Long-term success suggests that Shell will earn its "license to grow" by meeting acceptable environmental and social standards in a profitable way, [and] by becoming a "solutions provider," developing new cleaner products, and help to meet new international challenges. . . . [P]artnership and cooperation between government, international organizations, business, and local groups is essential in taking the sustainable development agenda forward.

Shell's "stakeholder journey" has involved changing needs, critical events, and new business strategies developed within an increasingly turbulent and challenging environment. Beginning with the international controversy surrounding the Rhodesian trade embargo in the 1960s and the subsequent pressure to withdraw from South Africa, Shell's management became increasingly aware that the modern corporation cannot remain isolated from world opinion and activism. The power of these forces to transform operating assumptions (see Figure 9.3) produced a management crisis when the twin problems of Brent Spar and Nigeria emerged in the mid-1990s and jolted Shell's leaders into action. The result has been a revolutionary shift in the company's premises: Central authority has replaced the company's traditional decentralized, independent local operating company model. "Planet Shell" has evolved into the "New Shell," a company that is immeasurably more engaged with societal stakeholders. Corporate purpose has been restated as an effort to help "build a better world." New methodologies have been developed for engaging stakeholders in meaningful dialogue. And an expanded global external affairs program has been established to implement these policy changes (Mirvis, 2000).

Shell's stakeholder journey can be summarized in the following themes:

- The strategic direction of the firm must be compatible with social and political conditions; ideally, the relationship will be harmonious.

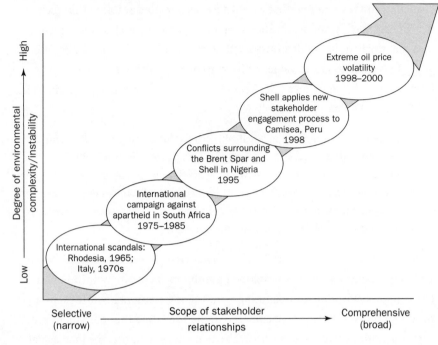

Figure 9.3   Shell's Stakeholder Journey.

- Forces from the periphery of the operating environment (such as the social-political arena) can be so powerful as to force a rethinking of the business mission in light of those conditions.

- The challenge of institutionalizing a stakeholder view into a large, complex global business requires that every system and lever of action (planning, budgeting, communication, training, evaluation, rewards, and so on) be used to infuse the organization with understanding and commitment to stakeholder management.

THE STAKEHOLDER VIEW: THEORETICAL IMPLICATIONS

Our research, along with much other current literature and commentary, confirms that the stakeholder view of the corporation is understood and accepted by some corporate managers, and has become the framework for long-term strategic decisions and policies in some major firms. Indeed, we believe that the

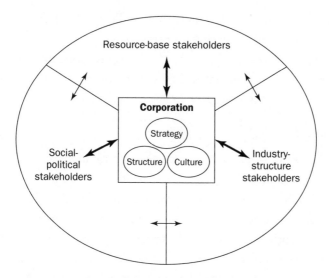

Figure 9.4   The Stakeholder View and the Corporate Core.

essential elements of the stakeholder view are much more widely recognized and utilized than most conventional managerial and financial rhetoric would suggest. The stakeholder view places the firm and its core of strategy, structure, and culture at the center of a web of stakeholder relationships, and shows how organizational wealth can be enhanced by favorable relations (and reduced by unfavorable relations) between the corporation the stakeholders within its resource base, industry setting, and social-political arena. (See Figure 9.4, which supplements Figure 2.3.) As the large arrows in Figure 9.4 suggest, the SHV emphasizes that stakeholders of all kinds have a direct impact on the corporate core. The small arrows emphasize that all stakeholders have connections and interactions with others in the corporation's stakeholder set.

The stakeholder view emphasizes the importance of an organization-wide commitment to humanistic values and ethical practices as a basis for "organizational morality." It is not competitive with other perspectives, but complementary and integrative. It embraces and supplements the explanations offered by both the resource-based view (RVB) and industry-structure view (ISV) as to the sources of organizational wealth. It emphasizes that relational assets may be created by constructive linkages with *all* stakeholders. It also stresses the potential impacts, both positive and negative, of actors and interests in the social and political environments.

In the following sections, we review the descriptive, instrumental, and normative contributions of the stakeholder view (SHV) to our understanding of the corporation and the concept of strategic management.

Descriptive

The stakeholder view makes two distinctive contributions at the descriptive level. First, it emphasizes the social and political dimensions of the firm's strategic environment. Second, it emphasizes the potential value of the humanistic, ethical, and behavioral aspects—in addition to transactional characteristics such as price and cost—of the firm's relationships with all stakeholders. Conventional strategic management models give little attention to the range of social and political considerations that confront managers on a daily basis, treating them (if at all) as anomalous or unique disturbances to an otherwise normal and orderly routine. These models also neglect the role of understandings and collaborative behaviors developed over time, which are important for all types of stakeholders, in the long-term success (or possibly failure) of the enterprise. Trust is a key element in all stakeholder relationships, whether within the firm or between it and outside parties; yet trust has no role in the conventional price-oriented RVB or the competition-oriented ISV. Dyer and Singh (1998) note that the strategic behaviors suggested by both the RBV and ISV for dealing with suppliers are diametrically opposed to the kind of close buyer-supplier collaborations that can lead to new technological developments and long-term cost reductions that benefit both parties.

Our analysis of challenges and responses at Cummins, Motorola, and Shell shows how organization-wide commitments to core values can lead to greater long-term profits. Because stakeholder relationships are more enduring than simple transaction relations, each of these companies changed their traditional behavior in dealing with customers, employees, investors, business partners, governments, and other stakeholders. Each engaged in learning—sometimes deliberately, sometimes of necessity—and changed in response. Sometimes the responses were incremental and adaptive; sometimes new challenges forced them into fundamental changes in corporate behavior.

But resource needs and competitive factors alone do not explain why Cummins collaborated with environmental regulators to create the precedent-setting Health Effects Institute (Chapter 5); why Motorola established a Scientific Advisory Board to oversee its bioinformatics operations (Chapter 8); or why Shell devoted such effort to stakeholder involvement in the Camisea Project in Peru (Chapter 6). Their actions showed how management recognized new and potentially important stakeholders from the social and political arena, outside the scope of conventional market-transaction and industry-structure relationships.

The stakeholder view (SHV) expands the strategic environment of the firm to include social and political dimensions not governed by transactional or industry structure relationships. The stakeholder view embraces both the RBV and the ISV, but goes beyond them. It more accurately describes the conditions confronting companies in real operating environments and provides a superior framework for strategic management analysis and practice.

Instrumental

The commitment to creating organizational wealth in a manner that is economically, technologically, and socially sustainable challenges conventional thinking about the nature and sources of corporate success. Strategic management theory typically addresses the question of why firms achieve different degrees of success in terms of their resource endowments (financial strength, technological know-how, etc.) and/or industry positions (market share, regulatory status, etc.). Without denying the relevance of these factors—indeed, while emphasizing their central role within the stakeholder framework—we believe that the stakeholder view offers a broader and more comprehensive perspective on the sources of business success, as well as greater insight into potential problems and failure.

The stakeholder view presents a comprehensive description of the wealth-creation process, with special emphasis on sources and value of "relational wealth." For Motorola and Cummins, the widespread recognition of their brand names, their well-known and long-established human resource management policies, and their reputations for technological leadership, product quality, and business integrity have proved to be increasingly valuable over the long-term. Moreover, both companies were able to draw upon these "relational assets" in responding quickly and successfully to adverse technological, market, and financial challenges. Shell's realization that its global industry leadership was threatened by forces that had little connection with its technological and economic expertise is equally instructive. The company recognized the need to build "relational wealth" in its contacts with key external groups and the general public, and launched a global program of organizational learning and change in its efforts to do so. As the specific examples discussed in this book make clear, strategic management is not a matter of simple "column A/ column B" choices. It involves the integration of strategy, structure, and culture in a relentless effort to adapt, renew, or transform the corporation to deal with a wide range of stakeholder issues within a changing environment.

The impact of social and political stakeholders on corporate success is often illustrated with negative examples, including "horror stories" about human and environmental tragedies, legal actions, political and regulatory attacks, and adverse media coverage. Incidents of that type are important in our analysis of the transformation of Shell in Chapters 6 and 8. However, our research also shows the favorable impact of mutually supportive stakeholder relationships within firms, within the market environment, and between firms and their external, non-market stakeholders. The experience of Motorola in China (Chapter 7) may represent the "fully mature" level of comprehensive stakeholder orientation, involving employees, customers, suppliers, governments, philanthropic organizations, and the general public.

We noted at the outset that we do not claim statistically reliable evidence to show that stakeholder management is positively associated with profitability, growth, stability, or other economic performance indicators. Still, there is every reason to believe that this is the case; and this belief is supported by many case studies and extensive executive testimony. Recognition of the importance of favorable stakeholder relationships by corporations is reflected in their increasing public commitment to broad societal objectives, as in the case of Shell's commitment to the "triple bottom line" of economic, environmental, and community impact. The growth of "balanced scorecard" reporting also highlights the managerial attention given to these concerns in many firms. More companies are making commitments to "sustainable development," with a focus on ecological and societal impacts, and publishing relevant factual data—not simply stating their good intentions—in their annual reports and elsewhere. All of these data point to managerial acceptance of the stakeholder view.

Many experts still deny that the interests of other critical stakeholders, beyond those of shareowners, contribute to corporate success over the long term. There is considerable evidence to the contrary. We believe that the stakeholder view offers a comprehensive perspective on the sources of organizational wealth, and therefore that stakeholder management will contribute to the long-term success of a corporation. Stakeholder management is a way to develop a corporation's relationships to those it depends on for its "license to operate" and for its ultimate success.

Normative

The stakeholder view (SHV) espoused in this book emphasizes the role of relational wealth and the strategic importance of the social and political environment. But it also emphasizes normative considerations and success criteria. The RBV and ISV focus on economic values, which imply that a corporation can succeed by accumulating resources and enhancing its competitive positions. This is true, up to a point. But the SHV model shows that other factors also contribute to success in the long term. A smart company is a good investment, employer, customer, supplier, and neighbor. Overt and transparent commitments to humanistic practices, honesty, and fair dealing contribute to the overall performance of the firm, just like commitments to technological leadership or astute financial management.

This book focuses on commitments and behaviors, not image or reputation, although the latter usually is an extension of the former. Economic resources can still be amassed through corruption, theft, and piracy, and market positions can be enhanced through bribery and predatory acts, even when concealed within the letter of law. But such practices, even if not technically illegal, violate the basic principles of the market economy and are inconsistent with long-term and sustainable conditions for business success. They violate the integrity of the humanistic commitments that stakeholder-oriented firms value and pursue. Favorable stakeholder relationships are not only essential for the ongoing operations of the corporation, they are a form of organizational wealth. They are visible, even if their "return" is hard to measure.

The stakeholder view of the corporation is fundamentally normative (Donaldson and Preston, 1995). The normative base precedes and underlies its descriptive accuracy and its instrumental contribution to corporate success. Corporate managers must know and respect *all* stakeholder concerns, but this does not mean that every stakeholder wish can or should be granted. Motorola's commitment to uncompromising integrity and respect for the individual, and Shell's commitment to listening and responding, involve recognition, disclosure, and fair dealing. These commitments are a matter of principle; but in practice as well as in theory, the stakeholder view rests on a commitment to core values that are constantly renewed and sustained through organizational learning.

THE STAKEHOLDER VIEW: IMPLICATIONS FOR PRACTICE

Chapter 3 addressed questions that are central to the research on which this book is based. What motivates stakeholder commitment? How does it evolve over time? How is it expressed and implemented? What impact does such commitment have on the stability and growth of corporations?

Cummins, Motorola, and Shell have embraced the stakeholder view of the corporation. They realize that good stakeholder relationships create wealth and otherwise enhance their performance. As such, these firms try to conduct their business affairs while considering the concerns and interests of all their stakeholders, not just those who own stock in the company or work for it. Following are some of the ways stakeholder management practices have favorably affected the long-term performance and status of the three companies we examined.

Implementation

Stakeholder management means committing to the integrity of individuals, groups of individuals, other organizations and interests, and the general public. To do this in an ever-changing environment requires a continuing process of learning and adaptation. Hence, *commitment* and *learning* are keys to organizational wealth through stakeholder management. Stable and supportive stakeholder relationships are built on experience that develops understanding and trust. These qualities are valuable in themselves, and they also encourage collaborative behavior that helps the corporation to respond to new problems and challenges.

In successful organizations, the three core elements of strategy, structure, and culture are aligned and respond to external forces and changing expectations. The relationships among the core elements are dynamic and adaptive, both in relation to each other and in relation to the overall fit between the corporation and its environment. A comprehensive orientation toward stakeholder management penetrates the core of the corporation; in the redefined corporation, all three elements and their alignment reflects the underlying humanistic commitment to the firm's stakeholders. A clear demonstration that management possesses and intends to implement a compelling vision of the enterprise—*Who we are, and what we stand for*—provides the essential foundation for effective stakeholder management.

According to the stakeholder view, the success of the enterprise requires the collaboration and support of all stakeholders. However, the role of particular stakeholders with respect to any specific issue depends on their level of involvement and how important the issue is to them. Not every stakeholder wish can be granted, but the legitimate concerns of all stakeholders require consideration, and ultimate decisions conflicting with specific stakeholder viewpoints need to be explained. Their concerns should be identified and monitored regularly; this should be a basic management responsibility. Open two-way communication and imaginative use of new technology can nurture stakeholder relationships and help build trust over time.

Proactive corporate behavior is better than reactive behavior, enabling the firm to anticipate (and perhaps avoid) problems before they develop and preserving managerial discretion. As the experience of Shell clearly shows, a reactive stance leaves management at the mercy of events. Proactive behavior includes ongoing concern and involvement with stakeholder interests. This also provides a basis for rapid and collaborative response to crises, when speed and flexibility are required. Stakeholders have come to expect open and comprehensible reporting of relevant information. Outside audits that assess social, environmental, and economic factors are useful in sharing data on current initiatives and in creating the foundation for fact-based decision making (Global Reporting Initiative, 2000).

Governance

Adopting the stakeholder view of the corporation does not mean that all stakeholders must be included when determining formal governance structures. But it does imply acceptance of the fact that many classes of stakeholders already have substantial influence on the activities of the corporations with which they are associated, and that this influence is usually legitimate. Obvious examples are the governance impacts of unions, local authorities, government regulators, and other institutions established by or recognized in law. More subtle impacts come from customer groups and organizations, trade associations (both those representing the firm's own industry and those representing other, either collaborative or competitive, interests), and other private organizations representing community members or activist issues. Insofar as these entities influence the decisions and actions of the corporation, they have a role in governance. And, just as any board member may differ from the majority, any of these stakeholders may espouse views or support projects that are incompatible with the interests of broader stakeholder coalitions. The reasonable attempts of various classes of stakeholders to exert a governance impact on the corporation have to be recognized as legitimate. The proposals involved, however—just like the proposals of conventional directors and shareowners—need not always be accepted, or (if totally infeasible) given detailed study.

A second implication of the stakeholder view for governance is that the formal governance processes of corporations should make strenuous efforts to include the views of major stakeholder groups within the framework of analysis and decision making. Again, this does not mean that any particular stakeholder group should have a seat or vote on the board. It does imply, however, that the board should make every effort to know what the concerns and interests of critical stakeholders may be with respect to any significant board decision, and to include these stakeholder perspectives in their own decision making. Many innovative ways have been developed recently to accomplish these purposes. Board committees often focus on specific stakeholder interests—customers, communities, employees, and others—and take responsibility for identifying critical issues and viewpoints from the perspective of their assigned clientele. In several industries, outside experts serving as representatives of specific labor groups and unions have been appointed to boards with full voting rights and responsibilities. Experience with these arrangements suggests that they are somewhat problematic, solving some problems while creating others. Whatever the means employed, the stakeholder view of the corporation definitely implies that a systematic effort should be made to identify critical stakeholders, to specifically recognize and take into consideration their interests within the formal governance process, and to engage them in a ongoing process. More innovative ways for achieving this result will undoubtedly emerge as experience with the concept evolves.

Impact

The impact of stakeholder management practices cannot be discerned in conventional financial data, which are influenced by many transient factors, as well as by macroeconomic and technological trends that are beyond management control. Moreover, these effects are widely distributed, involving employees, customers, communities, and others, as well as investors and lenders. Nevertheless, we believe that a long-term perspective reveals the favorable impact of stakeholder management on the three focal companies.

- *Sustained acceptance.* Cummins, Motorola, and Shell have survived in industries where many other companies have failed or been acquired by others since the 1980s. In highly competitive industries within a rapidly changing global economy, a firm's continued acceptance by its stakeholders, resulting in its survival over time, is not "nothing." These firms have not only survived, but have grown their lines of business, made acquisitions and entered into new alliances, while others in their respective industries have vanished or become integrated into other enterprises. Under these circumstances, business survival, growth, and stakeholder support have to be regarded as strong indicators of "success."

- *Avoided costs.* Our studies—as well as much other evidence—also indicate that failure to anticipate and respond to stakeholder concerns can generate significant costs. From strikes and boycotts to increased regulation and complete withdrawal of a firm's "license to operate," stakeholders have numerous ways to make life difficult and more costly for a firm. Firms that develop effective stakeholder management processes avoid, or at least reduce, these problems and their associated costs. Cummins avoided regulatory costs when it undertook to work with EPA in creating the Health Effects Institute. Motorola lowered corporate turnover costs and enhanced productivity when it became an "employer of choice" through progressive human resource management practices. Shell, having absorbed the costs of Brent Spar and Nigeria, chose to pursue new stakeholder management strategies in Camisea and elsewhere.

- *Favorable results and continued use.* One test of the effectiveness of any management process is management's own appraisal and continued use of it. Successive generations of managers at both Cummins and Motorola have embraced stakeholder management concepts and implemented them within their own spheres of responsibility. Cummins has consistently addressed the concerns of community stakeholders wherever it operates. Motorola has applied its traditional principles of uncompromising integrity and respect for the individual to the myriad challenges facing a global corporation in the 21st century. It has also used its experience in developing policy coalitions and shaping public opinion, first gained in the 1980s with a focus on Japan, more recently to influence trade relations with China. The company's traditional commitment to a stakeholder perspective is being renewed through the work of the Global Corporate Responsibility Task Force. Shell appears to be using the new stakeholder management approach developed in Camisea in other locations and projects, and is institutionalizing a broad "listening and responding" commitment throughout the entire organization. The continued and growing use of stakeholder management approaches suggests that, in the view of corporate managers, they yield positive results. In addition, it appears that both Shell and Motorola are becoming increasingly proactive in their use of stakeholder management (e.g., Motorola's creation of an advisory board in its bioinformatics business; Shell's "listening and responding" campaign). The "stakeholder way" has become the preferred way of doing business in these companies.

• *Attractiveness.* Each of the firms studied has attempted to distinguish itself as an attractive employer of choice, neighbor of choice, business partner of choice, and investment of choice in the eyes of its stakeholders. To the extent that a corporation's management is responsible for managing all of its resources well, recognition of the firm's attractiveness by key stakeholders is an affirmation of the policies and practices that characterize its behavior. Reputation, image, and brand equity are further expressions of the importance of attractiveness to an organization. Once again, economic measurement may be less precise than desired. But tools such as the balanced scorecard (Kaplan and Norton, 1996; 2000), triple bottom line (Elkington, 1997), and value reporting (PricewaterhouseCoopers, 2001) can help an organization's leaders, board members, and managers better understand how attractiveness to customers, employees, suppliers, communities, and other stakeholders is ultimately tied to the organization's long-term prosperity and success.

THE STAKEHOLDER VIEW AND THE NEW ECONOMY

The new economy of the 21st century is being shaped by two dominant forces—economic globalization and technological innovation. Neither of these forces is "new" in the world, but both have reached levels and rates of change that are transformative rather than simply evolutionary. The challenge of implementing stakeholder commitments in diverse and unfamiliar cultural environments was discussed in Chapter 7. Here we briefly note some of the implications of the stakeholder view for the global economy being shaped by electronic technology and the Internet.

The "new economy" is composed of firms engaged in telecommunications, information management, and electronic commerce, along with firms and individuals that develop and produce the physical and functional elements that permit these activities to take place. Motorola is clearly a participant in the new economy; its activities include not only the production of physical items (chips and communications devices) but also design and operation of global communication systems and networks. All major firms—including Shell and Cummins—are customers in the new economy, acquiring and using its products and services. In fact, the distinction between the "new" and "old" economies is declining in importance because companies in all industries are using new information and communications technologies to redesign their operations and expand the range and effectiveness of their stakeholder contacts.

Users of the new technology are not limited to persons or organizations that engage, or might engage, in market-level transactions with the firm. Every wired household or office in the world is a potential recipient of such services, even if there is no thought or possibility that a transaction involving exchange and payment might take place. The new economy is a "web" in the most literal sense. It is a global skein of inter-linked networks and relationships, both powerful and fragile, and only a small percentage of these relationships are currently understood. Several features of the new economy have direct bearing on the relationships between corporations and their stakeholders, and strongly suggest that stakeholder management will be essential for business success is the 21st century.

Much of the excitement surrounding new economy enterprise is related to the "break the rules" mindset of the entrepreneurs who are creating and shaping e-commerce businesses. The normative orientation of the stakeholder view is highly consistent with this new economy theme. Respect for the individual, and tolerance for divergent ways of doing things are central to new ventures that rely on the Internet. Recent studies of the cultures and norms in e-commerce firms underscore how respect, commitment, and knowledge define the "communities of practice" involved in these ventures (cf. Storck, 2000). Companies such as America Online and Yahoo!—archetypes of the new economy culture—have been characterized by openness, freedom, personal fulfillment, respect, and community.

Openness

The openness of the new economy provides stakeholders with more freedom of action because information is abundant and more readily accessible to individuals and organizations. These features enable organizations of all types (e.g., activists) to organize, raise funds, and apply pressure to businesses to respond to public concerns. Although many companies were slow to comprehend the potential of web-based communications, there has been a broad awakening to the potential of the Internet to enhance the development and implementation of constructive stakeholder relationships. Companies can improve their regular communications with key audiences, implement quick responses in times of crisis (e.g., computer viruses), and support their stakeholders with information, applications, and systems via the Internet. Technology is forcing companies to better understand—and become responsive to—substantive stakeholder needs and concerns. The Internet is creating a powerful "pull" force as stakeholders learn how to more effectively articulate and express their expectations of the companies that wish to interact with them.

Interactive Networks

The stakeholder view "redefines" the corporation as an entity embedded in a network of stakeholder relationships. The fact that these stakeholders have non-economic as well as economic interests in the firm mirrors the variety of Internet users. As more of the world's people and institutions make the Internet a part of the normal way they manage their affairs, the degree of interaction (both volume and intensity) can be expected to rise. It is been estimated that 500 million people will have had some direct experience with the Internet by 2002; some estimates suggest that 2 billion people (40% of the world's population) will have some Internet experience by 2005 (cf., Storck, 2000; Computer Industry Almanac, 2000). The trend is unmistakably toward an increasingly networked world.

Information Richness

Scarcity of information has been replaced by an abundance—perhaps an over-abundance—of information. Information is shared rapidly, and new ways of collecting, aggregating, and disseminating meaningful data is shaping resource, competitive, and social-political relationships with stakeholders. Of special importance are the extensive efforts being made to codify standards of social and environmental practice into codes, provide regular reports to all stakeholders, and engage stakeholders in a dialogue on the meaning and direction of "progress." (cf., Global Reporting Initiative, 2000)

This is the connecting point between the operation of corporations in the global economy and the worldwide concern for sustainable economic, environmental, and social practices.

Impact in Global Arena

These characteristics—openness, freedom of action, interdependence, and information richness—have particularly powerful impact in the global arena. Economic, social, and cultural globalization has been underway at an accelerating rate for more than half a century. Some of the key innovations of the new economy arose in response to demands for increased capacity and greater speed in global communications, and all have contributed to the globalization process. The result is that the network of potential stakeholders connected to any firm is vastly enlarged, both in number and in diversity. While the geographic location of major firms remains relevant for some purposes (Microsoft is actually located in Redmond, Washington, not just "everywhere"), firms in the new economy are involved with virtual communities of many different kinds all over the world. They may be unable to identify the actual persons and entities involved in myriad relationships, but they exist and are a source of organizational wealth.

One particular implication of these developments involves an enlargement of the familiar advice to "think globally, act locally." As Shell's experience specifically illustrates, the point is not simply the need to implement a global perspective at the local level; it is also necessary to consider the global impact of local actions. As the experience of companies in the apparel, toy, agriculture, and military weapons industries (to name a few highly visible examples) has shown, public expectations are rising, *and they matter*. Today, a growing portion of the global consumer market is interested to know that the products and services they purchase are both "made well" and "made appropriately" (cf.

Abernathy et al., 1999). Global expectations about a corporation's practices in *all* of its operating locations—and over a wide range of issues, from employment and working conditions to marketing and community relations—are changing rapidly, and people anywhere in the world have the ability to know about and comment upon these practices. The implications of these developments for stakeholder management are somewhat paradoxical. On one hand, stakeholder linkages are much easier to establish, and two-way communication is both quicker and cheaper, than ever before. On the other, the high information level available to all parties and the ease of severing/creating stakeholder links makes these networks more fragile. The potentials for new technological and business development, market access, identification and adaptation to customer preferences, and so forth, are vastly increased; and so are the opportunities for devastating short-run crises and failures. The Internet economy has established new levels of flexibility, speed, and innovation as prerequisites for business success. Relationships are temporary, responses to issues are lightning-quick, and formal planning has been replaced by rapid, adaptive capabilities. In the early 1990s, scholars attempted to capture the essence of how some major firms achieved sustainable success in the phrase "*built to last*" (Collins and Porras, 1994). By the end of the decade, the rapid development of new companies and technology helped produce a countertrend called "built to flip," where "flipping" involved creating a new business in order to sell it to another firm or to outside investors at a premium over the initial investment (Collins, 2000). But the crash of the dot.com economy provided a sober reminder that true business value lies in market and nonmarket relationships that are nurtured and sustained, not flipped and disregarded.

Several spectacular growth companies did emerge out of the new economy, and some large and powerful corporations have been created (e.g., the merger of America Online and Time Warner). Technology and global competition have made the economy of the twenty-first century highly competitive at every level—technological, financial, market, and communications—and the ability of firms to maintain control over scarce resources or reap exceptional rewards because of protected market positions is extremely limited. Within this setting, both long-term vision and quick short-term adaptation appear to be critical for business success. Stakeholder linkages are easy to establish and utilize (through two-way communication, for example), yet fragile and easy to sever as well. We believe that these circumstances strengthen the case for stakeholder management. As close and stable stakeholder relationships become rarer, they also become more valuable. Therefore, it will pay firms to recognize, create, and enhance stakeholder linkages. High customer, employee, supplier, and investor turnover imposes significant costs (financial and non-financial) on the firm; stable relationships, based on trust, are correspondingly cost-reducing and valuable. Imaginative use of newly available technologies should make it possible to ascertain the individual needs and concerns of investors, employees, customers and other critical stakeholders, and to adapt financial arrangements, compensation schemes, products and services, and other practices to them. Indeed, it appears that stakeholder links may already have become central to the value-creation process in many firms, placing new pressures on managers to build and maintain stakeholder relationships (Wilson, 2001).

CONCLUSION

For as long as business corporations have existed, their role in the economy and society has been a focus of attention and debate. The power of the corporation to influence the pattern of economic, social, and political development—along with its sometimes negative impact on specific employees, customers, and communities—has regularly been weighed against the capacity of the corporation to create new wealth. These conflicting relationships reveal the corporation to be both a contributor and a challenge to society. Each generation has asked, in its own terms, the fundamental question: *To whom and for what is the corporation responsible?* At the beginning of the 21st century, with the corporate system expanding all over the world, this question remains as important as it has ever been. The corporation is both a contributor to and a beneficiary of the larger social system within which it operates. It affects, and is affected by, law, public policy, and social expectations; it conforms to existing social standards and arrangements, and simultaneously alters them by its own independent initiatives and innovations.

The corporation is linked economically and socially, voluntarily and involuntarily with numerous stakeholders who may contribute to, or be impacted by, its success or failure. The stakeholder view of the corporation recognizes these reciprocal interdependencies, which constitute the stakeholder network of each firm. This network is the context for the firm's strategic decision making, as well as for its routine operations. Creation and preservation of organizational wealth in the modern economy depends on the development and maintenance of favorable relationships within this network.

The stakeholder view of the corporation (SHV) is a more comprehensive basis for strategic management than either the resource-based view (RBV) or the industry structure view (ISV). The stakeholder view integrates both of these perspectives, and adds the social-political environment as a critical third dimension. The result is a more realistic conception of the context, challenges, and opportunities of strategic management. In addition, the stakeholder view broadens the range of corporate performance criteria beyond short-term profitability and growth to include the long-term interests of multiple stakeholders that are critical to the firm's success.

Underlying values and cultural norms shape corporate policies and practices in the "new economy" just as in traditional industries and sectors. Our studies of Cummins, Motorola, and Shell show that fundamental commitments to humanistic values can help firms to become both responsive to stakeholder concerns and successful in the marketplace. Proactive stakeholder strategies can help firms avoid, reduce, and control costs over the long term. Such strategies may also increase the likelihood that creative and innovative responses to problematic situations will emerge over time. In short, adoption of the stakeholder view should increase the ability of managers to configure and implement combinations of strategy, structure, and culture that enhance organizational wealth.

Recognition of the importance of humanistic values is not only critical for the long-term success of the individual firm; it is even more important for the survival of the corporate system as a whole. The corporation has been a powerful instrument of economic and social development for centuries; but disregard of its normative impact and purpose has repeatedly led to criticism and to demands for social controls. The high level of global communication and awareness now available through new technologies has heightened criticism of corporate practices, even as it has opened up new business opportunities and lowered costs. Although the corporate system is currently expanding throughout the world, its future is by no means assured. To maintain its status as the preeminent institutional arrangement for the creation of wealth, the corporation must earn its "license to operate," both locally and globally, by demonstrating its respect for people and its contribution to building a better world. The wealth of the corporation is not merely the property it owns, the financial resources it accumulates, or even the intellectual property it develops. The corporation's most important asset—and the only one it cannot create or replace on its own—is its acceptance within society as a legitimate institution.

CASE STUDIES

The following section of Case Studies provides more detailed background about the history and evolution of Cummins, Motorola, and Shell. Each of these company profiles also contains a list of key events and developments related to the emergence of the company's stakeholder management approach.

A

CASE STUDY

Cummins

The research on Cummins was primarily conducted by Jeffery L. Cruikshank and David A. Sicilia in the course of preparing their official company history, *The Engine That Could* (1997). Sicilia provided us with research memoranda based on his original notes and supplementary material from both company and external sources, and we have made use of the company website (www.cummins.com). Sicilia also conducted, on our behalf, additional interviews with James A. Henderson (chairman and former CEO); Jack Edwards (executive vice president); Steven P. Knaebel (vice president, Cummins Mexico); and Adele J. Vincent (executive director, Cummins Engine Foundation). Our analysis of the Cummins history has been reviewed by Sicilia for accuracy.

HISTORY AND EVOLUTION

Thirteen men originally pooled their capital to form Cummins Engine Company. Two of them—William Glanton Irwin, who provided most of the capital, and Clessie Lyle Cummins, a mechanic-inventor who had the idea to build and sell diesel engines—became the moving forces in the company's early history. Cummins is a classic story of entrepreneurial zeal for an idea (diesel engines) that was new and exciting. The founders struggled through the 1920s and 1930s to improve technology, to persuade prospective customers that diesels could outperform gasoline engines, and to manufacture high-quality engines that would win customers and build loyalty to the Cummins brand name.

Cummins struggled for decades to identify a suitable domestic market for the untried diesel engine, experimenting with everything from stationary power for agriculture to luxury yachts. Finally, in the 1930s, the company focused on long-haul trucking, which exploited the diesel's power and low operating costs. It achieved its first profitable year in 1937. World War II provided opportunities for diesel manufacturers to demonstrate their technology and products, and the postwar economic expansion and highway development opened an enormous market for engines to drive the new fleets of trucks that were moving merchandise across the United States. Cummins became established as the largest independent engine manufacturer during this period. Rapid growth also emphasized the highly cyclical nature of the truck and engine markets. When business expansion was underway, orders for new trucks and engines soared; when the expansion stopped, orders slowed to a trickle. Cummins learned to adapt to these postwar "boom and bust" cycles, but suffered recurrent capital shortages whenever general economic recovery led to a rapid increase in demand.

The company's history is filled with examples of innovative behavior in response to sudden and unexpected shifts in demand, which continue to characterize the industry. Engine manufacturing is not only capital intensive but requires a skilled and experienced labor force. For long-term success, Cummins had to maintain access to the capital and labor required for periods of rapid expansion while avoiding insupportable costs during slack periods. These pressures have significantly shaped and influenced Cummins' stakeholder relations—its search for customers, investors, and operating partners on one hand, and its relationships with employees and communities on the other. The values and policies that Cummins originally developed in its home community and in the U.S. domestic market have been retained and proven successful, as it has expanded its production, marketing, and collaborative activities into the global economy.

Cummins retained its informal, family-business organizational structure for several decades, but realized the need for a larger and more professional management cadre during the rapid postwar expansion. By the early 1960s

Cummins was recruiting new MBAs for management careers. The company's geographic reach expanded during this same period, first within the United States and later abroad. It has been among the leading U.S. manufacturing exporters for many decades. It established a manufacturing plant in Scotland in the late 1950s, and subsequently set up "beachheads" in Europe and India from which it could export to other countries in each region. It also pioneered in the establishment of foreign joint venture and alliances. International sales now account for more than 40 percent of Cummins' revenues.

CULTURE

The culture of Cummins is highly personal, derived from the beliefs and attitudes of its leading executives, particularly J. Irwin Miller and Henry Schacht. Miller was educated in the humanities at Yale and Oxford; he held deep religious convictions and felt a responsibility for the impact of Cummins on individuals and on the community. Miller tried to maintain high levels of employment during the Great Depression and, unlike most employers at the time, welcomed the passage of the National Labor Relations Act (1936) as a protection of workers' ability to act in their own self-interest. All of Cummins' U.S. plants have been unionized for many years. In 1972 the company experienced a crippling strike, but for the most part union leaders and Cummins managers have acknowledged their common stake in the success of the enterprise. The most recent agreement between Cummins and the Diesel Workers Union, signed in 1993, was scheduled to extend for an unprecedented eleven years.

The Cummins culture also includes a broad, long-term social commitment, reflected in patterns of innovative philanthropy. For many years, it was one of only two U.S. publicly owned companies to contribute a full 5 percent of pretax net income to philanthropic purposes. The Cummins Foundation has been a leader in supporting innovative art, cultural, and civic improvement programs. Miller took active steps to promote racial integration in both the company and the local community well before the civil rights movement; and since the early 1970s Cummins has vigorously pursued workforce diversity through creative programs of affirmative action and recruiting. In short, the Cummins culture has blended a spirit of progressive humanitarianism with bottom-line thinking that has emphasized clear objectives and accountability for results. The language of "stakeholders," "doing the right thing," and "ethical standards" has never been foreign at Cummins. Its leaders, at every level of the company, have understood that such ideas are the sources of strength and creativity that enable the company to face its future boldly and with confidence.

RECENT DEVELOPMENTS

Cummins entered the 21st Century as a premier manufacturer of diesel engines. The company continues to develop leading-edge technology and engages in a variety of business alliances, partnerships, and joint ventures. In 2001, the company announced a joint venture to produce natural gas fuel systems for diesel engines. Cummins has led in the development of lower-emission products while providing customers with low life-cycle operating costs.

Cummins has grown its generator business in the United States and globally. In Brazil, for example, the company identified generators as a top growth opportunity because of power shortages. By 2001, generators were more than 40 percent of Latin American sales, up from 30 percent only a few years earlier. Cummins is poised for other regional markets that may run short of power. In Latin America, only 2 percent of generating capacity is protected by emergency back-up sources, compared to 15 percent in developed nations.

Table A.1
Cummins: Revenue, Assets, Employment

	1970	1975	1980	1985	1990	1995	1998	1999
Revenue (millions of U.S. dollars)	448	761	1,666	2,146	3,461	5,245	6,266	6,639
Assets (millions of U.S. dollars)	322	624	1,117	1,705	2,086	3,056	4,542	4,697
Employment (thousands)	14.5	17.9	21.2	19.6	24.9	24.3	28.3	28.5

Exhibit A.1
Cummins: Key Events

1919	Founding
1955	International sales reach more than 100 countries.
1956	Cummins Foundation provides services to Columbus, Indiana, school system.
1957	First overseas manufacturing facility opens in Scotland.
1961	Congress proposes differential taxes on diesel fuel and engines; Cummins opposes and wins.
1962	Joint venture to manufacture engines in India.
1972	Labor trouble; 57-day strike in Columbus is longest in Cummins history.
1972	Cummins creates Corporate Action Division to coordinate philanthropy, government relations, public affairs, community relations, human resources development, and affirmative action.
1977	Clean Air Amendments lead to major split among motor vehicle manufacturers.
1978	Cummins works with Environmental Protection Agency (EPA) to create Health Effects Institute to study health impact of various mobile sources of pollutants.
1980s	Cummins-Komatsu relationship changes from business partners to major competitors in Japan and United States. Cummins seeks new stakeholders through program of "building organizational capabilities"; joint venture with J. I. Case.
1983	Cummins begins manufacturing in China; China National Automobile Industry Corporation begins engine assembly from kits, expands to full manufacturing in 1985.
1984	First imports of Japanese diesel engines into United States occurs in 1984 at prices 40% below market. Cummins responds with price cuts, quality improvement, and marketing.

1988–89   Hanson PLC acquires 8.3% stake in Cummins for "investment purposes." Miller family buys back Hanson shares as "preventive philanthropy." Then Hong Kong–based Industrial Equity (Pacific) Ltd. (IEP) discloses significant ownership of Cummins stock; Cummins uses legal/political tactics to fight "greenmail."

1989   Cummins establishes employee stock ownership plan (ESOP) with 1.2 million shares ($75 million).

1989   Cummins attempts to stabilize equity ownership by adding Kubota Ltd. (Japan—5.4%), Tenneco (10.8%), and Ford (10.8%, with option to go to 20%) as investors.

1990s   Cummins moves to "team-based" work systems, leading to lengthy negotiations with Diesel Workers Union and precedent-setting 11-year contract with lifetime employment guarantee for current DWU workers, increased flexibility, skill-based performance system, health care cost sharing, and use of competitive economic measures for Cummins. (Contract approved April 24, 1993.)

1993   China becomes Cummins' third largest international market (behind United Kingdom and Canada), and 44% of sales come from outside United States. Cummins enters into joint venture with Tata Engineering and Locomotive Co., Ltd., India's largest manufacturer of commercial vehicles.

B

CASE STUDY

Motorola

Research on Motorola was primarily conducted by coauthors Preston and Post. Our study was authorized by executive vice president Glenn Gienko and facilitated by R. S. Moorthy, vice president and director of the Motorola Office of Knowledge Management. Motorola has been a case study in several books (such as Collins and Porras, *Built to Last*, 1994) and the subject of many articles, commentaries in leading business magazines and journals, and books.

A number of Motorola-sponsored publications have provided important chronological data: H. M. Petrakis, 1965/1995 (Motorola's official corporate history); R. W. Galvin, 1991; Moorthy and others, 1998; Peach, 1999; and Weisz, 1993. We had extensive access to Motorola archives and publications and were assisted by Eric Shuster, company historian, and the staff of the archives. Personal interviews were conducted with former CEO Robert Galvin, Glenn Gienko, R S Moorthy, and other Motorola employees. Jack Bradshaw, corporate vice president and director of ethics and compliance, provided additional assistance and supplementary materials, and Moorthy and Bradshaw reviewed draft materials for accuracy at various points throughout the process. As befits a firm so deeply involved in the telecommunications revolution, a great deal of Motorola's historical and current information is available on the company web site (www.motorola.com). A number of materials relating to Motorola in China, including the company's Chinese language web site, were translated by Guorong Zhu, a doctoral candidate at Boston University.

HISTORY AND EVOLUTION

Motorola was founded in 1928 as the Galvin Manufacturing Corporation in Chicago. Its first product was a "battery eliminator" that allowed radios to be operated directly from household electric current instead of batteries. In the 1930s the company manufactured car radios under the brand name Motorola, a neologism intended to suggest "sound in motion." During this period, the company also began producing home and police radios (Petrakis, 1965).

In 1947 Galvin changed its name to Motorola. The company did significant work for the U.S. Government during World War II and subsequently opened a solid-state electronics research laboratory in Phoenix, Arizona. At the time of Paul Galvin's death in 1959, Motorola was a leader in military, space, and commercial communications, had built its first semiconductor facility, and was a growing force in consumer electronics. Motorola's emphasis on frontier-shifting research originated with Dan Noble, formerly a professor of physics at the University of Connecticut, who established Motorola's research capability. His close relationship with the Galvin family meant that technological issues were consistently addressed at the most senior levels of the organization. Paul Galvin had strong moral commitments and a respect for human values that became embedded in the company when it was founded.

Under the leadership of Robert W. Galvin, Paul Galvin's son, Motorola expanded into international markets in the 1960s and began concentrating on high-technology products for commercial, industrial, and government customers. International growth continued throughout the 1970s, 1980s, and 1990s. Christopher Galvin, Robert Galvin's son, became president and COO in 1993, CEO in 1996, and chairman in 1998, but basic strategic directions remained unchanged. By 1998, 59 percent of Motorola's total revenues came from outside the United States, and the company had established an especially strong presence in Asia Pacific, China, and Europe.

TECHNOLOGY

Technological innovation has been Motorola's defining characteristic from the outset. Building on its wartime and postwar successes, Motorola anticipated the explosion of telecommunications and consumer electronics markets in the 1970s and 1980s and became the premier global supplier of cellular telephones. As a result of the wireless communications revolution, Motorola's sales rose from $3 billion in 1980 to more than $10 billion in 1990. Between 1990 and 1999, Motorola's worldwide employment increased to more than 140,000, and sales passed $30 billion in 1999. Throughout these decades of rapid growth, Motorola's commitment to leading-edge technology, product development, quality, and customer satisfaction has marked it as an exceptionally progressive, visionary firm. On several occasions, it has been named one of America's most admired companies.

A discussion of Motorola's activities during the 1990s would be incomplete without a mention of the Iridium project. Iridium was conceived as a global satellite communication system that would permit customers to connect with each other, anywhere in the world, by using a single wireless phone. The concept called upon all of Motorola's expertise, political as well as technological, as the satellite paths required approval of more than 150 national governments. Iridium was separately incorporated, but Motorola supported it with substantial loans, stock ownership, and a satellite service contract. Unfortunately, by the time all of the arrangements were completed, changing wireless technology and falling prices had eliminated the market for this highly sophisticated but expensive ($3000 per phone) system. The company filed for bankruptcy in 1999 and Motorola, its largest creditor, had to take large write-offs as a result.

Since its early years, Motorola has generated many more ideas for technological innovation than it could support financially. Its progress, therefore, has required careful priority setting and the development of innovative and adaptive financing arrangements. For example, at the end of World War II the company invested heavily in television and became a major manufacturer of consumer electronics. However, when competition in these markets increased and profit margins eroded (primarily due to Japanese competition), the entire consumer electronics business was sold and the resources involved were used to move into new technologies and into global production and marketing ventures that transformed the firm over subsequent decades. In 1980 three-fourths of the company's $3 billion total revenue came primarily from communications equipment and semiconductors, with government electronics, information systems, and other activities accounting for the remainder. At that time it began testing cellular phones in the Baltimore/Washington area, and also delivered 150 advanced paging units for testing in Japan. These products, and their expanded production and marketing overseas, brought about rapid change throughout the organization.

Motorola very early recognized the importance of Asia as both a production site and product market. In 1980 it entered into a joint venture with Toko, Inc. to produce semiconductors in Japan, opened a new assembly plant in Malaysia, and signed a production agreement with the government of Sri Lanka. In 1981 its Japanese subsidiaries were combined into Nippon Motorola, and a new corporate headquarters position was created for the management of this company, along with the Toko joint venture.

INTERNATIONAL EXPANSION

These changes in product emphasis and geographic focus altered Motorola's managerial perspective in other ways. Motorola executives had traditionally focused on three principal groups of stakeholders—customers, employees, and investors. Apart from experience during World War II, and the continuing importance of government customers, Motorola executives did not view public officials and political actors as primary stakeholders or important strategic contacts. However, the development of aggressive Japanese competition in the new electronics market brought a new awareness of the impact of public policy on the strategic environment, and Motorola sought federal government help in responding to the challenge of "Japan, Inc."

In 1982 Motorola submitted an antidumping petition to the U.S. International Trade Commission and the Commerce Department. This petition charged that Japanese firms were selling pagers in the United States at significantly lower prices than they were charging in Japan. Motorola was losing market share and executives were furious at what they viewed to be unfair competition. In January 1983, the Commerce Department set dumping margins on tone-only pagers, but the battle against unfair foreign competition would continue throughout the decade. Robert Galvin became a frequent visitor to Washington during this period and emerged as an important voice for fair and free trade.

Motorola's global growth strategy encountered other problems in the early 1980s. The strong dollar had a negative effect on international sales, and an economic crisis in Mexico resulted in cancellation of some orders. Competition became more intense in key markets. At the same time (1982), Motorola received its first major communications order from the People's Republic of China, and was accepted as a supplier of pagers to Nippon Telephone, shipping over 48,000 units. The company moved ahead in the cellular telephone market and put its DynaTac cellular telephone systems in place in 1983. These efforts enabled Motorola to become the only U.S. company to be designated a qualified cellular provider in Japan. The company opened a representative office in Beijing in 1987 and formed Motorola (China) Electronics, Ltd. (MCEL), now its most important foreign subsidiary, five years later.

The competitive battles of the 1980s (discussed in Chapter 5) turned Motorola into a stronger and healthier company in several respects. Motorola executives recognized that its markets were being transformed as companies engaged in more joint ventures, alliances, and ad-hoc business arrangements. The company's strong emphasis on "total quality" and its traditionally close association with its commercial and industrial customers enabled it to adapt as markets became more "relational" and less transaction oriented. Nevertheless, repeated organizational changes took place as the company searched for proper alignment of its technical, marketing, and business support resources with customer needs in a fast-changing global market. By 1998 another major reorganization was required; and, as in the case of Shell, the company's culture became a central element in the restructuring process.

VALUES AND CULTURE

Motorola's long-term commitment to "uncompromising integrity" and "respect for the individual" has evolved into a specific emphasis on "total customer satisfaction," which includes high quality standards as well as reliable service, open communication, and fair dealing. Motorola measures quality through what it calls the "Six Sigma" process. Six Sigma means having fewer than 3.4 defects per million manufactured parts, which translates into a 99.9997 percent perfection rating. Motorola's stated goal is to achieve a defect rate of zero for all manufactured products. All employees are expected to seek the highest levels of quality and to constantly challenge themselves toward improvement. The success of Motorola's quality commitment was recognized when the company received the first Malcolm Baldrige National Quality Award, the U.S. Government's highest award for quality achievement, in 1988.

A second important emphasis within Motorola's culture is employee training. Motorola believes that its employees must be well educated and continuously trained if they are to achieve the company's ambitious innovation and quality goals. To ensure that the skill level of all employees is high, the company makes large investments in training, much of which is done through Motorola University (MU). MU is highly regarded by training experts; by 1990 its programs reached all major Motorola locations in the United States and the principal operating sites in Europe, Latin America, and Asia.

Motorola values open communication and works to maintain a participatory atmosphere where management and employees can deal directly with each other. At the same time, an intense spirit of internal competition is fostered. Employees are rewarded for results, and major technological disagreements have led some observers to describe the company as a culture of "warring tribes." Such conflicts contributed to serious losses in the cellular telephone business during the 1990s, when the company resisted the move from analog to digital technology. The aftermath included a renewed commitment to team-based decision making.

At the end of the 20th century, Motorola stood as a clear leader in the global telecommunications industry, admired in many quarters for its technological expertise, management skill, and visionary leadership. In 1998, the company underwent a major reorganization that refocused its diverse technologies and geographic operations on wireless communications and embedded-solutions businesses. "Renewal" is a recurring theme among the three generations of Galvins who have led the company, each of whom has affirmed the company's core values—respect for the individual and uncompromising integrity—even while dealing with periodic crises and challenges. In fact, a commitment to continuous renewal, based on these core values, is at the heart of Motorola's culture.

RECENT DEVELOPMENTS

Motorola has been affected by rapid changes in the global business environment. Revenues reached $37 billion in 2000 and development of the Internet was seen as a promising opportunity. But in late 2000, the dot-com bubble burst, sharply affecting the telecommunications sector; sales and corporate earnings dropped. These problems were exacerbated by the September 11, 2001, terrorist attacks on the United States. These attacks killed thousands, destroyed billions of dollars worth of property, damaged consumer confidence, and precipitated economic effects that were broadly felt.

The two major components of Motorola's revenue stream, semiconductors and wireless phones, suffered sharp declines in 2001. The company undertook significant cost cutting and restructuring of its businesses, including termination of its semiconductor manufacturing; 30,000 jobs were eliminated. The company reaffirmed its focus on the telecom industry with a corporate-wide initiative, "Telecom Next, Telecom Now."

Table B.1
Motorola: Revenue, Assets, Employment

	1970	1975	1980	1985	1990	1995	1998	1999
Revenue (millions of U.S. dollars)	796	1,311	3,098	5,443	10,885	27,037	29,400	30,931
Assets (millions of U.S. dollars)	596	1,001	2,111	4,370	8,742	22,801	28,700	37,327
Employment (thousands)	36	47	71.5	90.2	105	142	140	121

Exhibit B.1
Motorola: Key Events

1928	Company founded in Chicago as Galvin Manufacturing Corp. to produce battery eliminators; soon diversified into AM home radios.
1930	Automobile radio successfully designed and marketed under "Motorola" name.
1936	Expanded into two-way mobile radios and central station equipment for police use; moved to FM in 1941.
1941	New technology for "walkie-talkie" units developed, refined and expanded for military use.
1947	Company name changes to Motorola; produces mobile and portable radios, transmitters, phonographs, and microwave systems; television set production begins.
1948	Expanded automobile radio production for Ford and other manufacturers.
1949	Phoenix facility established to begin work on transistors; large-scale production achieved by 1956.
1955	Radio pagers introduced.
1958	Transistor technology introduced.
1960s	Overseas expansion for semiconductor production and sales; later expanded into pagers and other products.
1964	Corporate campus at Schaumburg, Illinois, established.
1970	Space program involvement; television set production discontinued; gradually abandoned all consumer electronics to concentrate on microprocessors and other new technologies.
1981	"Meeting Japan's Challenge" campaign initiated the "chip wars." Quality crusade begins, with "total customer satisfaction" commitment. Robert Galvin testifies in Washington about Japan's competitive barriers and dangers to U.S. manufacturing. Motorola enters China.

1990s	Motorola expands in cellular communications; Iridium project initiated.
1997	Asian financial crisis hits Motorola core businesses; major restructuring and large-scale layoffs result in successful turnaround; stock price rises to all-time high. New Code of Ethics issued.
1999	Motorola agrees to acquire General Instrument; introduces "Digital DNA" for embedded technology uses. Iridium, previously spun off into separate company, eventually fails and files for bankruptcy.

C

CASE STUDY

Shell

Research on Shell was conducted by all three authors, with additional work by Ruth Schmitt and Daniel Peter, doctoral students at the University of Zurich. There is much literature on Shell, but the contemporary publications that were most useful to us are the following: Howarth, 1997; Schwartz, 1991; and de Geus, 1997. In addition, we examined many Shell publications, including annual reports and other documents from Shell Transport and Trading Company PLC (U.K.), Royal Dutch Petroleum Company (Netherlands), and Shell Oil Company (U.S.). Recent Shell International publications such as *Interchange* (the groupwide public affairs periodical), *Shell World* (an in-house magazine), annual editions of *The Shell Report,* the series of "Management Primers" on major public affairs topics, and a large collection of ad-hoc documents, speeches, and conference presentation materials were also used, along with material from the company web site (www.shell.com). Heinz Brodbeck, former vice president of Shell Switzerland, participated in many interviews and arranged our initial contacts with Shell International in London. Our principal contacts there were Tom Henderson, former manager of corporate identity communications, and Gerry Matthews, advisor on group policy development and external relations. In addition, we interviewed Robin Aram (vice president, external relations and policy development); Alan Detheridge (vice president; former manager of Shell operations in Nigeria); and Jeremy Frearson (external affairs advisor and formerly a Shell executive in China). Murray Jones, former manager of Camisea Project, provided information and assistance regarding the

Camisea Project; he is currently advisor on sustainable development and corporate health and safety for Shell Canada. John Simpson, vice president of external affairs for Shell Australia, provided valuable comments as a reader.

HISTORY AND EVOLUTION

The Shell Transport and Trading Company Ltd. was founded in 1897 by Marcus Samuel, who had previously headed a family business established by his father in 1834 to trade British machinery, textiles, and tools for the local products of various countries in the Far and Middle East. By the 1880s, Samuel was transporting and trading oil from the Dutch East Indies. However, the company fell heavily into debt, and in 1907 Samuel entered into an alliance with the Royal Dutch Petroleum Company, which had been founded in 1890 after the accidental discovery of oil in Indonesia. According to the merger agreement, the two parent companies—Shell Transport and Royal Dutch—remained separate, each with its own board and chairman. Royal Dutch would be responsible for production and refining, and Shell for transport, storage, and marketing. The two parent companies would have joint ownership, Royal Dutch with 60 percent and Shell with 40 percent, in the operating companies, which would be directed by a single directorate consisting of members of the other two boards. Since then, Shell has had dual headquarters located in London and The Hague.

War and political developments have shaped the global petroleum industry throughout its history. Shell's early development was closely linked to the colonial empires and strategic trading policies of the United Kingdom and Holland. Shell was an important supplier of the Allied Forces in World War I, and during World War II it administered the British Petroleum Board (the "Pool"), which coordinated worldwide acquisition, storage, and distribution of oil for all of the Allies. This gave Shell valuable experience in global systems management and facilitated its postwar expansion into new areas such as Nigeria, India, Venezuela, and China.

During the 1950–60s the global oil industry grew rapidly as economic expansion took place in North America, Western Europe, and Asia, often with little consideration of ecological and environmental impacts. The industry was dominated by large, vertically integrated, multinational companies—the so-called "Seven Sisters": Shell, Exxon, Mobil, British Petroleum, Texaco, Chevron, and ENI. Since the 1970s this structure has weakened because of the nationalization of oil resources and facilities in some countries, emergence of state-owned and domestically favored firms in other nations, and international agreements among petroleum exporting countries.

Just as these competitive changes were taking place, a new global awareness of the ecological and environmental impact of worldwide economic development was emerging. *The Limits to Growth*, a path-breaking report published in 1972 by a prestigious group of international business leaders organized as the "Club of Rome," argued that total world production and consumption of natural resources could not continue to expand at prevailing rates. This broad concern became sharply focused on the petroleum industry the following year, when the Six Day War between Israel and its Arab neighbors highlighted the dangers of global dependence on Arab oil. The simultaneous formation of a global oil cartel (the Organization of Petroleum Exporting Countries, OPEC) restricted production, forced oil prices to an all-time high, and plunged Europe and North America into a decade of inflation. The entire oil industry came under public scrutiny and criticism.

These external changes pushed many companies into diversification programs, most of which were eventually abandoned. The challenges of the 1970s, later followed by a long period of declining oil prices, also resulted in a series of large mergers and led the major firms to spread investment risks through joint ventures and alliances that sometimes mixed private and state-owned enterprises. The industry structure emerging from this process has been described as "coopetition."

ORGANIZATIONAL STRUCTURE

Unlike most of the major oil companies, Shell has never been led by a strong chief executive officer. According to the company's Statement of General Business Principles (SGBP), Shell is "a decentralized, diversified group of companies with widespread activities, and each Shell business unit (company) has considerable freedom of action" (1997). In contrast to its competitors, Shell did not undergo major structural change in the 1980s, when many oil companies changed from geography-based to product-based divisional structures. These companies tend to have centralized headquarters and to operate through three major operating divisions: upstream, downstream, and chemicals. Shell's regionally decentralized configuration had historically been responsive to local operating conditions and needs and was suited to the management of upstream (exploration and drilling) activities. However, for the management of downstream activities, where rapid information flows and quick market-adaptive decisions are vital, excessive decentralization proved to be a handicap. By 1994, Shell's economic performance, as measured by the rate of return on average capital employed (ROACE) was only 7–10%, in contrast to target rates of 12% ("acceptable") and 15% ("good"). Oil prices in inflation-adjusted terms had declined to pre-1970s levels, and several of Shell's major global competitors were becoming involved in merger negotiations.

Throughout its history, Shell has been a true multinational company, dealing with many different cultures and governmental systems and inevitably involved in complex interactions with social institutions and behavior, as well as with the physical environment all over the world. However, the company's decentralized structure and weak central management control meant that local relations were managed by country managers, known as powerful "barons." Two unrelated incidents in the 1970s revealed the dangers inherent in this arrangement. At about the same time, one Shell unit was accused of paying "protection money" to officials of the Italian government, and another was charged with violating international sanctions imposed against the white minority government of Rhodesia. The near-simultaneous occurrence of these events, and the media attention they attracted, suggested the need for more formal companywide policies relating to business conduct. This led to the creation of Shell's first Statement of General Business Principles, distributed internally in 1976 and externally published in 1984.

CULTURE AND CHANGE

Throughout its history, Shell has always been a technologically oriented company with a corporate culture dominated by scientific and technical expertise.

As former CEO Herkstroeter declared: "We are technological leaders and we are extremely proud of that, as we should be" (1996, p. 6). But Shell also has stated a commitment to humanistic principles. Since its publication in 1984, the Statement of General Business Principles has affirmed "honesty, integrity and respect for people" as core values.

Shell has historically been a leader in the development of sophisticated strategic planning techniques. The company pioneered the use of comprehensive global scenarios as the framework for planning. Introduced in the early 1970s, these scenarios challenged the mindset of Shell executives and enabled them to anticipate such large discontinuities as the oil shock of 1973 and the collapse of Communism in 1989. This approach emphasized the identification and impact of critical stakeholders and the importance of changes in stakeholder relationships.

By the early 1990s, Shell's scenario team realized that the company was confronted with dramatically new operating conditions, although it did not foresee all the emerging critical social challenges. The team had started to develop a "New Shell" model, including a major process of internal structural transformation, when problems with the disposal of the Brent Spar facility in the North Sea and Shell's relationship with Nigeria's repressive military regime revealed new levels of international public concern with the company's activities. These developments increased the importance of stakeholder relations and socioeconomic trend analysis within the "New Shell" organizational structure, as discussed in detail in Chapters 6 and 8 of this book.

RECENT DEVELOPMENTS

Shell has maintained its position as a leading global petroleum company. In 2000 revenues soared past $190 billion and net income exceeded $12 billion. Only Exxon-Mobil ranks larger among the superpowers of the oil industry. Shell continued global efforts to build corporate reputation and institutionalize stakeholder management practices. Benefits were realized when the company's community relationships enabled it to successfully clean up a serious oil spill in Sydney Harbor with a minimum of public outrage. The experience was touted within the company as a demonstration of the value of a sustained commitment to constructive stakeholder relationships.

Shell encountered difficulties with stakeholders in other venues however. An attempt to acquire Woodside Petroleum, Ltd., an Australian firm, failed when the government refused permission for the takeover. The bid was rejected because of national interest concerns amidst rising nationalism and a hostile political climate. In the United States, Shell was outbid in a $3 billion attempt to acquire Barrett Resources, a natural gas producer.

Shell's involvement in Nigeria continued to be trouble-filled. Refinery and transport operations were attacked amidst continuing violence in that nation. And in the United States, the U.S. Supreme Court refused to bar a lawsuit against the company for human rights violations in Nigeria. The decision permits four people to pursue claims in U.S. courts that they or their kin were imprisoned, tortured and in two instances killed by the Nigerian government and that Shell was complicit in those acts. The lawsuit was filed under a two century-old federal law that permits U.S. courts to hear suits by non-citizens claiming violations of international law (cf. Royal Dutch Petroleum v. Wiwa).

Table C.1
Shell: Revenue, Assets, Employment

	1970	1975	1980	1985	1990	1995	1998	1999
Revenue (billions of U.S. dollars)	11.1	30.7	78.9	94.6	132.4	150.6	138.2	149.7
Assets (billions of U.S. dollars)	12.8	40.6	42.2	42.3	59.4	74.6	71.4	71.9
Employment (thousands)	184	161	161	142	137	104	102	96

	Exhibit C.1 Shell: Key Events
1907	Founding by alliance of Shell Transport and Trading with Royal Dutch Petroleum.
1940s	During World War II, Royal Dutch Shell manages the "Pool" (Petroleum Board) to coordinate the oil supply to Allied forces around the world.
1957	McKinsey organization model is adopted, with service companies, operating companies, and committee of managing directors. This "three-dimensional matrix" structure will prevail for more than 35 years.
1958	Shell begins drilling operations in Nigeria.
1973	OPEC oil embargo pushes world oil prices to new levels.
1979	Shell is accused of paying "protection money" to Italian government officials. Shell is also accused of violating international sanctions imposed against Rhodesia because of its apartheid policies. Shell managing directors adopt the Statement of General Business Principles as operating guidelines.
1980	Shell reopens its operations in China.
1994	Shell is accused of complicity in the Nigerian government's suppression of human rights and the execution of 9 dissidents, including Ken Saro Wiwa.
1995	Brent Spar oil platform is occupied by environmental activists. Greenpeace organizes a boycott of Shell products in Europe. Shell is condemned by environmental and political groups for planning to sink the Brent Spar at sea rather than recycle materials.
1996	Shell "roundtables" are convened. 159 executives and 145 external participants engage in dialogue about what society expects from Shell.
1997	Revised Statement of General Business Principles is adopted by Shell managing directors. A new "core identity" is adopted by the company.

1998	Shell establishes "Renewables" as one of the company's five core businesses. Publication of "Profits and Principles: Does There Have to Be a Choice?"
1999	Social Report #2 issued.
1999–2000	Extreme fluctuations in oil prices; prices reach lowest point in 30 years, but then reach a new peak as OPEC cartel restricts production.
2000	Social Report #3 issued.

REFERENCES

INTRODUCTION

Ackerman, Bruce, and Joseph Alsott. 1999. *The Stakeholder Society.* New Haven, CT: Yale University Press.

Cruikshank, Jeffrey L., and David B. Sicilia. 1997. *The Engine That Could: Seventy-Five Years of Values Driven Change at Cummins Engine Company.* Boston: Harvard Business School Press.

Kaku, Ryuzaburo. 1997. "The Path of *Kyosei.*" *Harvard Business Review* (July–Aug.): 55–63.

Rosen, Daniel. 1999. *Behind the Open Door: Foreign Enterprises in the Chinese Marketplace.* Washington, DC: Institute for International Economics.

CHAPTER 1

Agle, Bradley R., Jeffrey A. Sonnenfeld, and Ronald K. Mitchell. 1999. "Managerial Determination of Important Stakeholders." *Academy of Management Journal,* 42(5): 507–525.

American Law Institute. 1992. *Principles of Corporate Governance: Analysis and Recommendations.* Philadelphia: American Law Institute.

Baumhart, R. 1968. *An Honest Profit: What Businessmen Say About Ethics in Business.* New York: Holt, Rinehart and Winston.

Berman, Shawn L., Andrew C. Wicks, Suresh Kotha, and Thomas M. Jones. 1999. "Who Matters to CEOs? An Investigation of Stakeholder Attributes and

Salience, Corporate Performance, and CEO Values." *Academy of Management Journal*, 42(5): 488–506.

Blair, Margaret. 1995. *Ownership and Control: Rethinking Corporate Governance for the Twenty-First Century*. Washington, DC: Brookings Institution, 1995.

Boatright, John R. 1996. "Business Ethics and the Theory of the Firm." *American Business Law Journal*, 34: 218–44.

Bowen, H. R. 1953. *The Social Responsibilities of the Businessman*. New York: Harper.

Brenner, S. N., and E. A. Molander. 1977. "Is the Ethics of Business Changing?" *Harvard Business Review*, 58(1): 54–65.

Burke, Lee, and Jeanne Logsdon. 1996. "How Corporate Social Responsibility Pays Off." *Long Range Planning*, 29(4): 495–502.

Carney, W. J. 1993. "The ALI's Corporate Governance Project: The Death of Property Rights?" *George Washington Law Review*, 61(4): 898–925.

Caux Round Table. 1994. *Principles for Business*. Washington, DC: Caux Round Table Secretariat.

Chappell, Tom. 1993. *The Soul of a Business: Managing for Profit and the Common Good*. New York: Bantam Books.

Clark, J. M. 1916. "The Changing Basis of Economic Responsibility." *Journal of Political Economy*, 24(3): 209–29.

Clarkson, Max B. E. ed. 1998. *The Corporation and Its Stakeholders: Classic and Contemporary Readings*. Toronto: University of Toronto Press.

Cummings, Jeffrey L., and Jonathan P. Doh. 2000. "Identifying Who Matters: Mapping Key Players in Multiple Environments." *California Management Review*, 42(2): 83–104.

Dodd, E. M. 1932. "For Whom Are Corporate Managers Trustees?" *Harvard Law Review*, 45(7): 1145–63.

Donaldson, Thomas E., and Lee E. Preston. 1995. "The Stakeholder Theory of the Corporation: Concepts, Evidence, and Implications." *Academy of Management Review*, 20(1): 65–91.

Drucker, Peter. 1946. *Concept of the Corporation*. New York: John Day Company.

Evan, W. M., and R. E. Freeman. 1993. "A Stakeholder Theory of the Modern Corporation: Kantian Capitalism." In T. Donaldson and P. H. Werhane, eds., *Ethical Issues in Business*. Englewood Cliffs, NJ: Prentice Hall: 166–71.

Follett, Mary Parker. 1918. *The New State: Group Organization, the Solution of Popular Government*. New York: Longmans Green.

Freeman, R. Edward. 1984. *Strategic Management: A Stakeholder Approach.* Boston: Pitman.

Frooman, J. 1997. "Socially Irresponsible and Illegal Behavior and Shareholder Wealth." *Business and Society,* 36(3): 221–49.

Griffin, J. J. 2000. "Stakeholder Research: An Organizing Framework." Presented at the Annual Meeting of the Academy of Management, Social Issues in Management Division, Toronto, Canada (Aug.).

Griffin, J. J., and J. F. Mahon. 1997. "The Corporate Social Performance and Corporate Financial Performance Debate: Twenty-Five Years of Incomparable Research." *Business and Society,* 36(1): 5–31.

Handy, Charles. 1997. "The Citizen Corporation." *Harvard Business Review,* 75(5): 7–8.

Hitachi Foundation. 1997. *Global Corporate Citizenship—Rationale and Strategies.* Washington, DC: Hitachi Foundation.

Jensen, Michael C. 2000. "Value Maximization, Stakeholder Theory and the Corporate Objective Function." In M. Beer and N. Nohria, eds., *Breaking the Code of Change.* Cambridge, MA: Harvard Business School Press: 37–57.

Jones, Thomas M. 1995. "Instrumental Stakeholder Theory: A Synthesis of Ethics and Economics." *Academy of Management Review,* 20: 404–37.

Jones, Thomas, and Andrew C. Wicks. 1999. "Convergent Stakeholder Theory." *Academy of Management Review,* 24(2): 206–21.

Jones, Tom, and Charles Hill. 1992. "Stakeholder Agency Theory." *Journal of Management Studies,* 29(2): 131–54.

Kaku, Ryuzaburo. 1997. "The Path of *Kyosei.*" *Harvard Business Review,* July–Aug.: 55–63.

Kay, John. 1995. *Why Firms Succeed.* New York: Oxford.

Kennedy, Allan A. 2000. *The End of Shareholder Value: Corporations at the Crossroads.* London: Perseus.

Kinder, Peter, Steven D. Lyndenberg, and Amy L. Domini. 1993. *Investing for Good: Making Money While Being Socially Responsible.* New York: HarperBusiness.

Kochan, Thomas, and Saul Rubenstein. 2000. "Toward a Stakeholder Theory of the Firm: The Saturn Partnership." *Organizational Science,* 11(4): 367–86.

Logsdon, Jeanne, and Patsy Llewellyn. 2000. "Stakeholders and Corporate Performance Measures: An Impact Assessment." In *Research in Stakeholder Theory, 1997–1998,* Toronto: Clarkson Centre for Business Ethics: 117–31.

Margolis, J. D., and J. P. Walsh. 2001. *People and Profits? The Search for a Link Between a Company's Social and Financial Performance.* Ann Arbor, MI: Lawrence Erlbaum.

Miles, Robert H. 1987. *Managing the Corporate Social Environment: A Grounded Theory.* Englewood Cliffs, NJ: Prentice-Hall.

Mills, Roger W., and Bill Weinstein. 2000. "Beyond Shareholder Value—Reconciling the Shareholder and Stakeholder Perspectives." *Journal of General Management,* 25(1): 79–93.

Mitchell, R. K., B. R Agle, and D. J. Wood. 1997. "Toward a Theory of Stakeholder Identification and Salience: Defining the Principle of Who and What Really Counts." *Academy of Management Review,* 22: 853–86.

Novartis. 1999. www.info.novartis.com/weare/overview.html.

OECD. 1999. *OECD Principles of Corporate Governance.* Paris: Organization for Economic Cooperation and Development. (See also *Corporate Governance: Improving Competitiveness and Access to Capital in Global Markets.* Report to OECD by the Business Sector Advisory Group on Corporate Governance, Apr. 1998.)

Posner, Barry Z., and Warren H. Schmidt. 1984. "Values and the American Manager." *California Management Review,* 26(3): 202–16.

Preston, Lee E., and D. P. O'Bannon. 1997. "Research Note: The Corporate Social-Financial Performance Relationship: A Typology and Analysis." *Business and Society,* 36(2): 113–22.

Preston, Lee E. 2002. "The Truth About Corporate Governance." In *Negotiations and Change: From the Workplace to Society,* Thomas Kochan and David Lipsky, eds. Ithaca, NY: Cornell University Press.

Roman, Ronald M., Sefa Hayibor, and Bradley R. Agle. 1999. "The Relationship between Social and Financial Performance." *Business & Society,* 38(1): 109–25.

Schilling, Melissa. 2000. "Decades Ahead of Her Time: Advancing Stakeholder Theory Through the Ideas of Mary Parker Follett." *Journal of Management History,* 6(5): 224–42.

Seidenberg, Ivan. 1998. "Ethics as a Competitive Edge." Sears Lectureship in Business Ethics, Center for Business Ethics. Bentley College, Waltham, MA, Apr. 13.

Steger, U. 1998. "A Mental Map of Managers: An Empirical Investigation into Managers' Perceptions of Stakeholder Issues." *Business and the Contemporary World,* 10(4): 579–609.

Suggett, Dahle. 2000. "Understanding the Business Case for Corporate Community Involvement." *Corporate Public Affairs*, 10(2): 1–3.

Sveiby, Karl Erik. 1997. *The New Organizational Wealth: Managing and Measuring Knowledge-based Assets.* San Francisco: Berrett-Koehler.

Ullmann, Arieh A. 1985. "Data in Search of a Theory: A Critical Examination of the Relationships among Social Performance, Social Disclosure, and Economic Performance of U.S. Firms." *Academy of Management Review*, 10(3): 540–57.

Verschoor, Curtis C. 1998. "A Study of the Link Between a Corporation's Financial Performance and Its Commitment to Ethics." *Journal of Business Ethics*, 17: 1509–16.

Wang, J., and H. D. Dewhirst. 1992. "Boards of Directors and Stakeholder Orientation." *Journal of Business Ethics*, 11: 115–23.

Wheeler, David, and Maria Sillanpää. 1997. *The Stakeholder Corporation: The Body Shop Blueprint for Maximizing Stakeholder Value.* London: Pitman.

Williamson, Oliver E. 1998. "The Institutions of Governance." *American Economic Review*, 88(2): 75–79.

Worthy, James C. 1984. *Shaping an American Institution: Robert E. Wood and Sears, Roebuck.* Urbana: University of Illinois.

CHAPTER 2

Aoki, Masahiko. 1984. *The Co-operative Game Theory of the Firm.* Oxford: Clarendon Press.

Barney, Jay. 1991. "Firm Resources and Sustained Competitive Advantage." *Journal of Management*, 17(1): 99–120.

Barney, J. B. 2001. "Is the Resource-Based 'View' a Useful Perspective for Strategic Management Research? Yes." *Academy of Management Review*, 20: 41–56.

Beccerra, M., and A. K. Gupta, "Trust Within the Organization: Integrating the Trust Literature with Agency Theory and Transaction Cost Economics." *Public Administration Quarterly*, 23(2): 177.

Blair, Margaret M., and Lynn A. Stout. 1999. "A Team Production Theory of Corporate Law." *Virginia Law Review*, 85(2): 247–328.

Brealey, Richard A., and Stewart C. Myers. 1996. *Principles of Corporate Finance.* New York: McGraw-Hill.

Coff, Russell W., and Denise M. Rousseau. 2000. "Sustainable Competitive Advantage from Relational Wealth." In Carrie Leana and Denise M. Rousseau, eds., *Relational Wealth.* New York: Oxford, pp. 27–48.

Condon, Bernard. 1999. "Gaps in GAAP." *Forbes.* January 25: 76–80.

Donaldson, Thomas, and Tomas W. Dunfee. 1999. *Ties that Bind: A Social Contracts Approach to Business Ethics.* Boston: Harvard Business School Press.

Dyer, Jeffrey H., and Harbir Singh. 1998. "The Relational View: Cooperative Strategy and Sources of Interorganizational Competitive Advantage." *Academy of Management Review,* 23(4): 660–79.

Dyer, Jeffrey H., and Wujin Chu. 2000. "The Determinants of Trust in Supplier-Automaker Relationships in the U.S., Japan, and Korea." *Journal of International Business Studies,* 31(2): 259–85.

Eccles, R. G., R. H. Merz, E. M. Keegan, and D. M. H. Phillips. 2001. *The Value-Reporting™ Revolution: Moving Beyond the Numbers Game.* New York: Wiley.

Economist. 1999. "A Price on the Priceless." June 12: 61–62.

Edvinsson, Lief, and Michael S. Malone. 1997. *Intellectual Capital: Realizing Your Company's True Value by Finding Its Hidden Brainpower.* New York: HarperBusiness.

Fombrun, Charles. 1996. *Reputation: Realizing Value from the Corporate Image.* Boston: Harvard Business School Press.

Fukao, Mitsuhiro. 1995. *Financial Integration, Corporate Governance, and the Performance of Multinational Companies.* Washington, DC: Brookings Institution.

Fukuyama, Francis. 1996. *Trust: The Social Virtues and the Creation of Prosperity.* New York: Free Press.

Ghoshal, Sumantra, and Peter Moran. 1996. "Bad for Practice: A Critique of the Transaction Cost Theory." *Academy of Management Review,* 21(1): 13–47.

Grant, Robert. 1996. "Toward a Knowledge-Based Theory of the Firm." *Strategic Management Journal,* 17(Special issue): 109–22.

Hatten, Kenneth J., and Stephen R. Rosenthal. 1999. "Managing the Process-Centered Enterprise." *Long Range Planning,* 32(3): 293–310.

Hatten, Kenneth, and Stephen R. Rosenthal. 2001. *Reaching for the Knowledge Edge: How the Knowing Corporation Seeks, Shares, and Uses Knowledge for Strategic Advantage.* New York: AMACOM.

Henderson, R., and W. Mitchell 1997. "The Interactions of Organizational and Competitive Influences on Strategy and Performance." *Strategic Management Journal,* 18(Summer Special Issue): 5–14.

Jeffries, Frank L., and Richard Reed. 2000. "Trust and Adaptation in Relational Contracting." *Academy of Management Review,* 25(4): 873–82.

Jennings, Ross, and Robert B. Thompson II. 1996. "Accounting for Intangibles in the United States." *Accounting Education*, 11(2): 491–95.

Kaplan, Robert S., and David P. Norton. 1996. *The Balanced Scorecard: Translating Strategy into Action*. Boston: Harvard Business School Press.

Keep, William W., Stanley C. Hollander, and Roger Dickinson. 1999. "The Challenge of Cooperative Business Relationships." *Global Outlook*, 11(1): 63–76.

Keller, Maryann. 1989. *Rude Awakening: The Rise, Fall, and Struggle for Recovery of General Motors*. New York: William Morrow.

Kochan, Thomas, and Saul Rubinstein. 2000. "Toward a Stakeholder Theory of the Firm: The Saturn Partnership." *Organizational Science*, 11(4): 367–86.

Leana, Carrie, and Denise M. Rousseau. 2000. "The Advantages of Stability in a Changing Society." In Carrie Leana and Denise M. Rousseau, eds., *Relational Wealth*. New York: Oxford, pp. 3–24.

Lev, Baruch. 2001. *Intangibles*. Washington, DC: Brookings.

Lev, Baruch, and P. Zarowin. Forthcoming. "The Boundaries of Financial Reporting and How to Extend Them." *Journal of Accounting Research*.

Lindberg, E. B., and S. A. Ross. 1981. "Tobin's q Ratio and Industrial Organization." *Journal of Business*, 54: 1–33.

Mayer, Roger C., James H. Davis, and F. David Schoorman. 1995. "An Integrative Model of Organizational Trust." *Academy of Management Review*, 20(3): 709–734.

Mills, D. Quinn, and G. Bruce Friesen. 1996. *Broken Promises: An Unconventional View of What Went Wrong at IBM*. Boston: Harvard Business School Press.

Mitnick, Barry M. 2000. "Moral Tethers." Presented at the Annual Meeting of the Academy of Management, Social Issues in Management Division, Toronto, Aug. 2000.

Nooteboom, Bart. 1999. "Trust as a Governance Devine." In M. C. Casson and A. Godley, eds., *Cultural Factors in Economic Growth*, chapter 1. Amsterdam: Springer Verlag.

Penrose, Edith. 1959. *The Theory of the Growth of the Firm*. White Plains, NY: Sharpe.

Peteraf, Margaret A. 1993. "The Cornerstones of Competitive Advantage: A Resource-Based View." *Strategic Management Journal*, 14: 179–91.

Porter, Michael E. 1980. *Competitive Strategy: Techniques for Analyzing Industries and Competitors*. New York: Free Press.

Priem, R. L., and J. E. Butler. 2001. "Is the Resource-Based 'View' a Useful Perspective for Strategic Management Research?" *Academy of Management*

Review, 26: 22–40; and "Tautology in the Resource-Based View and the Implications of Externally Determined Resource Value: Further Comments," 57–66.

Prusak, L., and D. Cohen. 2001. *In Good Company: How Social Capital Makes Organizations Work*. Boston: Harvard Business School Press.

Putnam, Robert D. 2000. *Bowling Alone: The Collapse and Renewal of American Community*. New York: Simon & Schuster.

Rindova, Violina P., and Charles J. Fombrun. 1999. "Constructing Competitive Advantage: The Role of Firm-Constituent Interactions." *Strategic Management Journal*, 20: 681–710.

Ring, Peter Smith, and Andrew H. Van de Ven. 1992. "Structuring Cooperative Relationships between Organizations." *Strategic Management Journal*, 13(7): 483–498.

Schendel, D. 1997. "Editor's Introduction to the 1997 Summer Special Issue." *Strategic Management Journal*, 18 (Summer Special Issue): 5–14.

Smith, Melvin L., Jeffrey Pfeffer, and Denise M. Rousseau. 2000. "Patient Capital: How Investors Contribute to (or Undermine) Relational Wealth." In Carrie Leana and Denise M. Rousseau, *Relational Wealth*. New York: Oxford, pp. 261–276.

Smithers, Andrew, and Stephen Wright. 2000. *Valuing Wall Street: Protecting Wealth in Turbulent Markets*. New York: McGraw-Hill.

Sveiby, Karl Erik. 1997. *The New Organizational Wealth: Managing and Measuring Knowledge-Based Assets*. San Francisco: Berrett-Koehler.

Teece, David J., Gary Pisano, and Amy Shuen. 1997. "Dynamic Capabilities and Strategic Management." *Strategic Management Journal*, 18(7): 509–33.

Webster, Frederick E. 1992. "The Changing Role of Marketing in the Corporation." *Journal of Marketing*, 56(4): 1–17.

Wernerfelt, B. 1984. "A Resource-Based View of the Firm." *Strategic Management Journal*, 5: 171–80.

Wheeler, David, and Maria Sillanpää. 1997. *The Stakeholder Corporation: The Body Shop Blueprint for Maximizing Stakeholder Value*. London: Pitman.

Wicks, Andrew C., Shawn L. Berman, and Thomas M. Jones. 1999. "The Structure of Optimal Trust: Moral and Strategic Implications." *Academy of Management Review*, 24(1): 99–116.

Williamson, Oliver E. 1975. *Markets and Hierarchies: Analysis and Antitrust Implications*. New York: Free Press.

CHAPTER 3

Chandler, Alfred. 1962. *Strategy and Structure: Chapters in the History of the American Industrial Enterprise.* Cambridge, MA: MIT Press.

Cruikshank, Jeffrey L., and David B. Sicilia. 1997. *The Engine That Could: Seventy-Five Years of Values-Driven Change at Cummins Engine Company.* Boston: Harvard Business School Press.

Davis, Stanley M. 1984. *Managing Corporate Cultures.* Cambridge, MA: Ballinger.

Deal, Terrence E., and Alan A. Kennedy. 1982. *Corporate Cultures: The Rites and Rituals of Corporate Life.* Reading, MA: Addison-Wesley.

De Geus. 1997. *The Living Company: Habits for Survival in a Turbulent Business Environment.* Boston: Harvard Business School Press.

Detert, James R., Roger G. Schroeder, and John J. Mauriel. 2000. "A Framework for Linking Culture and Improvement Initiatives in Organizations." *Academy of Management Review,* 25(4): 850–63.

Eisenhardt, K. M. 1989. "Building Theories from Case Study Research." *Academy of Management Review,* 14: 532–50.

Galvin, Robert. 1999. Comments at the 1999 Academy of Management annual meeting, Chicago, Aug.

Grant, Robert M., and Renato Cibin. 1996. "Strategy, Structure and Market Turbulence: The International Oil Majors, 1970–1991." *Scandinavian Journal of Management,* 12(2): 165–88.

Harrison, Jeffrey S., and R. Edward Freeman. 1999. "Stakeholders, Social Responsibility, and Performance: Empirical Evidence and Theoretical Perspectives." *Academy of Management Journal,* 42(5): 478–87.

Herkstroeter, Cors A. J. 1996. *Dealing with Contradictionary Expectations—The Dilemmas Facing Multinationals.* Amsterdam.

Jensen, Michael C. 2000. "Value Maximization, Stakeholder Theory, and the Corporate Objective Function." Harvard Business School Working Paper #00-058.

Khavul, Susanna. 2000. "Money and Knowledge: Sources of Seed Capital and the Performance of High Technology Start-Ups." Unpublished doctoral dissertation, Boston University.

Kolk, Ans, Rob van Tulder, and Carlijn Welters. 1999. "International Codes of Conduct and Corporate Social Responsibility: Can Transnational Corporations Regulate Themselves?" *Transnational Corporations,* 8(1): 143–80.

Lawrence, P. R., and J. W. Lorsch. 1967. *Organization and Environment.* Homewood, IL: Irwin.

Labovitz, George, and Victor Rosansky. 1997. *The Power of Alignment: How Great Companies Stay Centered and Achieve Extraordinary Things.* New York: Wiley.

Llewelyn, John T. 1998. "Evaluating Corporate Claims of Social Responsibility: Developing a Citizen Checklist." In J. E. Post, ed., *Research in Corporate Social Performance and Policy,* vol. 15, JAI Press, pp. 89–106.

Moore, James. 1996. "The Death of Competition." *Fortune,* 133(7) (Apr. 16): 142ff.

Motorola. 2000. www.Motorola.com

Nelson, Richard R., and Sydney G. Winter. 1982. *An Evolutionary Theory of Economic Change.* Cambridge, MA: Harvard University Press.

Nelson, Richard R. 1995. "Recent Evolutionary Theorizing About Economic Change." *Journal of Economic Literature,* 33(1): 48–90.

Ogbonne, Emmanuel, and Lloyd C. Harris, 2000. "The Dynamic Concept of Organizational Culture: Micro and Macro Applications." *Global Focus,* 12(2): 23–34.

Peach, Brian E., et al. 1999. *The Motorola Case.* Annual Meeting of the Academy of Management, Chicago, Aug. 9.

Petrakis, Harry Mark. 1965. *The Founder's Touch: The Life of Paul Galvin of Motorola.* New York: McGraw-Hill. Reprinted 1995, Schaumburg, IL: Motorola University Press (Motorola's official corporate history).

Penrose, E. 1959. *The Theory of the Growth of the Firm.* New York: Wiley.

Porter, M. E. 1979. "The Structure Within Industries and Companies' Performance." *Review of Economics and Statistics,* 61: 214–27.

Porter, M. E. 1980. *Competitive Strategy.* New York: The Free Press.

Porter, M. E. 1981. "The Contributions of Industrial Organization to Strategic Management." *Academy of Management Review,* 6: 609–20.

Porter, M. E. 1985. *Competitive Advantage.* New York: The Free Press.

Porter, Michael E. 1990. *The Competitive Advantage of Nations.* London: Macmillan.

Post, James E. 2000. "Global Codes of Conduct: Activists, Lawyers and Managers in Search of a Solution." In Oliver Williams, ed., *Global Codes of Conduct.* South Bend, IN: University of Notre Dame Press.

Post, James E., Anne T. Lawrence, and James Weber. 2002. *Business and Society: Corporate Strategy, Public Policy, Ethics,* 10th edition. New York: McGraw-Hill.

Preston, Lee E., and Danielle Mihalko. 1999. "Corporate Responsibility: Comparative Analysis of Current Documents." In *Principles of Stakeholder Management: The Clarkson Principles.* Toronto: Clarkson Centre for Business Ethics.

Putnam, Robert D. 2000. *Bowling Alone: The Collapse and Revival of American Community*. New York: Simon & Schuster.

Ruhli, Edwin, and Sybille Sachs. 1993/1994. "Towards an Integrated Concept of Management Efficiency." *Management International Review*, 33: 295–313.

Schein, Edgar H. 1990. "Organizational Culture." *American Psychologist*, Feb.: 110.

Shell. 1997. Statement of General Business Principles.

Thompson, J. D. 1967. *Organizations in Action*. New York: McGraw-Hill.

United Nations. 2000. www.unglobalcompact.org

Wack, Pierre. 1985. "Scenarios: Uncharted Waters Ahead (Part 1)." *Harvard Business Review*, 63(5): 72–90.

Wack, Pierre. 1985. "Scenarios: Shooting the Rapids (Part 2)." *Harvard Business Review*, 63(6): 139–51.

Williams, Oliver F., ed. 2000. *Global Codes of Conduct: An Idea Whose Time Has Come*. Notre Dame, IN: University of Notre Dame Press.

Yin, R. K. 1994. *Case Study Research: Design and Methods*, 2nd ed. Thousand Oaks, CA: Sage.

CHAPTER 4

Bollier, David. 1996. *Aiming Higher: 25 Stories of How Companies Prosper by Combining Sound Management and Social Vision*. New York: AMACOM and Business Enterprise Trust.

Boston Globe. 1999. "Home Depot's New Eco-Policy." Aug. 27: F2.

Boston University. 1995. *Site Visit Report to Motorola University, Schaumburg, IL*. Boston: Boston University Human Resources Policy Institute.

Burke, Edmund M. 1999. *Corporate Community Relations: The Neighbor of Choice Principle*. Westport, CT: Quorum Press.

Collins, James C., and Jerry I. Porras. 1995. *Built to Last: Successful Habits of Visionary Companies*. New York: HarperBusiness.

Cruikshank, Jeffrey L., and David B. Sicilia. 1997. *The Engine That Could: Seventy-Five Years of Values-Driven Change at Cummins Engine Company*. Boston: Harvard Business School Press.

Fireman, Paul. 1999. "Building a Culture of Commitment." Commencement address, Boston University School of Management, June 1999.

Gilmartin, Raymond. 1999. "Foreword," in E. M. Burke, *Corporate Community Relations: The Neighbor of Choice Principle*. Westport, CT: Quorum Press.

Hagel, John, and Arthur G. Armstrong. 1997. *Net Gain: Expanding Markets Through Virtual Communities.* Boston: Harvard Business School Press.

Hammer, Michael, and James Champy. 1993. *Reengineering the Corporation.* New York: HarperCollins.

Henderson, J. A. (interview). 1996. "How to Build Profits with Integrity." *Leaders Magazine,* 19(4): 3.

Kahn, Joseph. 2000. "Multinationals Sign U.N. Pact on Rights and Environment." *New York Times,* July 27, 2000: A1.

Kenan, Regina H. 1993. *Reproductive Hazards in the Workplace: Mending Jobs, Managing Pregnancies.* New York: Harrington Park Press.

Knaebel, Steve. 1994. "Getting Our Bearings Through Bench Marking." In Keith McGuiness, ed., *Charting the Mexican Labyrinth: A Practical Guide to Success in Mexico.* San Diego: HPH Partners.

Lindahl, Goran. 2000. "New Role for Global Business: Multinational Firms Must Make Protecting Human Rights a Priority." Time-Europe, 155(4).

Logan, David, D. Roy, and L. Regelbrugge. 1997. *Global Corporate Citizenship— Rationale and Strategies.* Washington, DC: The Hitachi Foundation.

Meredith, Robyn. 2000. "A Town Aspires to Landmark Status." *New York Times,* Jan. 2, 2000: 14.

Moorthy, R S 1996. "Motorola's Ethical Advantage and Challenge." *Impact,* 2: 3.

Moorthy, R S, et al. 1998. *Uncompromising Integrity: Motorola's Global Challenge.* Schaumburg, IL: Motorola University Press.

Prince of Wales Business Leaders Forum. 1996. *Business as Partners in Development.* London: Prince of Wales Business Leaders Forum.

Petrakis, Harry Mark. 1965. *The Founder's Touch: The Life of Paul Galvin of Motorola.* New York: McGraw-Hill. Reprinted 1995, Schaumburg, IL: Motorola University Press (Motorola's official corporate history).

Pfeffer, Jeffrey. 1998. *The Human Equation: Building Profits by Putting People First.* Boston: Harvard Business School Press.

Post, James E. 2000a. "Moving from Geographic to Virtual Communities: Global Corporate Citizenship in a Dot.Com World." *Business and Society Review,* 15(1): 27–46.

Post, James E. 2000b. *Meeting the Challenge of Global Corporate Citizenship.* Chestnut Hill, MA: Boston College Center for Corporate Community Relations.

Rawls, John. 1971. *A Theory of Justice.* Cambridge, MA: Belknap Press of Harvard University Press.

Reichheld, Frederick F. 1996. *The Loyalty Effect: The Hidden Force behind Growth, Profits, and Lasting Value.* Boston: Harvard Business School Press.

Sethi, S. Prakash. 1999. "Codes of Conduct for Global Business: Prospects and Challenges of Implementation." In *Principles of Stakeholder Management.* Toronto: Clarkson Centre for Business Ethics (University of Toronto).

United Nations. 2000. www.unglobalcompact.org

Williams, Oliver F., ed. 2000. *Global Codes of Conduct: An Idea Whose Time Has Come.* Notre Dame, IN: University of Notre Dame Press.

CHAPTER 5

Baron, David. 1995. "Integrated Strategy: Market and Nonmarket Components." *California Management Review,* 37: 47–65.

Baron, David. 1997. "Integrated Strategy, Trade Policy, and Global Competition." *California Management Review,* 39: 145–69.

Bhote, Keki R. 1989. "Motorola's Long March to the Malcolm Baldrige National Quality Award." *Productivity Review,* 8(4): 365ff.

Boddewyn, J. J., and T. L. Brewer. 1994. "International Business Political Behavior: New Theoretical Directions." *Academy of Management Review,* 19(1): 119–43.

Dertouzas, Michael, et al. 1989. *Made in America.* Cambridge, MA: MIT Press.

Dryfack, Kenneth, and Marc Frons. 1985. "Bob Galvin's Angry Campaign Against Japan." *Business Week,* April 15: 70ff.

Galvin, Robert. 1999. Authors' interview, Feb. 24, 1999, Schaumburg, IL.

Gienko, Glenn. 1999. Authors' interview, Feb. 24, 1999, Schaumburg, IL.

Industry Week. 1982. "Japan's Trade Efforts Draw Executives' Fire." Oct. 4: 26ff.

Kyodo News Service, Japan Economic Newswire. Oct. 27.

Mahon, J., and R. McGowan. 1996. *Industry as a Player in the Political and Social Arena: Defining the Competitive Environment.* Westport, CT: Quorum Books.

Moorthy, R. S. 1998. Personal interview, May 19, New York.

Murtha, T., and S. Lenway. 1994. "Country Capabilities and the Strategic State: How National Political Institutions Affect Multinational Corporations' Strategies." *Strategic Management Journal,* 15(Summer Special Issues): 113–29.

New York Times. 1981. "Is Japan's Challenge to American Industry Going Unanswered?" Aug. 10: D-7.

New York Times. 1999. "Motorola's Future." July 14: C1–2.

Pine, Art. 1989. "Motorola's Washington Lobbyists Keep Heat on Japanese Trade." *Los Angeles Times,* May 27: Business 1ff.

PR Newswire. July 31, 1986.

Shaffer, Brian. 1995. "Firm Level Responses to Government Regulation: Theoretical and Research Approaches." *Journal of Management*, 21: 495–514.

Yoffie, David. 1987. "Corporate Strategy for Political Action: A Rational Model." In A. Marcus, A. Kaufman, and A. Beam (eds.), *Business Strategy and Public Policy*. New York: Quorum Books, pp. 92–111.

CHAPTER 6

Duncan. 1995. "Wir werden uns ändern." *Frankfurter Allgemeine Zeitung*, June 27: 19.

Economist. 1995. "Multinationals and Their Morals." Dec. 2: 18.

Herkstroeter, Cors A. J. 1996. *Dealing with Contradictionary Expectations—The Dilemmas Facing Multinationals*. Amsterdam.

Howarth, Stephen. 1997. *A Century in Oil: The Shell Transport and Trading Company, 1897–1997*. London: Wiedenfeld and Nicolson.

Interchange. 1997. "Nigeria Issue Breaks New Ground." 2: 4.

Interchange. 1999. "Camisea: A Blueprint for the Future." 1: 13–15.

Jones, Murray G. 1997. "The Role of Stakeholder Participation: Linkages to Stakeholder Impact Assessment and Social Capital in Camisea, Peru." *Greener Management International*, 19(3): 87–97.

Jones, Murray G. 1998. "Environmental Impact Assessment Within a Multi-National Enterprise: Adaptive EIA in the Camisea Project." Paper presented at the Conference on Impact Assessment in the Development Process, University of Manchester (Oct. 23–24).

May, P., et al. 1998. *Corporate Roles and Rewards in Promoting Sustainable Development: Lessons Learned from Camisea*. Berkeley: Energy Resources Group, University of California-Berkeley.

Moody-Stuart, Mark. 1997. *It's More Than Just Business*. Konya.

Moody-Stuart, Mark. 1998. "A Force for Progress—The Royal Dutch/Shell Group in the 21st Century." CERA Conference, Houston.

New York Times. 1996. "Blood and Oil: A Special Report; After Nigeria Represses, Shell Defends Its Record." Feb. 13: 2.

Sethi, S. Prakash, and Oliver F. Williams. 2000. *Economic Imperatives and Ethical Values in Global Business: The South African Experience and International Codes Today*. Boston: Kluwer.

Shell. 1994. *Nigeria Brief: The Ogoni Issue*. Shell website: www.shellnigeria.com.

Shell. 1995. *Nigeria Brief: Community Developments.* London: Shell Petroleum Development Company of Nigeria.

Shell. 1995. *Nigeria Brief: The Environment.* Nigeria: Shell Petroleum Development Company of Nigeria.

Shell. 1996. Shell Business Framework (ed. 1).

Shell. 1997. "Investing in the Future." *Shell World,* Dec.: 8.

Shell. 1976–1997. *Statement of General Business Principles.* London: Shell.

Shell. 1998. *Business and Human Rights—A Management Primer.* London: Shell.

Shell Germany. 1998. "Das Camisea-Projeckt, Bericht über die Entwicklung des Camisea-Erdgasvorkommens in Peru." Hamburg, Jan.

CHAPTER 7

Antal, Ariane Berthoin, Meinolf Dierkes, and Lutz Marz. 1999. "Organizational Learning in China, Germany and Israel." *Journal of General Management,* 25(1): 17–42.

Benson, John, Philippe Debroux, and Masae Yuasa. 1998. "Labor Management in Chinese-Based Enterprises: The Challenge of Flexibility." *Business and the Contemporary World,* 10(4): 633–61.

Chen, Ming-Jer. 2001. *Inside Chinese Business.* Boston: Harvard Business School Press.

Cruikshank, Jeffrey L., and David B. Sicilia. 1997. *The Engine That Could: Seventy-Five Years of Values Driven Change at Cummins Engine Company.* Boston: Harvard Business School Press.

Economist Intelligence Unit (EIU). 1997. *Multinational Companies in China: Lessons from Winners and Losers.* Hong Kong: EIU.

Economist Intelligence Unit (EIU). 1995. *Moving China Ventures Out of the Red and into the Black.* Hong Kong: EIU.

Fung, Yulan. 1983. *A History of Chinese Philosophy.* Trans. and ed. Derk Bodde. Princeton: Princeton University Press.

Howarth, Stephen. 1997. *A Century in Oil: The Shell Transport and Trading Company, 1897–1997.* London: Wiedenfeld and Nicolson.

International Labor Rights Fund. 1999. "Mattel, Levi Strauss, and Reebok International Endorse Human Rights Principles for US Business in China." Press release, May 28.

Latham, Richard. 1997. Remarks at U.S.-China Business Council Meeting, Washington, DC, Jan. 13.

Lovett, Steve, Lee C. Simmons, and Raja Kali. 1999. "Guanxi versus the Market: Ethics and Efficiency." *Journal of International Business Studies*, 30(2): 231–48.

Luo, Yadong. 2000. *Multinational Corporations in China: Benefiting from Structural Transformation.* Copenhagen: Copenhagen Business School Press.

Mann, Jim. 1989. *Beijing Jeep.* New York: Simon & Schuster.

Matthews, Gerry. 1999. Personal interview conducted by Lee Preston.

Moran, Ted. 1998. *Foreign Direct Investment and Development.* Washington, DC: Institute for International Economics.

Motorola, Inc. 1997. *Motorola Milestones in China (1987–1997).*

Overholt, William H. 1993. *The Rise of China.* New York: Norton.

Prakash, Aseem, and Jeffery A. Hart. 1999. *Globalization and Governance.* London: Routledge.

Rosen, Daniel. 1999. *Behind the Open Door: Foreign Enterprises in the Chinese Marketplace.* Washington, DC: Institute for International Economics.

Santoro, Michael A. 1998. "Engagement with Integrity: What We Should Expect Multinational Firms to Do about Human Rights in China." *Business and the Contemporary World*, 10(1): 25–54.

Scarborough, Jack. 1998. "The Cultural Roots of China's Stance on Human Rights: A Caution Sign for Western Companies and Governments." *Business and the Contemporary World*, 10(3): 511–26.

Shanghai Foreign Investment Commission. 1998. *Guide to Investment in Shanghai.*

Spar, Debora L. 1998. "The Spotlight and the Bottom Line: How Multinationals Export Human Rights." *Foreign Affairs*, 77(2): 7–12.

Steidlmeier, Paul. 1997. "Human Rights in China: Multiple Agenda and Challenges for American Business." *Business and the Contemporary World*, 8(3/4): 86–103.

Wall Street Journal. 1998. "Motorola Expands Operations in China." June 12:A9.

Williams, Oliver F., ed. 2000. *Global Codes of Conduct: An Idea Whose Time Has Come.* Notre Dame, IN: University of Notre Dame University Press.

Xin, Katherine, and Jone L. Pearce. 1996. "Guanxi: Connections as Substitutes for Formal Institutional Support." *Academy of Management Journal*, 39(6): 1641–58.

Yan, Amin, and Yadong Luo. 2001. *International Joint Ventures: Theory and Practice.* Armonk, NY: Sharpe.

CHAPTER 8

Ackerman, Robert. 1973. "How Companies Respond to Social Demands." *Harvard Business Review*, July–August: 88–98.

Altman, Barbara W., and Deborah Vidaver-Cohen. 2000. "A Framework for Understanding Corporate Citizenship." *Business and Society Review*, 105(1): 1–8.

Argyris, Chris. 1977. "Double Loop Learning in Organizations." *Harvard Business Review*, Sept.–Oct.: 115–25.

Bollier, David. 1996. *Aiming Higher: 25 Stories of How Companies Prosper by Combining Sound Management and Social Vision*. New York: AMACOM and Business Enterprise Trust.

Bradshaw, Jack. 2000. Personal correspondence.

Cruikshank, Jeffrey L., and David B. Sicilia. 1997. *The Engine That Could: Seventy-Five Years of Values Driven Change at Cummins Engine Company*. Boston: Harvard Business School Press.

deGues, A. 1988. "Planning as Learning." *Harvard Business Review*, Mar.–Apr.: 70–74.

deGues, A. 1997. *The Living Company: Habits for Survival in a Turbulent Business Environment*. Boston: Harvard Business School Press.

Dixon, Nancy M. 2000. *Common Knowledge: How Companies Thrive by Sharing What They Know*, Boston: Harvard Business School Press.

Drucker, Peter. 1989. *The New Realities*. New York: Harper & Row.

Eccles, R. G., R. H. Merz, E. M. Keegan, and D. M. H. Phillips. 2001. *The Value Reporting™ Revolution: Moving Beyond the Numbers Game*. New York: Wiley.

Elkington, John. 1997. *Cannibals with Forks: The Triple Bottom Line of 21st Century Business*. London: Thompson.

Fiol, C. M., and M. A. Lyles. 1985. "Organizational Learning." *Academy of Management Review*, 10: 803–13.

Galvin, Robert. 1999. Authors' interview, Feb. 22.

Gienko, Glenn. 1999. Authors' interview, Feb. 22.

Hamel, Gary. 1996. "Strategy as Revolution." *Harvard Business Review*, July–Aug.: 69–82.

Hatten, Kenneth J., and Stephen R. Rosenthal. 1999. "Managing the Process-Centered Enterprise," *Long Range Planning*, 32(3): 293–310.

Hatten, Kenneth J., and Stephen R. Rosenthal. 2001. *Reaching for the Knowledge Edge: How the Knowing Corporation Seeks, Shares, and Uses Knowledge for Strategic Advantage*. New York: AMACOM.

Leonard-Barton, D. 1995. *Wellsprings of Knowledge*. Boston: Harvard Business School Press.

Marsden, Chris. 2000. "The New Corporate Citizenship of Big Business: Part of the Solution to Sustainability?" *Business and Society Review*, 105(1): 9–26.

Mirvis, Philip. 2000. "Transformation at Shell: Commerce and Citizenship." *Business and Society Review*, 105(1): 63–84.

Moorthy, R S, et al. 1998. *Uncompromising Integrity: Motorola's Global Challenge.* Schaumburg, IL: Motorola University Press.

Moorthy, R S 1999. Authors' interview, Feb. 22.

Motorola. 2000. www.motorola.com.

Peach, Brian. 1999. "Motorola Case Study." Presented at Annual Meeting of Academy of Management, Chicago, Aug. 9.

Post, J. E. 1978. *Corporate Behavior and Social Change.* Reston, VA: Reston Publishing.

Post, J. E., A. T. Lawrence, and J. Weber. 2002. *Business and Society: Corporate Strategy, Public Policy, Ethics,* 10th ed. New York: McGraw-Hill.

Rubinstein, S., and T. Kochan. 2000. *Learning from Saturn: Possibilities for Corporate Governance and Employee Relations.* Ithaca, NY: Cornell University Press.

Senge, Peter M. 1990. *The Fifth Discipline: The Art and Practice of the Learning Organization.* New York: Doubleday.

Senge, Peter M., ed. 1999. *The Dance of Change: The Challenges to Sustaining Momentum in Learning Organizations.* New York: Currency Doubleday.

Shell. 1997a. *Statement of General Business Principles.*

Shell. 1997b. *Shell World.*

Shell. 1998a. *Shell Report—Profits and Principles: Does There Have to be a Choice?* London: Shell International.

Shell. 1998b. *Business and Human Rights.* Pamphlet.

Shell. 1999a. *Listening and Responding—Dialogue with our Stakeholders.* London: Shell International. Comments of Mark Moody-Stuart.

Shell. 1999b. Comments of Jeroen van der Veer. "Globalisation, Ecology and Economy," Presentation at the Bridging Worlds Conference, Tilburg, Nov. 26.

Shell. 1999c. *Interchange.* (External affairs newsletter).

Shell. 1999d. *Shell Report—People, Planet and Profits.* London: Shell International.

Svendsen, Anne. 1998. *The Stakeholder Strategy.* San Francisco: Berrett-Koehler.

Watts, Phil. 2000. "Pursuing Sustainable Development." Speech at Oxford University, May.

CHAPTER 9

Abernathy, Frederick H., John T. Dunlop, Janice Hammond, and David Weil. 1999. *A Stitch in Time: Lean Retailing and the Transformation of Manufacturing: Lessons from the Apparel and Textile Industries.* New York: Oxford.

Andriof, J., and M. McIntosh (eds.). 2001. *Perspectives on Corporate Citizenship.* Sheffield, UK: Greanleaf.

Clarkson Centre for Business Ethics. 1999. *Principles of Stakeholder Management.* Toronto: Clarkson Centre for Business Ethics, University of Toronto.

Collins, Jim. 2000. "Built to Flip." *Fast Company,* March: 131–40.

Collins, J. C., and J. I. Porras. 1994. *Built to Last: Successful Habits of Visionary Companies.* New York: HarperBusiness.

Computer Industry Almanac. 2000. "The World's Online Populations." www.c-i-a.com.

Donaldson, Thomas E., and Lee E. Preston. 1995. "The Stakeholder Theory of the Corporation: Concepts, Evidence, and Implications." *Academy of Management Review,* 20(1): 65–91.

Dyer, Jeffrey, and Harbir Singh. 1998. "The Relational View: Cooperative Strategy and Sources of Interorganizational Competitive Advantage." *Academy of Management Review,* 23(4): 660–79.

Elsbach, Kimberly D., and C. B. Battachayra. 2001. "Defining Who You Are by What You're Not: A Study of Organizational Disidentification and the NRA." *Organization Science,* 12(4): 393–413.

Freeman, R. Edward. 1984. *Strategic Management: A Stakeholder Approach.* Boston: Pitman.

Global Reporting Initiative. 2000. *Sustainability Reporting Guidelines on Economic, Environmental, and Social Performance.* Boston: Global Reporting Initiative. See also www.globalreporting.org.

Henderson, Rebecca, and Will Mitchell, 1997. "The Interactions of Organizational and Competitive Influences on Strategy and Performance." *Strategic Management Journal,* 18(Special Issue): 5–14.

Investor Responsibility Research Center. 2000. *Social Issues Service.* Washington DC: IRRC. See also www.irrc.org.

Kaplan, Robert S., and David P. Norton. 1996. *The Balanced Scorecard: Translating Strategy into Action.* Boston: Harvard Business School Press.

Kaplan, Robert S., and David P. Norton. 2000. *The Strategy-Focused Organization: How Balanced Scorecard Companies Thrive in the New Business Environment.* Boston: Harvard Business School Press.

Leavy, Brian. 1998. "The Concept of Learning in the Strategy Field: Review and Outlook." *Management Learning,* 29(4): 447–66.

Mirvis, Philip H. 2000. "Transformation at Shell: Commerce and Citizenship." *Business and Society Review,* 105(1): 63–84.

Preston, Lee E., and James E. Post. 1975. *Private Management and Public Policy: The Principle of Public Responsibility.* Englewood Cliffs, NJ: Prentice-Hall.

Sen, Shankar, and C. B. Battachayra. 2001. "Does Doing Good Always Lead to Doing Better? Consumer Reactions to Corporate Social Responsibility." *Journal of Marketing Research,* May: 225–43.

Storck, John, and Patricia A. Hill. 2000. "Knowledge Diffusion Through Strategic Communities." *Sloan Management Review,* 41(2): 63–74.

van der Veer, Jeroen. 1999. "Earning the License to Grow: Globalisation, Ecology and Economy." Presentation at the Bridging Worlds Conference, Tilburg (Nov. 26).

Waddock, Sandra. 2002. *Leading Corporate Citizens: Meeting the Business in Society Challenge.* New York: McGraw-Hill.

Wilson, Ian. 2001. *The New Rules of Corporate Conduct: Rewriting the Social Contract.* Westport, CT: Quorum.

CASE STUDY: CUMMINS

Cruikshank, Jeffrey L., and David B. Sicilia. 1997. *The Engine That Could: Seventy-Five Years of Values Driven Change at Cummins Engine Company.* Boston: Harvard Business School Press.

CASE STUDY: MOTOROLA

Collins, J. C., and J. I. Porras. 1994. *Built to Last: Successful Habits of Visionary Companies.* New York: HarperBusiness.

Galvin, R. W. *The Idea of Ideas.* Schaumburg, IL: Motorola University Press, 1991.

Moorthy, R. S., et al. 1998. *Uncompromising Integrity: Motorola's Global Challenge.* Schaumburg, IL: Motorola University Press.

Peach, B. 1999. Presentation of Motorola Case Study at Annual Meeting of Academy of Management, Chicago, Aug. 9.

Petrakis, Harry Mark. 1965. *The Founder's Touch: The Life of Paul Galvin of Motorola.* New York: McGraw-Hill. Reprinted 1995 Schaumburg, IL: Motorola University Press (Motorola's official corporate history).

Weisz, W. 1993. *The Philosophy Memos: Articles, Speeches & Quotations.* Schaumburg, IL: Motorola University Press.

CASE STUDY: SHELL

Howarth, S. 1997. *The Empire of Oil.* London: Weidenfeld & Nicolson.

de Gues, Arie. 1997. *The Living Company.* Boston: Harvard Business School Press.

Schwartz, P. 1991. *The Art of the Long View.* New York: Doubleday.

ABOUT THE AUTHORS

JAMES E. POST, Professor of Management at Boston University, is senior coauthor of *Business and Society: Corporate Strategy, Public Policy, Ethics* (10th edition, 2002, McGraw-Hill) and series editor of *Research in Corporate Social Performance and Policy* (Elsevier/JAI). His 1975 book *Private Management and Public Policy* (Prentice-Hall), coauthored with Lee E. Preston and regarded as a defining contribution to its field of study, was honored with a 20th Anniversary Symposium at the Academy of Management Annual Meeting in 1995. During 1994–95, Post served as research director of business and society studies at The Conference Board. He is the author of more than 100 academic publications and has served as a consultant to international agencies, foundations, and business firms on the social aspects and impacts of business management.

LEE E. PRESTON, Professor Emeritus of the Robert H. Smith School of Business at the University of Maryland, is the author or editor of more than 150 academic publications in the fields of economics, marketing management, and public policy. His most recent book, *The Rules of the Game in the Global Economy: Policy Regimes for International Business* (Kluwer), was published in a revised second edition in 1997. His 1995 article "The Stakeholder Theory of the Corporation: Concepts, Evidence and Implications," coauthored with Thomas Donaldson, established a new basis for analysis and study of this topic. Between 1995 and 2000, he was codirector of the "Redefining the Corporation" project, funded by the Alfred P. Sloan Foundation.

SYBILLE SACHS is Associate Professor at the Institute for Research in Business Administration at the University of Zurich. Her habilitation thesis, "The Corporation's Role in Society," was published in 2000. She has published a number of research papers in German, and several recent articles in English. She has been a conference participant in Europe and North America, and is coleader (with Edwin Ruhli) of a field research project on social issues management for the RoyalDutch/Shell Group of Companies.

In addition to the authors, who are responsible for all aspects of this book, substantial input was received from David Sicilia, coauthor with J. L. Cruikshank of *The Engine That Could* (1997), a history of Cummins Engine Company, and Daniel H. Rosen, author of *Behind the Open Door: Foreign Enterprises in the Chinese Marketplace* (1999).

INDEX

4987